T0306054

How Ideas Move

This book builds on research in translation studies of change in organizations and demonstrates the implications and application of these findings for managing innovation and change.

When implementing ideas into practice in order to carry out innovative change, translation is key. From strategic and leadership changes to policy and health management decisions, abstract ideas such as 'LEAN', 'CSR', 'Sustainability', 'Public-Private Partnerships', 'Clinical Pathways' and 'AI' are introduced to improve organizational processes. However, in any company and organization, miscommunication and misinterpretation can lead to these ideas being modified, added to and appropriated in ways that make them unsuccessful. This book presents a case for change ideas in organizations being translated rather than "implemented" and offers a profound understanding of the translation processes needed in order for this to succeed.

This vital study is a must-read for researchers, students and practitioners including change agents, general and health care managers, public servants as well as strategic managers and policy decision-makers.

John Damm Scheuer, Master of Science in International Business, PhD, is Associate Professor in the Department of Social Sciences and Business, Roskilde University, Denmark.

RIOT!

Routledge Studies in Innovation, Organizations and Technology

How is Digitalization Affecting Agri-food?
New Business Models, Strategies and Organizational Forms
Edited by Maria Carmela Annosi and Federica Brunetta

Social Innovation of New Ventures
Achieving Social Inclusion and Sustainability in Emerging Economies and Developing Countries
Marcela Ramírez-Pasillas, Vanessa Ratten and Hans Lundberg

Sustainable Innovation
Strategy, Process and Impact
Edited by Cosmina L. Voinea, Nadine Roijakkers and Ward Ooms

Management in the Age of Digital Business Complexity
Edited by Bill McKelvey

Citizen Activities in Energy Transition
User Innovation, New Communities, and the Shaping
of a Sustainable Future
Sampsa Hyysalo

How Ideas Move
Theories and Models of Translation in Organizations
John Damm Scheuer

Managing IT for Innovation
Dynamic Capabilities and Competitive Advantage
Mitsuru Kodama

For more information about this series, please visit: www.routledge.com/
Routledge-Studies-in-Innovation-Organizations-and-Technology/
book-series/RIOT

How Ideas Move

Theories and Models of Translation
in Organizations

John Damm Scheuer

Routledge
Taylor & Francis Group
LONDON AND NEW YORK

First published 2021
by Routledge
2 Park Square, Milton Park, Abingdon, Oxon OX14 4RN

and by Routledge
605 Third Avenue, New York, NY 10158

Routledge is an imprint of the Taylor & Francis Group, an informa business

© 2021 John Damm Scheuer

British Library Cataloguing-in-Publication Data
A catalogue record for this book is available from the British Library

Library of Congress Cataloging-in-Publication Data
A catalog record has been requested for this book

ISBN: 9781138354807 (hbk)
ISBN: 9781032038117 (pbk)
ISBN: 9780429424540 (ebk)

Typeset in Bembo
by codeMantra

Contents

Figures

Tables

Preface

It took a few years to write this book. As when an artist looks at a piece of wood and discovers what kind of figure or statue may be in there, the ideas that were assembled in this book developed gradually. At first randomly and with no direction. Later more guided as my own ideas about translation processes matured and developed based on encounters with other researchers' work. I stand on the shoulders of giants like Michel Callon, Bruno Latour, Barbara Czarniawska, Francois Cooren, Kjell Arne Røvik and others who have contributed with valuable insights into how translation processes unfold in organizations. I thank them for their contributions and insights which have been very valuable to me and inspired my own research interests and work! I hope that my book will give something back to the small but also growing community of researchers interested in researching, theorizing and modeling translation processes in organizations. That it will also inspire practitioners to start thinking differently about change in their organizations! Writing a book like this is time consuming. When you write, it helps to be in nice surroundings. I will therefore send my warm thanks to the institutions that took me in and took good care of me while writing different parts of the book: Klitgaarden Refugium in Skagen, the Monastery of San Cataldo in northern Italy, the Quarry Refugium in Nexø, Bornholm. My good colleagues in the Department of Social Science and Business at Roskilde University continue to provide a warm and inspiring context within which research ideas may be cross-fertilized and grow. Just as my collaboration with the IT researchers Jesper Simonsen and Morten Hertzum has been very inspiring. As a bit of a nerd in translation studies, it is also always a pleasure to meet up with another nerd sharing your research interest. And my good friends Søren Obed Madsen and Niels Christian Nickelsen have always been up to the task! Also my family (my wife Anette and my daughters Rikke and Line) should receive my warm thanks for their patience with me during the long periods of time when I was away or busy in my office writing this book! Also the Region of Sealand should receive my thanks for their funding of IT research that ended up inspiring parts of the book. Finally, I would like to thank the editors from Routledge, Guy Loft and Alexandra Atkinson, for their patience with me and confidence in the relevance of this book project! And I will thank project manager Aswini Kumar from Codemantra for the help with setting up and preparing the book manuscript.

John Damm Scheuer
Department of Social Science and Business
Roskilde University
December 2020

Part 1

Introduction

1   Introduction

In school you may have played the game where children are sitting in a circle and one child tells a story at one end of the circle. Each child then has to whisper the story to the child sitting next to it until the story reaches the child sitting at the end of the circle. What always happens when the stories of the first child and the last child in the circle are compared is that it turns out that the story has changed. The reason is that the story was translated by each child as it moved through the circle. In organizations, innovative ideas and other tokens move (and are changed) in a similar way; strategy and leadership ideas move in order to be 'implemented'; policy ideas move in order to realize democratic policy decisions; ideas about concepts such as 'LEAN', 'TQM' and 'BPR' are introduced to improve organizational processes and knowledge about treatments in healthcare move, and they are supposed to make doctors change their behaviors just as innovative ideas from universities move out into industry in order to be turned into new forms of products and services. In all these situations, abstract ideas are moved and translated in order to achieve certain 'wished-for' aims. And in all these situations, what happens with the idea is in the hands of the next person translating it who may decide to let the token drop, modify it, betray it, add to it or appropriate it (Latour, 1986). Now, if change ideas and other tokens in organizations are translated rather than 'implemented', a profound understanding of such translation processes is needed. This book sums up and further develops the research conducted in translation studies of change in organizations and shows the implications of these findings for managing innovation and change. The book is thus relevant for researchers, PhD and other students, and practitioners including change agents, general managers, public servants as well as strategic managers and policy decision-makers.

In management and organization studies, it has become widely accepted that tokens – for instance, knowledge in the form of new ideas, practices, scientific developments and technologies – are not stable. Rather, studies have shown that knowledge both changes and retains characteristics when it is translated. Knowledge is thus blended, modified, adapted or reinvented as it defuses, flows or moves between individual human actors or groups of humans (Spyridonidis, Currie, Heusinkveld, Strauss, & Sturdy, 2016, p. 2).

Translation studies have moreover been characterized by different theories, which have created confusion and some ambiguity about the meaning and content of the concept of translation as well as of the nature of the translation process (Spyridonidis et al., 2016). If a researcher thus tries to review the literature in organizational translation studies, he/she will easily be confused. Several organizational researchers theorize, model and analyze organizational change processes as translation. However, many of them define the concept of translation and theorize or model the translation process differently. The similarities and differences between them have until recently not been very clear. Just as the key research questions and knowledge gabs in organizational translation studies have not been specified to a sufficient degree (O'Mahoney; 2016; Wæraas and Nielsen, 2016).

In 2016 a special issue in the *International Journal of Management Review* provided the first updated overview over different perspectives in organizational translation studies, summed up research conducted until now and identified areas where further research was needed (*Journal of International Management Reviews*, Vol. 18, Iss. 3, July 2016). Two reviews of the organizational translation literature were made: One by Wæraas and Nielsen (2016), and the other by O'Mahoney (2016). The insights derived from these reviews are summed up in Appendices 1 and 2. This book builds on this research, and its overall aim is to further develop the research by:

- Summing up former research in organizational change and innovation as translation processes
- Identifying gabs in former research and further research needed
- Exploring and demonstrating insights and use of the translation perspective in different areas of application
- Further developing translation studies by exploring its origins and developing new ways of theorizing translation processes in relation to organizational change and innovation
- Showing the implications of these findings for managing organizational innovation and change

In order to realize these aims, the book is divided into 24 chapters which are organized in four parts. In Part 1 'Introduction', the aims of and the background for the book, and research questions addressed as well as the methods used to perform the books literature review are presented. In Part 2 'Moving ideas – theories and models', diffusion theory and the most important theories about organizational translation are presented. Here, diffusion theory is included because translation theory and models partly developed as a critique of diffusion theory. In Part 3 'Translation in the meeting between idea and practice', a number of basic assumptions about how tokens (including ideas) materialize (Czarniawska & Joerges, 1996) in organizations are developed on the basis of former research, and a new model of translation is developed – the idea-practice-translation model. Finally, in Part 4 the consequences of the translation perspective for researchers and practitioners are discussed. To make researchers more aware of the consequences of the different philosophies of the social sciences on which different theories and models of organizational translation are built, four modes of researching organizational translation processes are identified: The science mode, the humanities mode, the actualist mode and the design mode. Moreover, the different ways these different modes produce 'truth statements' (Foucault, 1978) about the translation process, its outcomes and what may make the translation process 'work better' are identified and discussed. In chapter 24 about the practical consequences of the translation perspective, it is pointed out that practitioners' translation of tokens is influenced by many things, that translators need to do many different types of work in order to succeed with a translation, and that tokens change and have uncertain effects as they are translated just as other practically relevant insights are communicated.

The research questions the book is contributing to answer are the following:

1   What different theories of organizational translation exist?
2   How do they define, theorize and/or model the translation process?
3   What are the key focus points, research themes and key research questions of organizational translation theories/models across theories and models?
4   What influences translation processes according to these theories/ models?
5   To what degree are the theories and/or models different or similar in their views on translation processes?
6   How may translation and the materialization (Czarniawska and Joerges, 1996) of tokens (including ideas) be theorized and modeled in more detail?
7   What modes of doing social science do the different theories and models of translation build on?
8   How does these modes influence the way researchers produce 'truth statements' (Foucault, 1978) about the translation process and its outcomes, and what may make the translation process 'work better'?
9   What are the practical consequences of a translation perspective on the movement of tokens?

Research questions 1–5 are answered in Part 2 of the book. Research question 6 is answered in Part 3. Finally, questions 7, 8 and 9 are answered in Part 4.

The book's unique contribution to organizational translation studies is that it, for the first time, identifies what are the main theories and models of organizational translation in organization studies and then presents each of these theories in detail as well as compare them. No other publications have done this before even though a few reviews of some of the main research streams in organizational translation studies exist (O'Mahoney, 2016; Scheuer, 2006; Wedlin and Sahlin, 2017; Wæraas and Nielsen, 2016). Another unique contribution of the book is to identify for the first time what are the key focus points, research themes, key research questions, and knowledge gabs of organizational translation theories and models across different theories and models. In addition, the book identifies how the translation process influences the movement of tokens (including ideas) in and between organizations according to these theories and models. Finally, the book identifies some of the consequences that the different translation theories/model's philosophies of the social sciences have for researchers in organizational translation studies and points out some consequences for practitioners adopting a translation perspective on management and change in organizations.

Even though this book does not explore this issue, it contributes by giving other researchers a basis for further discussions: To what degree the different translation perspectives may cross-fertilize each other and/or be combined (Spyridonidis et al., 2016; Wæraas & Nielsen, 2016). This by presenting the most important and different theories in this area of research in detail. Readers interested in how different translation perspectives may cross-fertilize each other and/or be combined may read my presentation of Wæraas and Nielsen's (2016) literature review that focuses upon this theme in Appendix 1. Finally, the book contributes to translation studies by theorizing and modeling in more detail how ideas materialize (Czarniawska & Joerges, 1996) in organizations. Based on an analysis of former research, a number of assumptions about the materialization of tokens (ideas, practices, etc.) in organizations are developed and drawn together in the 'idea-practice-translation model'.

Wæraas and Nielsen (2016) noticed a lack of cross-references between the three perspectives (the actor-network, the knowledge-based and the Scandinavian institutionalist) of translation they identified in their literature review. And they noticed that there were ontological differences between the perspectives. They pointed out that these issues might suggest that the approaches they analyzed focused on three different phenomena, or were separate or incompatible research traditions altogether. The authors however concluded that they did not believe that this was the case. They instead suggested that the perspectives focused on different aspects of translation processes, and did so with different emphasis and terminology. The authors thus viewed the perspectives as complementary and as trying to say something about the same phenomenon: How an object changes from one state to another within and across organizational settings. This book (and its author) agrees with and builds on this view. Just as the supplementary literature review and study conducted when writing this book have turned out to support this view. Also note that the number of different perspectives on translation in organization studies have increased from 3 in Wæraas and Nielsen's review to 13 in this book (diffusion theory and the 'idea-practice-translation model' excluded). When analyzed in detail, these theories and models translate the concept of translation differently. Some of the theories and models however share common basic assumptions and philosophies of the social sciences.

The methods used when conducting the literature review

In order to be included in Part 2 of the book, a text needed to (1) study the movement of tokens (ideas, knowledge or other tokens) in one or more organizations, and (2) use the concept of translation as a main concept when trying to understand, theorize or model how the movement of the token took place. This meant that the vast research literature related to the translation of texts (for instance books, technical texts, etc.) from one language to another that did not deal explicitly with the movement of and translation of tokens in and/or between organizations was excluded. Theories and models of organizational translation that were included in the study (and thus Part 2 of the book) were selected based on the following criteria:

• The degree to which the theory/model was cited by other researchers
• The degree to which the theory/model was different from other researchers' ways of theorizing or model translation in organizations

This in order to identify the most important as well as the different ways organizational translation has been theorized and modeled in organizational translation studies. Therefore, some of the theories and models that have been included in Part 2 are highly cited and recognized as main theories/models in organizational translation studies. While other theories/models have not received the same level of attention from other researchers but have original other ways to theorize and model translation processes that may also inform researchers as well as practitioners interested in this area of study.

The selection criteria mentioned above meant that the research evidence supporting (or not supporting) each of the theories and models of organizational translation that were selected and included in Part 2 has not been looked into. This is a limitation of the research that has been conducted. But performing such a study represented a research task that was beyond the scope of this book because of the huge amount of empirical research that has been produced using a translation view on the movement of tokens in organizations. The book however contributes by providing a platform for and an outset from which such research may be performed by other researchers in the future within the limits of each of their preferred modes and philosophies of the social sciences (see Chapter 23).

The research to the book started out from existing reviews of the research literature in organizational translation studies, including reviews by Scheuer (2006), Wedlin and Sahlin (2017), Wæraas and Nielsen (2016) and O'Mahoney (2016). These reviews were supplemented with an additional literature review conducted especially to support the research conducted when writing this book. In this literature review, the most cited theories and models in different areas of organizational translation studies were identified as well as theories/models that represented different definitions and understandings of translation and the translation process. Organizational translation studies conducted in the following areas of research were identified and analyzed in the literature review: Organization studies generally, actor-network theory, Scandinavian institutionalism, symbolic interactionist studies, linguistic studies, policy translation, strategy translation and studies of translation in relation to innovation.

By inserting data from the queries in these areas in Web of Science into the CitNetExplorer software, a visual map showing which authors and theories/models were cited the most by other researchers in each query was produced. Another output from inserting the data into CitNetExplorer was a list that described which authors (and thus theories/models) were cited most in each query. The visual maps and lists were then used to identify the authors, theories and models that most other researchers referred back to and cited in each of the above-mentioned research areas. And they were used to find research contributions that represented different ways to theorize and model translation in organizations. This was done by looking through the titles and abstracts of articles that the visual maps and lists of research articles produced by the CitNetExplorer software in each area suggested may live up to the selection criteria described above. How this process was handled technically is described in detail in Appendix 3. Before being selected to be included in Part 2 of the book, the different theories and models identified through this process were compared with authors, theories and models that earlier reviews (O'Mahoney, 2016; Scheuer, 2006; Wedlin and Sahlin, 2017; Wæraas and Nielsen, 2016) had identified as important and belonging to the area of organizational translation studies.

Finally, it should be noticed that Everett Rogers (2003) theory about the diffusion of innovations was included in Part 2 even though it is not based on a translation view on how ideas move in and between organizations. The reason is that the translation perspectives on the movement of tokens in organizations partly originated from Latour's (1986) critique of the diffusion perspective. Moreover, Everett Rogers theory about diffusion of innovations includes elements that may very well be relevant for translation researchers to explore in the future. For instance, whether characteristics of receivers of tokens (ideas) – such as whether they are innovators, are early adopters, belong to the early or late majority, or are laggards (Rogers, 2003, pp. 279–285) – influence the translation process? What is the role of opinion leaders in translation processes? Or whether factors that Rogers believes are important for the adoption rate of innovations may also influence translation of tokens in and between organizations; perceived attributes of the token (innovation) such as its relative advantage, compatibility, complexity, trialability and observability, the type of decision process used to introduce the token, the communication channels used to communicate knowledge about the token, the norms and values of the social systems involved and change agents' efforts to promote the token.

References

Czarniawska, B., and Joerges, B. (1996). Travels of ideas. In B. Czarniawska and G. Sevon (Eds.), *Translating organizational change* (pp. 13–48). Berlin: de Gruyter.

Foucault, M. (1978). Politics and the study of discourse. *Ideology and Consciousness, 3*, 7–26.

Latour, B. (1986). The powers of association. In J. Law (Ed.), *Power, action and belief – A new sociology of knowledge?* London: Routledge & Kegan Paul.

O'Mahoney, J. (2016). Archetypes of translation: Recommendations for dialogue. *International Journal of Management Reviews, 18*(3), 333–350.

Rogers, E. (2003) *Diffusion of innovations* (5th ed.). New York, NY: Free Press.

Scheuer, J. D. (2006). About the translation of the concept of translation-An analysis of the Scandinavian neo-institutionalists translation of the concept of translation. *Nordic Organization Studies, 8*(4), 5–41.

Spyridonidis, D., Currie, G., Heusinkveld, S., Strauss, K., & Sturdy, A. (2016). The translation of management knowledge: Challenges, contributions and new directions. *International Journal of Management Reviews, 18*, 231–235.

Wedlin, L., & Sahlin, K. (2017). The imitation and translation of management ideas. In R. Greenwood, C. Oliver, & B. Thomas (Eds.), *The SAGE handbook of organizational institutionalism*. London: Sage Publications Ltd.

Wæraas, A., & Nielsen, J. A. (2016). Translation theory 'translated': Three perspectives on translation in organizational research. *International Journal of Management Reviews, 18*(3), 236–270.

Part 2

Moving ideas – theories and models

2 Introduction to Part 2

Table 2.1 gives an overview of all theories and models of translation in organizations that have been included in this book – including the 'idea-practice-translation model' that is developed in Part 3 of the book. The latter model will be developed and presented in Part 3 of the book. This chapter will present the theories and models of translation in organizations that are either highly cited by researchers in organizational translation studies or represent different ways of theorizing and modeling translation in organizations. Part 2 ends with a chapter (Chapter 18) that identifies focus points, research themes, research questions and knowledge gabs across theories and models of translation in organizations. The aim of the chapter is to answer research questions 1–5 presented in the introduction. The theory of the diffusion of innovations will not be included in this discussion because it is not a translation perspective on the movement of ideas in organizations.

Table 2.1 Theories and models of diffusion and translation

	Diffusion	ANT	The idea model	Symbolic interactionist models
Token that is moved	New ideas	Different tokens	Management ideas	Knowledge
How does the token move?	1 An innovation is 2 Communicated through certain channels 3 Over time 4 Among members of a social system	The token is associated with human and non-human elements that form actor-network that performs it	1 Idea is translated into an 2 Object then 3 Action and if repeated into 4 An institution	Translation and coordination through construction of meanings in and between groups facilitated by boundary spanning and boundary objects
Factors influencing the translation (or diffusion) process	1 Attributes of innovation 2 Type of innovation decision 3 Communication channels 4 Social system 5 Change agents' efforts 6 Characteristics of adopters (laggards or innovators?)	Are identified empirically by: a Following the actor b Following the controversy	What human actors attend to before and during the translation process	The meanings constructed by groups of people belonging to different social and cultural worlds Transfer, translation and negotiation of meanings across boundaries Boundary objects
Key actors	Opinion leaders Change agents Adopters	Humans Non-humans Translators	Humans Objects Translators	Humans Groups Translators
Measure of outcome	Desirable/undesirable Direct/indirect Anticipated/unanticipated	Outcome= The effect of related actants' work	Degree of institutionalization (repetition of typified actions over time)	Knowledge translated in a way that is meaningful to involved groups
Key concepts	Diffusion, adoption	Actant, actor-network, translation	Idea, translation, dis- and re-embedding, fashion	Boundary spanning and boundary objects, meaning, transfer, translation and negotiation
Philosophy of the social sciences	Scientific	Actualist	Humanistic	Humanistic

	The theory of action nets	*Strategy translation*
Token that is moved	Ideas	Strategy texts (from text to text, from text to talk, from talk to text and from talk to talk)
How does the token move?	1 Ideas are translated into an 2 Object then 3 Action and if repeated into 4 An institution: Typified actions repeated over time 5 That are or may then become part of an action-net Action-nets consist of all interconnected actions that perform the organization (investing, buying, selling, producing, transporting, etc.) Constructing action-nets involves translation work: Translating from ideas to narrative forms that makes sense; managing texts by translating, editing and inscribing them; budgeting; constructing machines; writing institutionalized codes; creating norms; etc.	When translators do (or do not): a Communicate the meaning of the text b Translate it in a way that makes the text work as intended and assure that it c Is understood in another culture while still d Reflecting the interests and ideology of the translator
Factors influencing the translation process	When people's local frames of reference and ideas in residence clash and cause friction with travelling ideas that they encounter	The translators' degree of loyalty to: – The content – The intention – The context – The ideology and/or interests of the strategy text
Key actors	Ideas about organizing/new actions needed People with local frames of references and ideas Translators	Strategy text(s) Translators
Measure of outcome	Products and services, social order, formal organization, informal networks, macro-actors, etc. appear	The degree to which a strategy text is translated as intended
Key concepts	Action-net Translation	Language related, functional, cultural and ideological ways of translating texts
Philosophy of the social sciences	Humanistic	Humanistic

(Continued)

	Policy translation	Instrumental theory of translation
Token that is moved	Policy ideas	Knowledge about ideas and practices
How does the token move?	Through a semiotic communication process where: 1 Policy ideas are communicated to 2 Receivers who may continuously interpret, re-interpret and construct the ideas and act in many different ways depending on their local context 3 And where the 'power of the idea' depends on the number of people acting on behalf of it	First the knowledge is: 1 De-contextualized and given an abstract representation (an image, words/texts, etc.) in a source context. Then it is 2 Contextualized by being turned into materialized practices in a recipient context
Factors influencing the translation process	The collaborative multi-actor co-construction of policy through actors: – Ascribing meaning to ideas – Reflexive learning – Interaction, competition bargaining and negotiation	1 Characteristics of the source (including its translatability) 2 The transformability of the knowledge construct 3 The degree of similarity and difference between recipient and source context 4 Translators competences 5 Translation rules (should idea be reproduced, modified or altered?)
Key actors	Policy makers Actors/translators receiving and acting on policy ideas	The knowledge construct The translator(s)
Measure of outcome	Policy ideas are translated in a way that actors/ translators find meaningful	Whether idea/practice is translated in a way that achieve organizational ends
Key concepts	Interactive, collaborative policy-making Translation	The idea/practice/knowledge construct, source and receiving context, translator and his/her competences, rules
Philosophy of the social sciences	Humanistic	Humanistic

(Continued)

	Knowledge translation in healthcare	The linguistic model of translation
Token that is moved	Knowledge aimed at improving health services	Knowledge
How does the token move?	Through interplay between a and b: a Knowledge creation cycle consisting of knowledge: – Inquiry – Synthesis – Tools/products (tailored) b Action cycle: – Identify problem – Adapt knowledge to local context – Assess barriers to knowledge use – Select, tailor, implement interventions – Monitor knowledge use – Evaluate outcomes – Sustain knowledge use	Translators translate knowledge from a source context/social network to receivers in another social network (from one cross-cultural team to another). Translation: – Is a sensemaking activity – Is subject to personal cognition and interlingual transfer of knowledge into social networks – Is subject to constraints
Factors influencing the translation process	a Barriers related to knowledge creation cycle: Volume of and access to research, lack of time and skills to read and appraise evidence b Barriers related to action cycle: May be structural, organizational, related to peer group, professional, patient-related, etc.	– Degree of translators' understanding of and the uncertainty and ambiguity of the source knowledge – Translators' language related errors and lack of equivalent words and concepts when translating – His/her ability to make tacit knowledge explicit, combine new and local explicit knowledge and to internalize and make new knowledge tacit again. – The translatability and convertibility of the knowledge – Whether the idea is generally, sufficiently, mostly or fully conveyed to the receivers
Key actors	Researchers/doctors producing 'evidence' Users/doctors using the evidence	The translator The cultural group from which the knowledge originates and the cultural group which receives it
Measure of outcome	Health services delivered are in accordance with evidence-based knowledge	The successful translation of knowledge from one domain/language group to another
Key concepts	Knowledge creation and action cycles Knowledge translation	Ambiguity of source, interference, lack of equivalence, socialization, externalization, combination and internalization, translating/converting knowledge
Philosophy of the social sciences	Scientific	Humanistic

(Continued)

	Translation through design	The middle manager as translator
Token that is moved How does the token move?	Knowledge Through design as a translation mechanism in open innovation processes where: a Design is tied to problems of interpretation and translation of varying stakeholder, user and expert perspectives that b Unfold as a complex process riddled with negotiations d Where the designer acts as intermediary between disparate ideas, viewpoints and goals and translate and integrate many things and where e Design artifacts are used to ease communication	Ideas (knowledge, practices, strategies, rules and technologies) Middle managers translate ideas through different micro-practices: 1 Idea acquisition 2 Appropriation of translation role 3 Legitimation of role 4 Enrollment of actors in networks 5 Idea variation 6 Alignment of actors 7 Idea stabilization
Factors influencing the translation process	The ideas, viewpoints and goals of stakeholders including users and experts The ability of the designer to use design artifacts and to translate, integrate, mediate and negotiate with stakeholders	Contingencies related to each of the seven phases Inability of middle managers to move forward through or from one or more phases
Key actors	Stakeholders participating in open innovation The designer who translates Design artifacts	The middle manager
Measure of outcome	Innovative design outputs that combine and integrate the ideas, knowledge and competencies of the different stakeholders and solve the problem at hand	Middle manager succeeds (or does not) with identifying relevant ideas, gets the task of translating it/them as well as succeeds with enrolling and aligning actors so that the idea may be stabilized as a new shared pattern of action and interaction (a routinized practice)
Key concepts	Open innovation Design as a translation mechanism	Micro-practices Translation
Philosophy of the social sciences	Design	Humanistic

(Continued)

	The consultant as translator	*The knowledge translation value chain*
Token that is moved	Ideas that produce noise, and disturbs and disrupts order	Knowledge
How does the token move?	Through consultants' use of language he/she translates and introduces ideas that introduce noise, and disturb and disrupt order in both the senders' and the receivers' language systems. The translation at the same time both creates new links that did not exist before and modifies the two agents: It comprises what exists and what is created. It creates a 'third' type of language through that process.	Research-based knowledge is: 1 Developed and reported in research journals and books 2 Translated through theory-to-practice experiments, where its meanings and suggested strategies for engaging with practice are reported in practitioner-oriented journals 3 Resulting in translation and engagement with users and 4 Further translation through production and distribution of texts and evidence designed to engage a greater number of users (info about savings achieved, reports, becoming part of curriculum at universities, etc.) 5 Leading to widespread dissemination, translation and involvement of user groups through sector reports aimed at whole industry and groups of stakeholders and use of journalists 6 And finally translation through production of usable outputs like teaching materials, textbooks tools, web publications and software Researchers' ability to participate in interactive knowledge translation processes with relevant stakeholders and to produce boundary objects that may then later be translated and turned into other forms of knowledge and outputs by other translators along the knowledge–translation value chain
Factors influencing the translation process	The language system (game) that is introduced	The researcher
Key actors	Senders and receivers The consultant as translator	Potential users of the research
Measure of outcome	That the language-based order in senders and receivers is disrupted and changed	That research-based knowledge is translated and used in practice
Key concepts	Language Noise, disruption Translation	The knowledge-translation value chain
Philosophy of the social sciences	Humanistic	Humanistic

(Continued)

The idea-practice-translation model

Token that is moved	Ideas
How does the token move?	Translation through:
	• Ventriloquizing and learning from actants
	• Use of symbolic and socio-material tools
	• Designing relations and interactions of humans, objects and contexts
	• Handling relational inertia
	Resulting in an assembly including a narrative about it
Factors influencing the translation process	Communication: The body-internal and external humans and non-humans that the translator(s) mobilize and make speak. And the body-internal and external humans and non-humans that mobilize and makes the translator(s) speak
Key actors	The translator
	Humans
	Non-humans
Measure of outcome	Aim of socio-technical design effort is accomplished
Key concepts	Translation, assembly, ventriloquism, design, learning and relational inertia
Philosophy of the social sciences	Design

3   Diffusion of innovations

According to Everett Rogers' (2003) communication, diffusion and social change are closely related. He suggests that diffusion is a special type of communication, in which the messages are concerned with a new idea. In addition, it is the newness of the idea in the message content of communication that gives diffusion its special character. The newness means that some degree of uncertainty is involved (Rogers, 2003, p. 6). He suggests that diffusion is a kind of social change – defined as the process by which alteration occurs in the structure and function of a social system (Rogers, 2003, p. 6). He claims that social systems are going through a gradual learning process regarding an innovation, as the aggregated experience of the individuals with a new idea builds up and is shared among them through interpersonal networks.

Communication is the core process in Everett Rogers theory about the diffusion of innovations. He defines communication as 'a process in which participants create and share information with one another in order to reach a mutual understanding' (Rogers, 2003, p. 5). Everett Rogers (2003, p. 11) now defines diffusion as the process by which:

1   An innovation
2   Is communicated through certain channels
3   Over time
4   Among the members of a social system.

In the following sections, these elements of the innovation diffusion process will be analyzed in further detail. The innovations communicated through certain channels among the members of social system are the independent variables that influence the dependent variable – the time individuals or other adoption units use to adopt an innovation. Therefore, points 1, 2 and 4 will be presented before the third element – time below.

The Innovation

An innovation is understood as 'an idea, practice, or object that is perceived as new by an individual or other unit of adoption' (Rogers, 2003, p. 11).

According to Everett Rogers, an innovation will always result in a feeling of uncertainty among the receivers of the innovation. In order to reduce this uncertainty, the adoption unit/the individual will try to reduce the uncertainty related to the advantages and disadvantages of the innovation. It is assumed that a decision about adoption or rejection will not be taken before the feeling of uncertainty has been reduced to an acceptable level. The adoption rate and thus the speed with which the innovation is adopted will be affected by how the adoption unit perceives the innovation. The adoption unit/individual will especially evaluate these characteristics of the innovation in that connection (Rogers, 2003, pp. 15–16):

1   The relative advantage of the innovation/idea compared to former ideas or alternatives
2   The degree to which an innovation is perceived as being consistent with the existing values, past experiences and needs of potential adopters
3   The complexity of the idea and thus the degree to which an innovation is perceived as difficult to understand and use
4   Trialability is the degree to which an innovation may be experienced and tried out on a limited basis
5   Observability is the degree to which the results of using an innovation are visible to others

Everett Rogers assumes that the adoption unit or an individual may also reinvent the innovation. With the concept of reinvention, he understands 'the degree to which an innovation is changed or modified by a user in the process of its adoption and implementation' (Rogers, 2003, p. 17).

Communication channels

Communication of an innovation takes place through certain channels. They connect a sender of an innovation with its receivers. A communication channel is defined as 'the means by which a message gets from one individual to another' (Rogers, 2003, p. 18). Everett Rogers distinguishes between mass media and interpersonal communication channels. Mass media channels are 'all those means of transmitting messages that involve a mass medium, such as a radio, television, newspapers, and so on, which enable a source of one or a few individuals to reach an audience of many' (Rogers, 2003, p. 18). Interpersonal channels 'involve a face to face exchange between two or more individuals' (Rogers, 2003, p. 18). Mass media and interpersonal channels can be local and thus within the social system or Cosmopolitical and thus found outside the social system. Whether people are alike or different in terms of beliefs, education and socio-economic status (homophily) is suggested to influence the degree to which they communicate and transfer innovative ideas (Rogers, 2003, p. 19).

The social system

Everett Rogers defines a social system as 'a set of interrelated units that are engaged in joint problem solving to accomplish a common goal' (Rogers, 2003, p. 23). The members or units of a social system may be individuals, informal groups, organizations and/or subsystems. According to Everett Rogers, there are certain characteristics of social systems that influence the diffusion of an innovation (Rogers, 2003, pp. 23–31). These include:

- The social structure
- Opinion leaders and change agents
- Norms and values
- The type of innovation decision used and
- The consequences of an innovation

Everett Rogers distinguishes between a formal and informal structure of a social system and relates the latter to the social system's communication structure. The communication structure is defined as the differentiated elements that can be recognized in the patterned communication flows in a system (Rogers, 2003, p. 24). The social structure of social systems may both hinder and facilitate the diffusion of an innovation. Social systems whose members are closely connected through communication networks are characterized by faster diffusion and adoption of innovations. A communication network consists of interconnected individuals who are linked by patterned flows of information (Rogers, 2003, p. 27). In such a network, the communication is more effective when sender and receiver are alike and share the same kinds of meaning structures, beliefs and types of language. Concerning adoption or rejection of an innovation, Everett Rogers emphasizes the following: 'In deciding whether or not to adopt an innovation, we all depend mainly on the communicated experience of others much like ourselves who have already adopted. These subjective evaluations of an innovation mainly flow through interpersonal networks' (Rogers, 2003, p. 293).

Rogers now suggests that opinion leaders play an especially important role in the diffusion of innovations. Opinion leadership is defined as 'the degree to which an individual is able informally to influence other individuals' attitudes or overt behavior in a desired way with relative frequency' (Rogers, 2003, p. 27). Rogers theorizes the communication of innovations as a two-step process where information about the innovation first reaches the opinion leaders who then inform, communicate with, and influence other persons in their communication network.

A change agent is an individual who influences clients' innovation decision in a direction deemed desirable by a change agency (Rogers, 2003, p. 27). Change agents are experts who are brought in from outside the social system. They often collaborate with opinion leaders. They create a need for change by combining the clients' problems and needs with new solutions to the problem, make a more precise diagnosis of the client's problem and translate it into action. They contribute to the adoption of the innovation and try to prevent its rejection.

Values and norms also influence the diffusion of an innovation. Values are the criteria employed in selecting the goals of behavior (Scott, 1991, p. 16). Norms are the established behavior patterns for the members of a social system (Rogers, 2003, p. 26). An innovation that is not in accordance with the norms and values of a social system will not be adopted as fast as if the opposite was the case. Adoption sometimes depends on a previous adoption of a new value system.

The diffusion of an innovation is also influence by the type of innovation decision that is used. Everett Rogers distinguishes between three types of innovation decisions: Optional decisions where the individual can choose to adopt or reject an innovation him/herself. Collective decisions are based on consensus between the members of a social system and authority decisions where the decision is made by relatively few individuals in the social system who have power, status or technical expertise (Rogers, 2003, pp. 28–29). Contingent decisions are based on a combination of these types of decisions.

Finally, Rogers suggests that the consequences of an innovation will influence its diffusion. Consequences are defined as the changes that occur to an individual or to a social system because of the adoption or rejection of an innovation (Rogers, 2003, p. 31). He distinguishes between three types of consequences: (1) desirable versus undesirable consequences, (2) direct versus indirect consequences and (3) anticipated versus unanticipated consequences. The change agent will usually introduce an innovation that has consequences that are perceived as having desirable, direct and anticipated consequences for the client or social system. The problem with innovations is however that they sometimes have unanticipated, indirect and undesirable consequences. The consequences of the innovation will therefore influence its diffusion.

Time

The diffusion of innovations takes time. According to Everett Rogers, this may be explained in at least three ways:

1   The innovation-decision process takes time
2   An adoption unit/an individual may be more or less innovative and therefore slow or fast to adopt
3   The adoption rate may vary from one social system to another

The innovation-decision process

An innovation-decision process is defined as the process through which an individual (or other decision-making unit) passes from first knowledge of an innovation, to forming an attitude toward the innovation, to a decision to adopt or reject, to implementation of the new idea and to confirmation of this decision (Rogers, 2003, p. 20). Rogers assumes that news about the innovation reaches the individual or adoption unit through mass media or interpersonal communication channels. When it does the individual or adoption unit is assumed to go through five phases (Rogers, 2003, pp. 20–22):

1 Knowledge where an individual/adoption unit becomes aware of and acquires knowledge about the innovation and possible need for change
2 Persuasion where an opinion leader, a change agent or the individual or decision unit itself evaluates the innovation and is or is not persuaded
3 Decision where the decision unit decides to adopt or reject the innovation
4 Implementation where the adoption unit carries out or implements the decision and
5 Confirmation where the adoption unit confirms or rejects the decision

Characteristics of adopters

Concerning the individual person or adoption unit, Everett Roger divides them into five ideal typical categories depending on how innovative they are compared to a statistical standard distribution of adopters. What is focused upon is the degree to which an individual or unit of adoption is relatively earlier in adopting new ideas than other members of a social system (see Rogers, 2003, pp. 279–285).

Innovators are defined as the first 2.5% who adopt an innovation. They are characterized by being venturesome, able to understand and apply complex technical knowledge, and willing to take risks and handle uncertainty. Early adopters are the next 13.5% who adopt an innovation. They decreases uncertainty about a new idea by adopting it, and then they convey a subjective evaluation of the innovation to near peers through interpersonal networks. They are respected individuals who often play the role as opinion leaders and missionaries for the innovation in their local social systems. The early majority is defined as the next 34% who adopt an innovation. The early majority typically seek advice from opinion leaders among the early adopters. They provide interconnectedness in the social systems interpersonal networks and are not the first to try out a new idea nor the last to lay the old aside. The late majority is defined as the next 34% who adopt an innovation. They are characterized by being skeptical toward innovations. Most of the uncertainty about a new idea will have to be removed before the late majority feel that it is safe to adopt the innovation. The pressure of peers is necessary to motivate adoption. Laggards are defined as the last 16% who adopt an innovation. They hold a traditional view where the point of reference is the past and they are therefore suspicious toward innovations and change agents. They exercise no opinion leadership, but they are local in their outlook and relatively isolated in their social systems.

The adoption rate of social systems

Everett Rogers now brings together all the above-mentioned elements in a model that explains the adoption rate of social systems and thus 'the relative speed with which an innovation is adopted by members of a social system' (Rogers, 2003, p. 23). The adoption rate model (see Rogers, 2003, pp. 221–223) describes these relationships.

The first factor that influences the members of a social system when they decide whether to adopt an innovation or not is the perceived attributes of the innovation. It is thus important how they perceive the relative advantage, compatibility, complexity, trialability and observability of the idea. The specific content of these categories was explained above.

Another factor that influences the adoption rate of the social system is the type of innovation-decision process used when introducing the innovation. Here, Everett Rogers distinguishes between three types of innovation decisions: Optional decisions where the individual can choose to adopt or reject an innovation him/herself, collective decisions that are based on consensus between the members of a social system, and authority decisions where relatively few individuals who have power, status or technical expertise make the decision in the social system.

Moreover, the communication channels that are used to communicate the innovative idea influence the adoption rate. Everett Rogers distinguishes between mass media and interpersonal communication channels. He suggests that mast media channels are good at communicating knowledge about an innovation, while interpersonal channels are more effective in the persuasion phase. This is however not always the case. Thus, the more complex an innovation is the more effective interpersonal communication channels are to diffuse it.

The characteristics of the social system that affects the adoption rate are the norms and values as well as the communication structure of the social system. Here, it is important whether the norms and values of the social system are in accordance with or are in conflict with the innovation. The general attitude toward change among members of the social system may also be important. Furthermore, the degree of homogeneity or heterogeneity among persons in the social network in relation to values, norms, attitudes, education and social status is important.

Everett Rogers suggests that the degree of connectedness of the communication structure is positively related to the adoption rate. Finally, opinion leaders may affect the adoption rate since they can activate a positive or negative attitude toward the innovation. The last variable that may determine the rate of adoption is the extent of change agents' promotion efforts. These efforts include (Rogers, 2003, pp. 369–370):

1   Developing a need for change
2   Establishing an information exchange relationship

3   Diagnosing problems
4   Creating an intent to change in the client
5   Translating an intent into action
6   Stabilizing adoption and prevent discontinuance
7   Achieving a terminal relationship where the client is able to maintain the change himself/herself/themselves

References

Rogers, E. (2003). *Diffusion of innovations* (5th ed.). New York, NY: Free Press.
Scott, R. W. (1991) *Organisations - rational, natural and open systems.* Englewood Cliffs, NJ: Prentice Hall.

4   Actor–network theory

Actor-network theory (ANT) was developed by researchers in the sociology of scientific knowledge and the social construction of technology in the beginning of the 1980s. David Bloor and Barry Barnes from the Edinburgh school started studying basic research in the natural sciences using a social constructivist perspective. They suggested that all knowledge developed in the natural sciences as well as elsewhere is socially constructed and proposed a principle of symmetry stating that 'all beliefs are on par with one another with respect to the causes of their credibility' (Barnes & Bloor, 1982, p. 23). Thus, regardless of whether a sociologist evaluates a belief about nature or social entities as true or rational, or as false and irrational, he/she must search for the causes of its credibility. To account for the genesis of a belief or knowledge, it is necessary to identify the constraints under which it was formulated as much as the factors which led to their plausibility. It is necessary to ask, not merely why anyone should believe that, but how that belief came to be expressed, articulated or conceptualized in the specific form, which it assumes (McGrath, 1990, p. 101).

ANT was developed as a critique of and an alternative to the social constructivist approach to studying the construction of scientific knowledge by researchers associated with the Centre de Sociologie de L'innovation at Ecoles des Mines de Paris (Michel Callon, Bruno Latour), and a researcher from the University of Keele (John Law) (Callon, 1986; Latour, 1986; Law, 1987). According to these researchers, the Edinburgh sociologists neglected the influence of physical and material entities upon the construction of scientific knowledge. The basic thesis in ANT thus was that knowledge about the reality is not socially constructed, but rather co–constructed by human as well as nonhuman actors. The association of social as well as natural or technical elements was theorized as a part of the construction of scientific as well as other types of knowledge:

> scientists and engineers are bricoleurs. They work by linking bits and pieces together. Heterogeneous bits and pieces. Human and nonhuman.
> (Callon & Law, 1997, p. 168)

This meant that knowledge construction was assumed to be a network-building activity. A scientific as well as any other knowledge claim, idea or token has to be picked up or translated by humans to become powerful. During the process an ever-longer chain of humans and nonhumans are convinced and enrolled into a socio-material network that through its work and 'actions' realizes the knowledge claim, idea or token. As a consequence the construction of scientific knowledge should be studied based on a principle of 'general symmetry' that allows humans as well as nonhumans to be the sources of actions in the co-construction of scientific knowledge.

Thus, instead of studying the social construction of scientific and other types of knowledge, the actor-network researchers suggested that a researcher should focus upon analyzing the network-building activities that construct knowledge about the social as well as the material world:

> our general symmetry principle is thus not to alternate between natural realism and social realism, but to obtain nature and society as twin results of another activity, one that is more interesting to us. We call it network building, or collective things, or quasi-objects, or trials of force.
>
> (Callon & Latour, 1992, p. 348)

The actor-network researchers translated their demand for studies based on general symmetry to a demand for a language or vocabulary that might be used to analyze the construction of knowledge about natural as well as social phenomena in the world. This language and vocabulary was constructed on the basis of concepts adopted from the structuralist semiotician Greimas (Greimas & Courtès, 1982) who contributed with the concept of the 'actant'; Michel Callon and Bruno Latour who inspired by Gabriel Tarde contributed with the concept of the actor-network (Callon & Latour, 1981); and Michel Serres who provided the concept of translation (Serres, 1974).

The result was the development of a theory where the meaning of an entity as a knowledge claim, an action, a technology, an idea, an actor or an organization is assumed to be performed in the specific episodes where the entity is realized. And where to realize is assumed to happen through translation processes, where people as well as things or objects are mobilized, associated and convinced, forced or in other ways influenced to perform the work that is necessary to realize the phenomenon in question. Another outcome was the development of a number of theoretical concepts and a vocabulary that may be used to study how such phenomena were made possible through translation processes and human and nonhuman actors work.

When John Law was once asked to describe ANT, he answered by writing an article showing how different researchers had translated and used ANT differently in each of their studies (see Law, 2008). The point was to show how ANT is constantly being translated and used in different ways by different researchers and that it is therefore a theory 'on the move' rather than a stable entity. It does therefore not make sense to try to present a final or authoritative version of ANT. What does make sense however is to present a description of the basic theoretical ideas, concepts and vocabulary that has been developed by ANT researchers. The following sections will not provide a complete overview of the ideas, concepts and vocabulary that has been developed by ANT researchers but will focus upon those that are necessary to understand how the concept of translation was theorized by them.

The theory of actor-networks

To really understand ANT, it is important to remember that it was originally developed to study the construction of scientific knowledge in a symmetrical way – a way where both humans and nonhumans were assumed to do the work that realized the phenomenon that we call 'scientific knowledge'. Bruno Latour (1996) explains that actor-network researchers achieved that aim by fusing three unrelated strands of preoccupations:

– A semiotic definition of entity building
– A methodological framework to record the heterogeneity of such a building
– An ontological claim on the 'networky' character of actants themselves

He emphasizes that 'the limits of these three unrelated interests are solved when, and only when, they are fused together into an integrated practice of study'. ANT thus took its point of departure in a semiotic understanding of entity building, introduced an ontology based on the idea that entities in the world are actant-networks, and proposed a semiotic and methodological framework and vocabulary that may be used to study and tell stories about how such heterogeneous entities are built. This theory and method (or practice of study) was then later used by ANT and other researchers as a general theory and method to track and describe the symmetrical construction of other 'tokens' and phenomena in the world including in as varied scientific areas as social medicine (Berg, 1997), art studies (Hennion, 1989), political science (Barry, 2001), city planning (Bowler, 1999) and organization studies (Czarniawska & Hernes, 2005; Czarniawska & Sevôn, 1996).

In the following sections, the most important concepts of ANT will be presented.

The actor as an actant

The structuralist semiotician Algirdas Julien Greimas developed the actantial model. The model is a tool that can theoretically be used to analyze any real or thematized action, but particularly those depicted in literary texts or images. In the actantial model, an action may be broken down into six components, called actants: A subject and an object, helpers and opponents, and senders and receivers. Actantial analysis consists of assigning each element of the action being described to one of these actantial classes (Hébert, 2019, p. 49). The actantial model thus suggests that both humans (like princes, princesses and kings) and nonhumans (like magic swords, horses and dragons) may be described as being the source of actions. In a similar way, Bruno Latour defines an actor as an actant:

> An 'actor' in AT is a semiotic definition -an actant, that is, something that acts or to which activity is granted by others. It implies no special motivation of human individual actors, nor of humans in general. An actant can literally be anything provided it is granted to be the source of an action.
>
> (Latour, 1996, p. 7)

Therefore, an actor in ANT is not a human actor in a social network of other human actors. Rather, it is something, human or nonhuman, that may be described as the source of an action in a narrative about how different actors' work constructs and makes phenomena as ideas, scientific knowledge, researchers like Pasteur, organizations, hotel keys and speed-bumps (and many more) powerful and 'real' in the world.

Actor-network

Like the concept of the 'actant', the concept of 'actor-network' is also a semiotic concept (Law, 1992). The aim of the concept is to make it possible for ANT researchers to write up symmetrical narratives about how assemblies or collectives of actors (actants) through their concrete work construct and make entities and tokens powerful and able to perform effects in the world.

Saussure suggests that the meaning of a word is not related to its reference to an external reality but to the specific differences between this word and other words in language. The word 'man' thus gets its meaning from its difference from other words such as 'woman' and from the differences between the words 'man' and 'woman' compared to words such as 'children' or 'animals'. The word 'man' thus gets its meaning from the sum of its relations to other words (Elgaard, 2003, p. 6). ANT lends this point from semiotics and suggests that no entity or token has an essence, which may be identified as powers or some characteristics, vested within the entity or token itself. Rather, the power or characteristics of this entity or token like the meaning of words is fully defined by its relationships with other actants in a network. As a consequence, an actant is thus at the same time both an actant and an actor-network. Michel Callon explains:

> The actor network is reducible neither to an actor alone nor to a network... The entities it is composed of, whether natural or social, could at any moment redefine their identity and mutual relationships in some

new way and bring new elements into the network. An actor network is simultaneously an actor whose activity is networking heterogeneous elements and a network that is able to redefine and transform what it is made of.

(Callon in Bijker, 1987, p. 93)

In another text, Bruno Latour (Latour, 1996) compares actor-networks with Deleuze's concept of rhizomes. When used in relation to plants rhizomes are modified stems running underground horizontally. They strike new roots out of their nodes, down into the soil. They also shoot new stems up to the surface out of their nodes (Spruce.com). Latour explains that an actor-network is like a rhizome and that the consequence of this metaphor is that instead of thinking in terms of surfaces – two dimensions- or spheres – three dimensions – one should think of actor-networks in terms of nodes that have as many dimensions as they have connections (like you find in rhizome plants root networks) (Latour, 1996).

In ANT then an actor-network may be defined as the humans, non-humans and the relations and interactions between them that construct a given entity or token. What an entity or token 'is' is theorized as an effect of the collective work done by the human and nonhuman actants that are related to, interact and through these activities 'realize' this entity or token. Since actants are nodes that have as many dimensions as they have con-nections, the type of relationships and interactions between actants in an actor-network that realizes an entity/token and creates its effects is always an empirical question. The entity's or token's actor-network and the kind of work it performs will have to be carefully analyzed and described in a symmetrical narrative by the ANT researcher if he/she wants to answer questions about what the characteristics and effects of the entity or token are or were.

A consequence of this way of theorizing is that the power of an entity or token is an effect of the number of actants that have been mobilized and made do the work necessary to construct and realize the entity/token and its effects. The more the actants that have been mobilized the more powerful an entity/token becomes while the less the actants mobilized the less powerful the entity/token is.

Now however another question arises – namely, through what process are actor-networks created, changed and reproduced? In ANT, the answer to this question is that it happens through translation processes.

Translation

Michel Serres theorizes translation as both communication and invention (Brown, 2002). He points out that the very opening of a message involves the risk of failure. Communication may be disturbed by 'noise', be thwarted or 'betrayed' by the medium through which it passes. At the receivers' end, this failure or betrayal may however also be seen as a process of invention and the creation of something new (Brown, 2002, p. 6). Michel Callon draws upon Michel Serres when he suggests that translation takes place on a common site where varied significations, concerns and interests commingle (Brown, 2002, p. 5). Callon further suggests that there is a loose structure or network of associations between ideas, things, people and resources around which and through which translation processes are enacted. The acts of making something new, whether that be a discovery of an object or the formulation of a theory, occurs through the forging of novel associations, almost a kind of bricolage (Callon, 1986; Callon, Law & Rip, 1986; Latour, 1987). In agreement with Michel Serres ideas about the role of 'noise', John Law (1997) notes that translation can also be seen as a kind of distortion. To translate is to transform, and in the act of transforming, a breaking of fidelity toward or a betrayal of the original source is necessarily involved.

ANT researchers' different ways of explaining and defining what translation is originates from the above-mentioned ideas. In the text 'Unscrewing the big Leviathan – How actors macro-structure reality and how sociologists help them to do so', Michel Callon and Bruno Latour define the concept of translation in a way that emphasizes the kind of work that a translator (or force) has to do (negotiate, calculate, persuade, etc.) to mobilize actants, construct the network and thus become a spokesperson for a performative and thus powerful actor-network:

> by translation we understand all the negotiations, intrigues, calculations, acts of persuasion and violence, thanks to which an actor or force takes, or causes to be conferred on itself, authority to speak or act on behalf of another actor or force.
>
> (Callon & Latour, 1981, p. 279)

They also emphasize that if the translator succeeds he/she will no longer only speak on behalf of him- or herself but on behalf of the collective of actants that he or she has mobilized and now represents. He/she will thereby have become stronger and more powerful. He/she will have become an obligatory passage point – someone who must be taken into account because he/she represents the entity or token in question:

> 'our interests are the same', 'do what I want', 'you cannot succeed without going through me'. Whenever an actor speaks of 'us', s/he is translating other actors into a single will, of which s/he becomes spirit and spokesman. S/he begins to act for several, no longer for one alone. S/he becomes stronger. S/he grows.
>
> (Callon & Latour, 1981, p. 279)

It may be noted then that what happens through the above-mentioned process is that the number of actants that are associated with an entity or token and 'act on its behalf' grows and that as a consequence the power of that entity and token as well as its spokesperson(s) grows.

Callon's model of translation

In accordance with this, Michel Callon suggested a model of translation that focused upon the work that translators need to do in order to mobilize and enroll (increasing numbers of) actors (actants) in a performative actor-network. He did this in the paper 'Some elements of a sociology of translation: Domestication of the scallops and the fishermen of St. Brieuc Bay' (Callon, 1986). In the text, Michel Callon follows and studies three marine biologists in their attempt to establish a network-alliance (an actor-network) between an innovative Japanese idea and method to grow scallops, scallops and their larvae, fishermen in the bay of St. Brieuc in northern France and some scientific colleagues. The aim of the research and development project was to find out whether a Japanese method for growing scallops could be used in the sea around France and thus by the scallops industry in France. The understanding of the translation process that came out of this study theorized the translation process related to translators building up of a performative and powerful actor-network in this way:

1   One or more human actors define a problem in a way that makes it an obligatory passage point for other human and nonhuman actors. Through defining the problem in a certain way, actors are given reasons for becoming interested in searching for solutions to the problem and thereby associating themselves with the actor-network
2   The translator then starts locking or associating a certain group of alliance partners with the network by using plans and devices that make them interested. An actor (actant) A makes actor B interested by cutting of and weakening all the connections between B and other entities who wish to associate themselves with B or define B's identity differently than actor A's
3   After actors B, C, D, etc. have become interested, actor A tries to enroll them in his project by defining and ascribing roles to them that they need to accept – perhaps after negotiation. If the phase of making actors interested succeeds, the actors/representatives of the alliance partners will have become enrolled in the actor-network
4   Finally, the translator mobilizes his/her representatives and alliance partners. The translator now needs to know whether the spokespersons with whom he has been negotiating are in fact representatives for the alliance partners. Some of the questions that will have to be decided in this connection are: Who speaks in whose name? Who represents who? Will those who are represented follow their representative? The answers to these questions are central for the further development of the translation process

Latour's model of translation

In another paper by Bruno Latour (1986) 'The Powers of Association', he contrasts the diffusion model with the model of translation. What constitutes power in the two models is analyzed and compared. In the diffusion model, what constitutes power is explained as follows:

> Clearly, when it is used as a cause to explain collective action, the notion of power is considered in terms of the diffusion model: what counts is the initial force of those who have power; this force is then transmitted in its entirety; finally, the medium through which power is exerted may diminish the power because of frictions and resistances (lack of communication, ill will, the position of interests groups, indifference).
>
> (Latour in Law, 1987, p. 267)

In contrast, Bruno Latour describes the characteristics of the translation model as follows:

> The model of diffusion may be contrasted with another, that of the model of translation. According to the latter, the spread in time and space of anything-claims, orders, artefacts, goods -is in the hands of people: each of these people may act in many different ways, letting the token drop, or modifying it or deflecting it, or betraying it, or adding to it, or appropriating it.
>
> (Latour in Law, 1987, p. 267)

Bruno Latour thus emphasizes that the movement in time and space of entities or tokens is in the hands of people. He moreover emphasizes that it is people who decide what will happen with a given entity or token when they translate it because they may translate it in many different ways. They may let the token drop, modify it, deflect it, betray it, add to it or appropriate it. As a consequence – as also pointed out by Michel Serres and John Law – some distortion, transformation and thus betrayal of the moving entity/token (or source) may occur as it is translated (Law, 1997).

Thus, while Michel Callon's model of translation focused upon the work that translators need to do in order to mobilize and enroll actors (actants) in a performative actor-network, Bruno Latour's model of translation focused upon how an entity or token is translated and often transformed as it moves among people.

References

Berg, M. (1997). Rationalizing medical work: Decision support techniques and medical practice. Cambridge, MA: MIT Press.

Bowler, I. R. (1999). Recycling urban waste on farmland: An actor-network inter-pretation. *Applied Geography, 19,* 29–43.

Callon, M. (1986). "Some elements of a sociology of translation: Domestication of the scallops and the fishermen of St. Brieuc Bay". In J. Law (Ed.), *Power, action and belief – A new sociology of knowledge?* London: Routledge & Kegan Paul.

Callon, M., & Latour, B. (1981). "Unscrewing the big Leviathan: How actors macro-structure reality and how sociologists help them to do so". In K. Knorr-Cetina & A. V. Cicourel (Eds.), *Advances in social theory and methodology, toward an integration of micro and macro-sociologies.* Boston, MA: Routledge & Kegan Paul.

Callon, M., & Latour, B. (1992). Don't throw the baby out with the bath school! A reply to Collins and Yearley. In A. Pickering (Ed.), *Science as practice and culture* (pp. 343–368). Chicago, IL: University of Chicago Press.

Callon, M., & Law, J. (1997). After the individual in society: Lessons on collectivity from science, technology and society. *Canadian Journal of Sociology, 22* (2), 165–182.

Callon, M., Law, J., & Rip, A. (1986). *Mapping the dynamics of science and technology: Sociology of science in the real world.* Basingstoke: The Macmillan Press LTD.

Czarniawska, B., & Hernes, T. (2005). *Actor-network theory and organizing.* Copenha-gen: Liber & Copenhagen Business School Press.

Czarniawska, B., & Sevôn, G. (1996). *Translating organizational change.* Berlin/New York, NY: Walter de Gruyter.

Barnes, B., & Bloor, D. (1982). Relativism, rationalism and the sociology of sci-ence. In M. Hollis & S. Lukes (Eds.), *Rationality and relativism* (pp. 21–47). Oxford: Blackwell.

Barry, A. (2001). In the middle of the network. In J. Law & A. Mol (Eds.), *Science, technology and medicine.* Durham, NC: Duke University Press.

Bijker, W. B. (1987). The social construction of Bakelite: Toward a theory of inven-tion. In W. E. Bijker, T. P. Hughes, & T. Pinch (Eds.), *The social construction of tech-nological systems – New directions in the sociology and history of technology.* Cambridge, MA, London: The MIT Press.

Brown, S. D. (2002). Michel Serres. Science, translation and the logic of the parasite. *Theory, Culture & Society, 19*(3), 1–28.

Elgaard, T. E. (2003). Actor-network-theory – A sociology of facts, carracks and scallops, Papers in Organization, No. 48, New Social Science Monographs, De-partment of Organization and Industrial Sociology, Copenhagen Business School.

Greimas, A. J., & Courtès, J. (1982). *Semiotics and language. An analytical dictionary.* Bloomington: Indiana University Press.

Hébert, L. (2019). The actantial model. In: L. Hebert (Ed.), *Tools for text and image analysis: An Introduction to applied semiotics.* New York: Routledge.

Hennion, A. (1989). An intermediary between production and consumption: The producer of popular music, science. *Technology and Human Value, 14,* 400–424.

Latour, B. (1986). The powers of association. In J. Law (Ed.), *Power, action and belief – A new sociology of knowledge?* London: Routledge & Kegan Paul.

Latour, B. (1987). *Science in action.* Cambridge, MA: Harvard University Press.

Latour, B. (1996). On actor-network theory A few clarifications. *Soziale Welt,* 47 Jahrg., H.4, 369–381.

Law, J. (1987). Technology and heterogeneous engineering: The case of Portuguese expansion. In W. Bijker, T. Huges, & T. Pinch (Eds.), *The social construction of tech-nological system.* Cambridge, MA: MIT Press.

Law, J. (1992). Notes on the theory of the actor-network: Ordering, strategy and heterogeneity. *Systems Practice, 5*, 379–393.

Law, J. (1997). Traduction/trahison: Notes on ANT. Department of Sociology, Lancaster University. Retrieved from http://www.lancaster.ac.uk/sociology/stslaw2.html

Law, J. (2008). Actor network theory and material semiotics. In: B. S. Turner (Ed.), *The new Blackwell companion to social theory* (3rd ed., pp. 141–158). Oxford: Blackwell.

Mcgrath, A. E. (1990). *The genesis of doctrine: A study in the foundations of doctrinal criticism.* Cambridge, MA: Basil Blackwell Inc.

Serres, M. (1974). La Traduction, Hermès lll, Collection Critique. Paris: Les Èditions de Menuit.

5 The travel of ideas

Studying isomorphism and heterogeneity in organizational fields

Czarniawska and Joerges' (1996) theory about the travel of ideas originated from neo-institutional theory. According to this stream of research in organizational studies, organizations are socially embedded in organizational fields that influence organizational members' ways of organizing their companies/public organizations. DiMaggio and Powell (1991) suggested that an organizational field is created as a result of a structuration process (Giddens, 1984), where organizational actors gradually start interacting with each other and develop a shared consciousness or understanding suggesting that they somehow belong together. DiMaggio and Powell (1991, p. 65) thus defined the concept of organizational field in this way:

> by organizational field we mean those organizations that, in the aggregate, constitute a recognized area of institutional life; keys suppliers, resource and product consumers, regulatory agencies and other organizations that produce similar services or products.

and suggested that organizational fields are formed through this process:

> an increase in the extent of interaction among organizations in the field; the emergence of sharply defined inter-organizational structures of domination and patterns of coalition; an increase in the information load with which organizations in a field must contend; and the development of a mutual awareness among participants in a set of organizations that they are involved in a common enterprise.
> (DiMaggio & Powell, 1991, p. 65)

Based on a thorough review of the literature related to the emergence of organizational fields, Granqvist (2007, pp. 51–52) later specified that organizational fields are formed through five phases. (1) The starting point is individuals and their perceptions of some need for change of an existing institution. (2) These perceptions become interpreted and shared as meanings within a community which are (3) mobilized and disseminated further in relational networks of actors within and between communities. (4) Gradually, some commonalities begin to emerge and some meanings and understandings become more salient than others. This depends on the capacity of the actors to make their particular view or framing 'sticky' in the changing institutional context. (5) Eventually, the most persistent meanings become sedimented as institutions, which again are under constant pressure for change. Both individual and collective actions thereby play a role in the different processes that are crucial to the emergence of organizational fields.

Neo-institutional theory thus suggests that shared meanings are developed among people who are socially embedded in organizational fields. As they start to interact and communicate with each other, they over time develop shared meanings that are characteristic of the fields in which they are embedded. Institutionalized and legitimate meanings created at the field level are given priority over individually developed and not collectively shared meanings. As a consequence, much research in neo-institutional theory has focused upon explaining isomorphism – that is the process through which organizations become alike or similar in organizational form in organizational fields through adaptation to 'rationalized myths' (Meyer & Rowan, 1977) or regulative, normative or imitative pressures (Scott, 1995) from the environment. Another part of this research has focused upon explaining how new ideas and meanings emerge and become collectively shared and institutionalized in organizational fields and thus upon how variation, divergence or heterogeneity in organizational forms are created. Here one puzzling question has been how it is possible for human actors who are socially embedded and share similar institutionalized and legitimized meanings to come up with new ideas that may then become the origin of new organizational forms and thus divergence and heterogeneity in organizational fields (Lounsbury and Crumley, 2007).

What is the role of actors and how do ideas move in organizational fields?

Like Everett Rogers (2003) in his theory about the diffusion of innovative ideas, researchers in neo-institutional theory have tried to theorize how similar and/or new ideas move in organizational fields. In order to understand how that happens they have developed their own ways of theorizing the movement of innovative ideas. Instead of writing about the diffusion of ideas, they write about the travel and translation of fashionable ideas. According to Christensen and Karnoe (1997), the Scandinavian neo-institutionalists addressed a critique that had been raised by neo-institutional researchers: That neo-institutionalists do not make clear what is the role of actors and actions in relation to the creation, diffusion and stabilization of organizational practices:

> .... Since its inception, internal participants (DiMaggio, 1988; Zucker, 1977) and external critics alike have worried that neo-institutionalists do not make clear the role of actors and action in the creation, diffusion and stabilization of organizational practices. Some charge, in effect, that neo-institutionalists have re-placed the invisible hand of the market with the invisible hand of culture.
>
> (Christensen & Karnoe, 1997, p. 392)

They also addressed a gap in neo-institutional research related to how collective rules and ideas moved from the field level into organizations as well as from organizations into the organizational field:

> American research on institutional ideas has been strong in demonstrating that collective rules and ideas of various sorts do in fact travel down into particular organizational structures and sometimes their practices. It has been weaker on showing the processes involved in the rise of the ideas in question, the transformations these ideas go through over time at the collective level, the further transformations they go through as they travelled down into particular organizations, and the nature of the social processes involved in adoption or incorporation.
>
> (Meyer, 1996, p. 242)

During the 1980s and 1990s, many organizational researchers noticed that organizations were picking up popular ideas and tried to incorporate them into their formal structures. Mainly, diffused ideas appeared to be fashionable management ideas that were often introduced by consultants or other proponents of improved management and had labels such as TQM (total quality management), BPR (business process re-engineering), MBO (management by objectives), SPC (supplied change management) and NPM (new public management) (Wedlin & Sahlin, 2017). According to Scandinavian neo-institutionalists, organizational members adopted such management ideas, not because they were rational actors but rather because they were socially embedded beings, who adapted to what seemed socially appropriate and fashionable in the organizational field (Wedlin & Sahlin, 2017). The adoption of innovative ideas was thus hypothesized to be influenced by field-related fashion waves in the organizations' environment. According to Abrahamson (1996), fashionable management ideas came in waves and followed a bell-shaped curve as they spread. Czarniawska and Joerges (1996) now introduced a new theory about how fashion waves and fashionable management ideas influenced change and institutionalization processes in organizations. The title of their chapter in the edited volume *Translating Organizational Change* (1996) was 'Travels of Ideas'.

The travel of ideas

Communication and translation

Czarniawska and Joerges (1996) agree with Everett Rogers about the importance of communication in the spreading of ideas and their movement in time and space:

> the application of ideas takes place through acts of communication. Tracing repeated communication, we ask where ideas travel, and all though this question is formulated in spatial terms, the movement of ideas involves of cause both time and space.
>
> (Czarniawska & Joerges, 1996, p. 20)

The ideas they have about how and why ideas move between people and among groups of people are however different from the view of Everett Rogers. According to Czarniawska and Joerges (1996), the purpose of the idea model is to substitute metaphors as diffusion, planned change, innovation and adaptation to the environment with a metaphor of the materialization of ideas. The purpose is also to explain how fashionable ideas are created and move among socially embedded actors in institutional fields. The authors take their point of departure in a social constructionist and narrative approach characterized by 'blurred genres' (Czarniawska & Joerges 1996, p. 16). The authors thus introduced Bruno Latour's concept of translation to explain the process through which ideas move. Bruno Latour explains:

> the spread in time and space of anything-claims, orders, artefacts, goods-is in the hands of people; each of these people may act in many different ways, letting the token drop, or modifying it, or deflecting it, or betraying it, or adding to it, or appropriate in it.
>
> (Latour, 1986, p. 267)

Citing Latour (1993), Czarniawska and Joerges point out that translation means creation of a new link not existing before that modifies the two agents: Those who translated and that which is translated. In addition, they emphasize that that is what makes the concept attractive to them:

> it comprises what exists and what is created; the relationship between humans and ideas, ideas and objects, and humans and objects – all needed in order to understand what in shorthand we call 'organizational change'.
>
> (Czarniawska & Joerges, 1996, p. 24)

They also point out that translation is not just happening between two or three people but also when ideas are spread out through mass media technologies and through that process becomes the material basis for fashion and institutionalization:

> translation is speeded up, made continuous and magnified by technology: more specifically, by a mass storage, mass reproduction and mass media technologies. It is this hybridized humans/technologies network, which is the material basis for more complex translation mechanisms: fashion and institutionalization.
>
> (Czarniawska & Joerges, 1996, p. 24)

How ideas travel – A process model

What follows next is a process model, explaining how ideas travel among people and groups of people in institutional fields. The model describes the translation process of an idea as follows:

1   An idea is selected and attended to in moment/place A
2   The idea is translated into an object (a text, a picture, a prototype) which is then translated into
3   Action which is translated, repeated and stabilized into
4   An institution, which is then followed by further translations

When an idea has become objectified in a text or a prototype in moment/place A, it may be dis-embedded and move in time and space. It may start traveling among people in the institutional field. Some people in the institutional field may then re-embed the idea in another moment/place B (in for instance an organization) in the institutional field. The details of this process model are introduced in the following sections.

An idea is selected and attended to in moment/place A

Czarniawska and Joerges (1996) define an idea as 'images which become known in the form of pictures or sounds (words can be either one or another)' (Czarniawska & Joerges, 1996, p. 20). According to the authors, most ideas circulate somewhere most of the time. Therefore, processes of attention are more important than information processes (Czarniawska & Joerges, 1996, p. 26). To perceive presupposes the existence of categories. Thus, a system of categories or typification (Schütz, 1973) needs to be in place in the actor beforehand, which expresses his or her life experience for an actor to be able to relate what is perceived to certain categories. Czarniawska and Joerges (1996) now point out that 'this means that we cannot perceive something unless it somehow relates to what we already know' (Czarniawska and Joerges, 1996, p. 27). When the categories are in place, we focus our attention upon some categories but not others. The choice depends however on 'the purpose at hand' (Czarniawska and Joerges, 1996, p. 28).

According to Schütz (1973, p. 9), 'the purpose at hand selects those elements and among all the others contained in a situation which are relevant for this purpose'. The choice depends on the purpose at hand. Sometimes the encounter with an idea results in a reformulation of the purpose at hand. Ideas are discovered (Bruner, 1961), networks of beliefs are reconfigured or re-contextualized (Rorty, 1991) and translator as well as that which is translated is changed (Latour, 1992). Czarniawska and Joerges sum up:

> we approach an idea in terms of what we already know, and sometimes the encounter barely confirms it; at other times an idea re-arranges our beliefs and purposes as we translate it; the act of discovery creates a new idea and a new actor. This is the meaning of change on the phenomenological level.
>
> (Czarniawska & Joerges, 1996, pp. 28–29)

According to Czarniawska and Joerges (1996), a number of factors influence what ideas are attended to in an organization. They suggest that fashion and institutionalization processes in organizational fields are interconnected and interdependent. Fashion challenges the institutionalized order of things and is an institutional playfield where new practices can be tried out and disposed of or become institutionalized (Czarniawska & Joerges, 1996, p. 25). Cultural assumptions and political structures which are taken for granted in the local context means that there are themes and ideas that will never be put on the agenda unless they are by some reason changed (Czarniawska & Joerges, 1996, p. 29). Ideologies and discovery guided by learning-oriented leaders may also influence which ideas are attended to and put on the agenda in an organization. Moreover, it may be important what the market or the public attend to because organizational members may be forced to take these themes, issues and ideas into consideration. There are thus many reasons to why an idea may become noticed and an object of attention in organizations.

The idea is translated into an object

When an idea becomes the center of attention and is selected, it is translated into a quasi-object and later into an object: 'ideas that have been selected and entered the chain of translations acquire almost physical, objective attributes; in other words, they become quasi-objects, and then objects' (Czarniawska & Joerges, 1996, p. 32). Ideas are objectified in different ways. They may be translated into labels, metaphors or platitudes. They may also be translated into design for instance if ideas/images of ideas are translated into graphical form. When an idea has been translated into an image or sound, it can materialize as objects or actions, which results in change:

> they (ideas) can then be materialized (turned into objects or actions) in many ways: pictures can be painted or written (like in stage setting), sounds

can be recorded or written down (like in a musical score) and so on and so forth. There materialization causes change: unknown objects appear, known objects change their appearance, practices become transformed.

(Czarniawska & Joerges, 1996, p. 20).

The idea is translated into action

Czarniawska and Joerges (1996) assume that the translation of an idea into actions presupposes that the actors who translate it take the positive aspects of the idea for granted. They also assume that the decision to translate an idea is an act of will, prompted by positive expectations concerning the process itself (Czarniawska & Joerges, 1996, p. 41). They conceptualize an idea's translation into actions as 'idea materialization':

> this magic moment when words become deeds is the one that truly de- serves to be called materialization, whether performed mostly by human actors or mostly by material artifacts.
>
> (Czarniawska & Joerges, 1996, p. 41)

For an idea to be translated into actions, it has to be supplemented with an image of action that can guide the process. An idea must thus be sup- plied with an 'image of action', 'a verbal or graphic picture of possible ac- tion' (Czarniawska & Joerges, 1996, p. 40). The authors draw upon Miller, Galanter and Pribram (1960) when describing the process through which an image of action is translated into deeds:

> the cognitive process, fronted by acts of will, moves...... towards cali- brating images of action into something more like detailed plans of ac- tion and then into deeds.
>
> (Czarniawska & Joerges, 1996, p. 41)

Actions are translated into institutions

According to Czarniawska and Joerges (1996), ideas that are selected repeti- tively become institutions:

> from our point of view, a time and space collective constantly selects and de-selects among a common repertoire of ideas plans for action, and the ideas repetitively selected acquire institutional status.
>
> (Czarniawska & Joerges, 1996, p. 38)

In addition, as mentioned earlier fashion waves are important in this con- nection; 'fashions give birth to institutions and institutions make room for other fashions' (Czarniawska & Joerges, 1996, p. 39). Therefore, the important questions are 'which ideas become fashionable and which remain forever local?' (Czarniawska & Joerges, 1996, p. 25), and 'which ideas brought about by fashion are institutionalized and which are not?' (Czarniawska & Joerges, 1996, p. 25).

The process through which ideas become institutionalized is described as follows:

> fashions bring in a variety of ideas: organizations within a field, try them out, creating fashion by following it, but also creating institutions by persevering in certain practices, by refusing to reject previous fashions, or by hailing a new fashion as the final solution. Generally, one might say that what remains unaffected, after one fashion has changed into another, acquires the status of institutionalized action, the more so the longer it survives.
>
> (Czarniawska & Joerges, 1996, pp. 38–39)

The institutionalization of fashionable ideas now creates both stability and an outset for critique and development of new ideas:

> the economy of effort provided by institutionalization create room for new ideas, which will eventually upset old institutions; a strong identity provides a basis for innovative experiments and social control creates, among other effects, social unrest and disorder. Creativity grows out of routine. Rationality breeds irrationality.
>
> (Czarniawska & Joerges, 1996, p. 39)

How objectified ideas travel in time and space

When an idea has become objectified in for instance a text or a prototype, it may be dis-embedded and start moving from one time/place A – that is it may start traveling – until the idea is re-embedded in a new time and place B. Czarniawska and Joerges (1996) describe the process as follows:

> we begin by tracing ideas along the course of local time: how, at a given moment, do individuals and groups at certain place happened to notice an idea? We watch the ideas become quasi-objects, transgressing the barriers of local time and entering translocal paths, becoming "dis-embedded", in Giddens terms. We watch them again, landing in various localities, becoming "re-embedded", materialised in actions, and-when judged successful -becoming institutions, only to occasion anew the generation of ideas.
>
> (Czarniawska & Joerges, 1996, p. 22)

References

Abrahamson, E. (1996). Technical and aesthetic fashion. In B. Czarniawska & G. Sevon (Eds.), *Translating organizational change* (pp. 117–138). Berlin: de Gruyter.

Bruner, J. S. (1961). The act of discovery. *Harvard Educational Review, 31,* 21–32.

Christensen, S., & Karnoe, P. (1997). Actors and institutions: Editors' introduction. *American Behavioral Scientist, 40*(4), 392–396.

Czarniawska, B., & Joerges, B. (1996). Travels of ideas. In B. Czarniawska & G. Sevon (Eds.), *Translating organizational change* (pp. 13–48). Berlin: de Gruyter.

Dimaggio, P. J., & Powell, W. W. (1991). The iron cage revisited: Institutional isomorphism and collective rationality in organizational fields. In W. W. Powell & P. J. DiMaggio (Eds.), *The new institutionalism in organizational analysis.* Chicago, IL and London: The University of Chicago Press.

Giddens, A. (1984). *The constitution of society.* Berkeley: University of California Press.

Granqvist, N. (2007). *Nanotechnology and nanolabeling – Essays on the emergence of new technological fields.* PhD dissertation, Helsinki School of Economics.

Latour, B. (1986). The powers of association. In J. Law (Eds.), *Power, action and belief* (pp. 261–277). London: Routledge and Kegan Paul.

Latour, B. (1992). Technology is society made durable. In J. Law (ed.), *A sociology of monsters: Essays on power, technology and domination.* London: Routledge.

Latour, B. (1993). *Messenger talks, Lund: The Institute of Economic Research,* Working Paper, No.9.

Lounsbury, M., & Crumley, E. T. (2007). New practice creation: An institutional perspective on innovation. *Organization Studies, 28*(7), 993–1012.

Meyer, J. W. (1996). Otherhood: The promulgation and transmission of ideas in the modern organizational environment. In B. Czarniawska & G. Sevon (Eds.), *Translating organizational change* (pp. 241–252). Berlin: de Gruyter.

Meyer, J. W., & Rowan, B. (1977). Institutionalized organizations: Formal structure as myth and ceremony. *American Journal of Sociology, 83,* 340–363.

Miller, G. A., Galanter, E., & Pribram, K. H. (1960). *Plans and the structure of behavior.* New York, NY: Holt, Rinehart and Winston.

Rogers, E. (2003). *Diffusion of innovations* (5th ed.). New York, NY: Free Press.

Rorty, R. (1991). Objectivity, relativism and truth. In *Philosophical Papers* (Vol. 1). New York, NY: Cambridge University press.

Schütz, A. (1973). Common-sense and the scientific interpretation of human action. In M. Natanson (Ed.), *Collected papers* (Vol. 1, pp. 3–47). The Hague: Martinus Nijhoff.

Scott, W. R. (1995). *Institutions and organizations.* Thousand oaks, CA: Sage.

Wedlin, L., & Sahlin, K. (2017). The imitation and translation of management ideas. In R. Greenwood, C. Oliver, & B. Thomas (Eds.), *The SAGE handbook of organizational institutionalism.* Thousand oaks, CA: Sage Publications Ltd.

6 Symbolic interactionist models

A stream of research has developed that theorizes translation as happening between social worlds (Strauss, 1978). This stream of research builds on the basic assumptions of symbolic interactionism (O'Mahoney, 2016; Wæraas & Nielsen, 2016). According to Ritzer (2000, p. 357), the basic principles of symbolic interactionism are given as follows:

1 Human beings, unlike lower animals, are endowed with the capacity for thought
2 The capacity for thought is shaped by social interaction
3 In social interaction, people learn the meanings and the symbols that allow them to exercise their distinctively human capacity for thought
4 Meanings and symbols allow people to carry on distinctively human action and interaction
5 People are able to modify or alter the meanings and symbols that they use in action and interaction based on their interpretation of the situation
6 People are able to make these modifications and alterations because, in part, of their ability to interact with themselves, which allows them to examine possible courses of action, assess their relative advantages and disadvantages, and then choose one
7 The intertwined patterns of action and interaction make up groups and societies

Because of the above-mentioned assumptions, translation is theorized as happening between people and groups of people belonging to different social worlds (Strauss, 1978). Social worlds are typically remote from each other culturally as well as in time and space. This now creates problems whenever collaboration and coordination of several groups of people are needed in order to achieve common social goals. In this stream of research, questions related to how people and groups of people are coordinated and collaborate across boundaries of social worlds through translation of boundary objects have been focused upon (Star & Griesemer, 1989). Moreover, how knowledge is translated and thus transferred over boundaries of social worlds has been studied (Carlile, 2002, 2004).

Translating to manage knowledge across boundaries

Prior organizational research has contributed to studies of cross-boundary coordination and knowledge sharing and the challenges that arise from differences in meanings, norms and interests between groups of people or communities of practice (Wenger, 1998). Various approaches have been proposed for dealing with these differences, including transfer mechanisms that rely on a common lexicon and standard protocols, forms of translation that create shared understandings, and transformation processes that generate integrative knowledge and boundary objects (Bechky, 2003; Carlile, 2002, Dougherty, 1992). As pointed out by Kellogg, Orlikowski and Yates (2006, p. 22), this research has yielded important insights into cross-boundary interactions and the 'artful integrations' (Suchman, 1994) often required to accomplish coordinated work across structural, cultural and political boundaries.

Carlile (2002, 2004) examines the management of knowledge across structural, cultural and political boundaries in settings where innovation is desired. He develops a framework that explains how transfer, translation and transformation of knowledge happen across syntactic, semantic and pragmatic boundaries of different groups of people during innovation processes. He does this by linking these categories to information-processing, interpretive and political perspectives in organization theory (Carlile, 2004, p. 564). He suggests that if groups of people and communities of practices are similar, knowledge may be transferred easily. While if they are different, the knowledge also needs to be translated and negotiated.

He thus points out that if differences and dependencies between actors are known, a common lexicon is developed that is sufficient to share and assess knowledge at a boundary. The process may be understood as an information processing process where knowledge is simply '**transferred**' as described by Shannon and Weawer (1949). The techniques used to make it happen are a shared syntactic capacity, shared taxonomies as well as storage and retrieval technologies.

If something new is created during an innovation process, however, it is not sufficient to share and assess knowledge across a boundary. In such case a new situation arises that creates a semantic boundary that necessitates a **translation** or interpretive approach. Novelty thus generates some differences and dependencies that are unclear – different interpretations exist. Common meanings are developed to create shared meanings and provide an adequate means of sharing and assessing knowledge at the boundary. In that situation the different communities of practice engage in translating knowledge in order to create shared meanings. During this process, the techniques used are the development of the semantic capacity of different groups, cross-functional interactions and teams as well as boundary spanners and translators.

However, to create common meanings to be able to share and assess knowledge often also requires creating new agreements and thus involves a political dimension. Novelty thus generates different interests between actors that impede their ability to share and assess knowledge. Common interests are therefore developed to transform knowledge and interests and provide an adequate means of sharing and assessing knowledge at a boundary. Knowledge is therefore not just translated but also negotiated and through that political process it is **transformed**. The techniques required by actors involve an ability to be pragmatic, to use prototyping and other kinds of boundary objects that can be jointly transformed. To share and assess knowledge thus requires significant practical and political effort.

The fourth and last characteristic of managing knowledge at a boundary is that it requires multiple iterations. Thus,

> addressing the consequences cannot be resolved with one try, but requires an iterative process of sharing and assessing knowledge, creating new agreements, and making changes where needed. As the actors participate in each iterative stage, they get better at identifying what differences and dependencies are of consequence at the boundary; they improve at collectively developing more adequate common lexicon, meaning, and interests. Through this iterative capacity the invested and path -dependent nature of knowledge can be transformed.
>
> (Carlile, 2004, p. 563)

Translation thus becomes related to how different groups or communities of practice engage in translating knowledge in order to create shared cultural meanings. But that however only as part of a broader process that also includes these groups creating a shared lexicon and making (political) agreements about involved actors' and groups' interests as they try to innovate. According to Carlile (2002, 2004), boundary objects assist in the transfer, translation and transformation of knowledge across syntactic, semantic and pragmatic boundaries.

Cooperating in the absence of consensus

Susan Leigh Star (2010, p. 5) explains that her initial framing of the concept boundary objects was motivated by a desire to analyze the nature of cooperative work in the absence of consensus:

> many models, in the late 1980s and continuing today, of cooperation often began conceptually, with the idea that first consensus must be reached, and then cooperation could begin. From my own fieldwork among scientists and others, cooperating across disciplinary borders and to historical analysis of heterogeneous groups who did cooperate and did not agree at the local level, it seems to me that the consensus model was untrue. Consensus was rarely reached and fragile when it was, but cooperation continued often unproblematically. How might this be explained?
>
> (Star, 2010, p. 5)

Susan Leigh Star and James R. Griesemer (1989) introduced the concept of 'boundary objects' to explain this mystery. In their article, they researched the collaboration between amateurs and professionals in Berkely's Museum of Vertebrate Zoology. Joseph Grinnell was the first director of the Museum. He worked on problems of speciation, migration and the role of the environment in Darwinian evolution. Grinnell's research required the labor of (among others) university administrators, professors, research scientists, curators, amateur collectors, private sponsors and patrons, occasional field hands, government officials and members of scientific clubs. Some objects of interests to but also used differently by these people and groups included:

- Species and subspecies of mammals and birds
- The terrain of the state of California
- Physical factors in California's environment (such as temperature, rainfall and humidity)
- The habitats of collected animal species.

Based on their case analysis, Star and Griesemer concluded that the success of the museum and Joseph Grinnell in coordinating all these diverse groups work in a way that produced scientific knowledge was achieved through methods' standardization and the management of boundary objects. Grinnell's managerial decisions about the best way to translate the interests of all these disparate social worlds shaped not only the character of the institution he built, but also the content of his scientific claims. His elaborate collection and curation guidelines established a management system in which diverse allies could participate concurrently in the heterogeneous work of building a research museum. Boundary objects played a key role in that connection. In their original article, Star and Griesemer explain and define the concept of boundary object as follows:

> Boundary objects... Is an analytic concept of those scientific objects, which both inhabit several intersecting social worlds and satisfy the informational requirements of each of them. Boundary objects are objects, which are both plastic enough to adapt to local needs and the constraints of the several parties employing them, yet robust enough to maintain a common identity across sites. They are weakly structured in common use, and become strongly structured in individual site use. These objects may be abstract or concrete. They have different meanings in different social worlds but their structure is common enough to more than one world to make them recognizable, a means of translation. The creation and management of boundary objects is a key process in developing and maintaining coherence across intersecting social worlds.
>
> (Star & Griesemer, 1989, p. 393)

Star (2010, pp. 5–6) later explained in more detail what characterizes boundary objects and the process of how people interact with them:

- The object (remember, to read this as a set of work arrangements that are at once material and processional) resides between social worlds (or communities of practice) where it is ill-structured
- When necessary, the object is worked on by local groups who maintain its vaguer identity as a common object, while making it more specific, more tailored to local use within a social world and therefore useful for work that is not interdisciplinary
- Groups that are cooperating without consensus tack back and forth between both forms of the object

Translation mediated by boundary objects

The introduction of the concept of translation in the discussion of how different professional groups or communities of practice use boundary objects to succeed with cooperative work in the absence of consensus starts out with what seems to be a betrayal of the original meaning of the concept of translation presented by ANT. Thus, instead of being part of a semiotic vocabulary and practice that researchers may use when doing symmetrical studies of how entities and tokens are created through the (translation) work of humans and nonhumans, the concept is presented as a way to understand how empirically identified human actors belonging to different social worlds cooperate and coordinate even though they translate and thus interpret meanings, symbols and objects that they use in action and interaction differently. As in symbolic interactionism the meaning of objects becomes the interpreted meaning of humans, ANTs' semiotic actants become human actors and heterogeneous actor-networks become social networks. Star and Griesemer (1989:389) thus interpret the relation between Joseph Grinnells' attempt to organize groups of human actors around his museum in a way that makes production of scientific knowledge possible and Latours, Callons and Laws' concepts of actor-networks and translation as follows:

> The problem of translation as described by Latour, Callon and Law is central to the kind of re-conciliation described in this paper. In order to create scientific authority, entrepreneurs gradually enlist participants (or in Latour's word, 'allies') from a range of locations, reinterpret their concerns to fit their own programmatic goals and then establish themselves as gatekeepers (in Law's terms, as "obligatory points of passage"). This authority may be either substantive or methodological. Latour and Callon have called this process interessement, to indicate the translation of the concerns of nonscientists into those of the scientists.
>
> (Star & Griesemer, 1989, p. 389)

They further elaborate however that

> a central feature of this situation is that entrepreneurs from more than
> one social world are trying to conduct such translations simultaneously.
> It is not just a case of interessement from nonscientist to scientists. Un-
> less they use coercion, each translator must maintain the integrity of the
> interests of the other audiences in order to retain them as allies yet this
> must be done in such a way as to increase the centrality and importance
> of that entrepreneur's work.
>
> (Star & Griesemer, 1989, p. 389)

Star and Griesemer thus conclude that the challenge intersecting social worlds
pose to the coherence of translations cannot be understood from a single
viewpoint. If professional groups or communities of practice succeed with
cooperative work in the absence of consensus, it does not happen through
a process where social actors and social networks are mobilized through a
process of problematization, interessement, enrollment and mobilization as
Michel Callon (1986) suggests. Rather, it happens through a process where
vaguely defined boundary objects make such coordination and cooperation
possible because each group translates common boundary objects in a way
where they are weakly structured in common use, and become strongly
structured in individual site use.

As a consequence of this symbolic interactionist way of reasoning, the
meaning of objects became interpreted as the meaning ascribed to objects
and especially boundary objects by humans who coordinate and collaborate
across social and time-space boundaries without having a consensus. ANTs'
semiotic actants became understood as human actors and heterogeneous
actor-networks became identified as social networks. Finally, translation became associated with 'the flow of objects and concepts through the network
of participating allies and social worlds' (Star & Griesemer, 1989, p. 389) that
makes such a non-consensus based type of cooperation between social groups
and communities of practice possible.

Knowledge translation between center and periphery

Yanov (2004) reflects upon the translation of knowledge between social
groups of which some of them are situated within the boundaries of the
organization while others have connections to and perform practices with
groups situated within as well as outside the organizational boundaries. Using three in-depth case studies of how groups of people share knowledge and
learn in a company selling and operating copy machines (Orr, 1992, 1996), a
national-level government corporation in Israel aimed at community development of educational, social and recreational services (Yanow 1993, 1996)
and in workers' communities of practices (Wenger, 1998), she tries to explain
why relevant local and practice-based knowledge is considered less valuable
than knowledge of hierarchically centrally placed experts.

Yanov (2004) distinguishes between managements' more scientific and technical way of knowing and workers' more intuitively based know-how in that connection and explores what are the problems of translating knowledge across the boundaries of these groups. Referring to the first two case studies that she analyses, Yanov states that what they have in common is that organizationally relevant local knowledge learned and held by organizational members located hierarchically and geographically removed from the center of the organization is not ascribed the same value as centrally placed managers' expert knowledge.

The work practices of these groups in the periphery entailed interacting with clients, customers or other members of the public beyond the organizations borders, including delivery van drivers, bakery shop owners, copier techs, machine operators, and employees with residents and professional counterparts at other agencies (Yanov, 2004, p. 14). Yanov states that what emerges from her mapping of the actors in the cases is a bi-directional 'center-periphery' axis. In a structural sense, these workers move on the periphery of their organizations in two dimensions, and they operate at the intersections of this double periphery. Vertically, within the organization, they work at a hierarchical periphery at lower levels of the organization. They are removed geographically from perceived centers of authority, decision-making and other sources of power and status according to bureaucratic values. Horizontally and in a spatial sense, they are crossing its borders and are moving outside the organization; they intersect with non-members at a geographic periphery which is also at a distance from the presumed centers of organizational operations.

Yanov (2004) points out that aside from the local knowledge expertise these peripheral workers develop as border-crossers; in their interactions among clients and customers, they also develop a form of practice expertise as they act, in some respects, as bicultural translators. Moreover, as she emphasizes, translating requires expert, local knowledge of at least two settings and practices. And one does not translate language per se; one translates meaning. Or as Yanov explains:

> Translating builds on 'a feeling for the organism' (Keller, 1983), a kinesthetic and even aesthetic sense for the object or practice whose meaning one is trying to render into a context different from its "native" habitat. Translation is never just a neutral, procedural matter of recognizing or identifying meaning 'as such' and finding the right word in the target language with which to render that meaning from its source language. There are many more dimensions -psychological, cultural-at play. Translation is affected and shaped by the translator, and both person and process shape the outcome.
>
> (Yanov, 2004, p. 15)

Yanov (2004) explains that translation of practices is about rendering meaning from a source language in terms of some other language. When people translate practices, they however also draw on their knowledge of cultural contexts including sets of meanings and ways of doing things. In addition, when you translate you intend to render the original meaning faithfully and without intentional distortion, yet in ways that make it understandable in a different context. However, in translating organizational practices, the meaning is not fixed. The target culture and potentially the source culture actively interpret and act on the knowledge in translation, often as the translator is rendering it. The value of the translation is evaluated on the basis of whether a given practice is understood and on the basis of its utility for action. According to Yanov:

> translation in practice is interactive, bound up with action, practice, doing: the translator translates "culture for culture" (or meaning-for-meaning) rather than word-for-word.
>
> (Yanov, 2004, p. 15)

Yanov (2004) suggests that the employees working at the vertical and horizontal/ geographical peripheries of their organizations master three domains of 'linguistic' expertise:

> the translators have three domains of 'linguistic' expertise: that of their work practice; the organizational context within which that practice resides; and practice of the extra organizational domain. In other words, they master three cultures: internally, they learn how to operate with in their employing organization, as well as how to conduct their own practice, whether truck driving and delivery or the technical expertise of fixing copiers or the professional practice of community organizing: and they also learn the language, customs and mores of the other organizations or groups external to their home organization with whose members they interact.
>
> (Yanov, 2004, p. 16)

Yanov (2004) suggests that the knowledge that employees working at the vertical and horizontal/geographical periphery of their organizations acquire ought to be considered valuable by their organizations but that most often the formal "expert" knowledge of centrally placed managers is prioritized instead. The peripheral workers are thus being prevented from participating more fully, not as individuals but as a category, in the sense that their collective knowledge is systematically kept at arm's length from organizational policy and decision-making. It is not only that their local knowledge is not seen and appreciated as expertise; their role as translators also remains largely invisible to the organization (Yanov, 2004, p. 22).

Consequently, Yanov concludes:

> Perhaps, the organizational learning that needs to take place is a phenomenological learning: in order to escape the pitfalls of denigrating

peripheral workers knowledge and modes of knowing, organizations – executives, managers, and others alike – need to learn to see organizational life 'multiculturally', not in a race ethnic or other trait sense, but in a work practice and knowledge system sense.

(Yanov, 2004, p. 23)

References

Bechky, B. (2003). Sharing meaning across occupational communities: The transformation of understanding on the production floor. *Organization Science, 14,* 312–330.

Callon, M. (1986). Some elements of a sociology of translation: domestication of the scallops and the fishermen of St. Brieuc Bay. In J. Law (Ed.), *Power, action and belief – A new sociology of knowledge?* London: Routledge & Kegan Paul.

Carlile, P. R. (2002). A pragmatic view of knowledge and boundaries: Boundary objects in new product development. *Organization Science, 13,* 442–455.

Carlile, P. R. (2004). Transferring, translating, and transforming: An integrative framework for managing knowledge across boundaries, *Organization Science, 15*(5), 555–568.

Dougherty, D. (1992). Interpretive barriers to successful product innovation in large firms. *Organization Science, 3,* 179–202.

Keller, E. F. (1983). *A feeling for the organism.* San Francisco, CA: W. H. Freeman.

Kellogg, K. C., Orlikowski, W. J., & Yates, J. A. (2006). Life in the trading zone: Structuring coordination across boundaries in postbureaucratic organizations. *Organization Science, 17*(1), 22–44.

O'Mahoney, J. (2016). Archetypes of translation: Recommendations for dialogue. *International Journal of Management Reviews, 18*(3), 333–350.

Orr, J. (1996). *Talking about machines: An ethnography of a modern job.* Ithaca, NY: Cornell University Press.

Orr, J. (1992). Ethnography and organizational learning: In pursuit of learning at work. Paper for the NATO Advanced Research Workshop, 'Organizational Learning and Technological Change', Siena, Italy, September 22–26.

Ritzer, G. (2000). *Sociological theory* (5th ed.). New York: McGraw Hill Higher Education.

Shannon, C., & Weawer, W. (1949). *The mathematical theory of communications.* Urbana, IL: University of Illinois Press.

Star, S. L. (2010). This is not a boundary object: Reflections on the origin of a concept. *Science, Technology, & Human Values, 35*(5), 601–617.

Star, S. L., & Griesemer, J. (1989). Institutional ecology, 'translations', and boundary objects: Amateurs and professionals on Berkeley's museum of vertebrate zoology. *Social Studies of Science, 19,* 387–420.

Strauss, A. (1978). A social world perspective. *Studies in Symbolic Interaction, 1,* 119–128.

Suchman, L. (1994). Working relations of technology production and use. *Computer Supported Cooperative Work, 2,* 21–39.

Wæraas, A., & Nielsen, J. A. (2016). Translation theory 'translated': Three perspectives on translation in organizational research. *International Journal of Management Reviews, 18*(3), 236–270.

Wenger, E. (1998). *Communities of practice: Learning, meaning and identity.* Cambridge: Cambridge University Press.

Yanov, D. (2004). Translating local knowledge at organizational peripheries. *British Journal of Management, 15,* 9–25.

Yanow, D. (1993). The communication of policy meanings: Implementation as interpretation and text. *Policy Sciences, 26,* 41–61.

Yanow, D. (1996). *How does a policy mean? Interpreting policy and organizational actions.* Washington, DC: Georgetown University Press.

7 The theory of action nets

Defining action nets

According to Czarniawska (2014), construction is a process by which something is being built from existing materials (in contrast to creation, which, at least in principle, starts from nothing). She has a performative view on the organization based on the following assumptions (Czarniawska, 2014, p. 7):

- A definition of an organization arises from social perceptions that change with the context
- Actors constantly construct an organization through their actions and their interpretations of what they themselves and the others are doing
- Knowledge of an organization resides in the first place with the actors; observers may have knowledge about an organization, which does not result from any privileged access to reality
- There can be many descriptions of the same organization that can be compared according to pragmatic or aesthetic criteria
- the purpose of research is to capture and describe practices

According to Czarniawska (2014), organizations are constituted by the actions of people related to them. People and groups of people thus construct organizations through their interconnected actions. Czarniawska uses the term 'action nets' when she theorizes these interconnected actions (Lindberg & Czarniawska, 2006, p. 293):

> the concept of the action net is based on the assumption that organizing (and it's special case: management) requires that several different collective actions be connected according to a pattern that is institutionalized at a given time and in a given place. The collective actions concerned need not necessarily be performed within the bounds of a specific organization. On the contrary, an action net may involve a great variety of organizations or organized groups of people of a loose or temporary nature.

Action nets thus consist of all the interconnected actions of people and groups of people necessary to perform the organization including the actions of investing, constructing, producing, buying, selling, transporting, collaborating, etc.

The travel and translation of ideas

According to Czarniawska and Joerges (1996), 'travel of ideas' model ideas need to be translated from ideas and into institutionalized patterns of actions to be 'implemented' in organizations.

> The spread in time and space of anything – claims, orders, artefacts, goods – is in the hands of people; each of these people may act in many different ways, letting the token drop, or modifying it, or deflecting it, or betraying it, or adding to it, or appropriating it.
>
> (Latour 1986, p. 267)

Thus, there is no initial energy moving an idea. Ideas do not diffuse by themselves: It is people who pass them on to each other, each one translating them according to their own frames of reference. The encounters between traveling ideas and people's local frames of reference or 'ideas in residence' may cause friction. In such situations, the idea is checked out and influenced by habits, routines and institutionalized behavior present in the local context in advance. And such encounters may sometimes result in an energizing clash between ideas in residence and traveling ideas, leading to the transformation of both (Czarniawska, 2014, p. 106).

Forming and stabilizing action nets

However, how are ideas translated into institutionalized and thus stabilized patterns of interactions or action nets? To understand how action nets form, Czarniawska refers to Berger and Luckmann's (1966) description of how the forming of institutions takes place. According to this view, people first perform some kind of collective action. Then if people repeat that action, it becomes an action pattern that is taken for granted by the group members. This regular action pattern may now be identified by an external observer who may ask the group members: Why do you act like this? In that situation, the group members will present a normative explanation of why they act as they do in which case the action pattern has become an institution or been 'institutionalized' (Czarniawska, 2014, p. 22).

Czarniawska (2014) emphasizes that the symbolic, the practical and the political aspects are woven together in organizing processes; they do not exist in three separate domains that occasionally meet. The same hammer can serve as an ideological symbol, and objects to threaten someone or to defend oneself with, but also a tool for pounding a nail into a wall (Czarniawska, 2014, p. 53). She also suggests that people in organizations use storytelling and an appropriate repertoire of historically developed and shared collective interpretive templates to transmit knowledge to people and groups of people in a way that makes sense to them (Weick 1996) (Czarniawska, 2014, p. 33). Thus, if you want to tell a story about the change that is going to happen, you need to do it in a way where you build on what people in the organization already know if you want the change to make sense to them. She also thinks that texts are important for organizing because they stabilize connections in an action net. She emphasizes however that texts are not alone in fulfilling this task: There are texts written with numbers (like budgets), and there are pictures and images; but there are also other stabilizing artifacts, such as tools and machines (Czarniawska, 2014, p. 51). And all these different actors or act-ants are translated and play a role in the construction and stabilizing of action nets. Ideas are translated into narratives, objects and actions, and stabilized/institutionalized as intra- or inter-organizational patterns of actions through which 'the organization' is performed.

The types of translation work involved in accomplishing this include the following:

- Translating ideas into a narrative form that makes sense to organiza-tional actors according to local frames (Goffman, 1974) and interpretive templates (schematic plots that can be used for weaving disparate events in a meaningful whole) (Czarniawska, 2012, 2014, p. 37). Frames, as in film and photography, serve as a classifying device ('this is sexual harass-ment'). Interpretative template helps people to find a way of explaining the clue ('men in higher hierarchical positions tend to exploit their fe-male subordinates'), and may suggest a proper script or response ('I must report it to the equality ombudsman') (Czarniawska, 2014, p. 40).
- Managing through texts by translating, editing and inscribing them: During the process, texts are translated from and to technical, economic, legal and everyday language; from and to local languages (of a given department, of a given organization, of a given country); from words to pictures to numbers; and from numbers to words and pictures. Editing of the text reflects different (political and other) interests and viewpoints. Finally, the text is inscribed into a more permanent form which serves as a proof of the successful completion of the two other actions and stores their result in a form (a handwritten page or a formal document) that lasts across time and space (Czarniawska, 2014, p. 42).
- Budgeting: Translating actions and events into numbers and then num-bers into actions in order to control, resulting in various types of actions being connected to one another, including actions undertaken in distant places and at distant times thus contributing to constructing and stabiliz-ing action nets (Czarniawska, 2014, p. 29).
- The construction of machines that help in producing and maintaining the institutional order. Machines used to manage people, and people who wish to manage machines by using codes supposed to aid both attempts (Czarniawska, 2014, p. 69).

- Organized work where only legal persons – companies, associations or authorities – are allowed to 'write in' the institutionalized code where the code through a circular process becomes law (Czarniawska, 2014, p. 66).
- Creation of norms prescribing machine behavior (A4 paper in the printer, 220 V in Europe, etc.) and regulating environmental issues (limits to air, water pollution, pesticides in foot, etc.) that refer to measuring systems and complex theories and instruments and include cybernetic machines used to control human actions (Czarniawska, 2014, p. 67).

And the outcomes of the translation processes are many: Products and services, social order, formal organizations, informal networks, macro-actors and much more (Czarniawska, 2014, p. 31).

Leadership as a service

According to Czarniawska, managers are needed in professional organizations not only to propagate the professionals' achievements outside, but also to organize work for others, rather than organize others' work. It is in this sense that she refers to leadership as service: Managers who deliver services and the services are 'precisely the acts of organizing' (Czarniawska, 2014, p. 87). Czarniawska suggests this analogy to describe the effective leader in a professional organization:

> the closest analogy I can think of is that between an effective leader in a professional organization and an effective chairperson at a big meeting. An effective chairperson sees to it that all participants can say what they want without either anybody dominating the floor or feeling excluded, that the participants do not tire one another, and with everyone feeling that they had taken a step forward. Good chairpersons do not exploit their positions, either by forcing their own opinions or by favorite members of the group. Perhaps the best test for a potentially effective leader is to see if the candidate is able to lead the way to a collective decision that goes against his or her judgement.
>
> (Czarniawska, 2014, p. 89)

Drawing upon Mary Follett (1927), Czarniawska theorizes the relationship between bosses and their subordinates as co-working (Czarniawska, 2014, p. 88) and emphasize the following characteristics as important to being a leader in an organization with professionals:

- Co-workers' talents are fully used
- The leader interacts and communicates with his co-workers because professional work may seem individual but it is, in fact, embedded in action nets, networks and multiple interactions

- The leader integrates knowledge and experience that belongs to individuals so that the whole organization can use it for common purposes
- The leader demonstrates an ability to pattern recognition – that is an ability to distinguish the formation of new patterns in the chaotic multitude of events that we are confronted with daily
- Leadership is practiced through taking an organizing role in sensemaking, in distinguishing between figure and ground, in enactment of the environment and in interpreting what is happening. It also means taking an organizing role in sense-giving and sense-taking

References

Berger, P., & Luckmann, T. (1966). *The social construction of reality*. New York, NY: Doubleday.

Czarniawska, B. (2012). New plots are badly needed in finance: Accounting for the financial crisis of 2007–2010. *Accounting, Auditing and Accountability Journal, 25*(5), 756–775.

Czarniawska, B. (2014). *A theory of organizing* (2nd ed.). Cheltenham, UK, Northampton, MA: Edward Elgar Publishing Limited.

Czarniawska, B., & Joerges, B. (1996). Travels of ideas. In B. Czarniawska & G. Sevon (Eds.), *Translating organizational change* (pp. 13–48). Berlin: de Gruyter.

Follett, M. P. (1927/1941). *Leader and expert in dynamic administration: The collected papers of Mary Parker Follett*. New York, NY: Harper and Bros.

Goffman, E. (1974). *Frame analysis*. Boston, MA: Northeastern University Press.

Latour, B. (1986). The powers of association. In J. Law (Eds.), *Power, action and belief* (pp. 261–277). London: Routledge and Kegan Paul.

Lindberg, K., & Czarniawska, B. (2006). Knotting the action net, or organizing between organizations. *Scandinavian Journal of Management, 22*, 292–306.

Weick, K. E. (1996). *Sensemaking in organizations*. Thousand Oaks, CA: Sage.

8 The linguistic model of translation

Holden, Harald and Kortzfleisch (2004) argue that concepts from linguistic translation research provide useful analogies that may be used to understand the nature of the transfer of knowledge between cross-cultural teams. Knowledge transfer between cross-cultural teams is particularly challenging because knowledge 'is generated in different language systems, (organizational) cultures, and (work) groups. And, if the context changes (culture), knowledge also changes' (Vensin, 1998). They suggest that 'translation…is by far the oldest universal practice of conscientiously converting knowledge from one domain (i.e., a language group) to another' and that 'it is worthwhile exploring the relationship between international knowledge transfer and translation because the two are very much the same thing!' (Holden et al., 2004, p. 129). Holden et al. first introduce a number of insights from linguistic translation theory which they think may inform knowledge transfer research focusing on knowledge transfer between cross-cultural teams. These insights are given as follows:

- Translation is not just about the linguistic transcoding from one language to another but about integrating the translation into a wider network of social relations.
- The quality of the final product and the translation process itself is what should be focused on. The first aspect deals with issues of quality, accuracy and impact on readers; the second focuses on cognitive issues and the competencies of translators.
- The level of accuracy of a translation is important. It may be communicated in four different ways: (1) the general idea is conveyed, (2) sufficient information is conveyed, (3) most of the information is conveyed and (4) virtually all the information is conveyed (Pinchuk, 1977).
- There are constraints on the production of good translations. They may be influenced by ambiguity (confusion at the source), interference (intrusive errors originating from one's own background) and a lack of equivalence (an absence of corresponding words or concepts).

Concerning the ambiguity of translations, Holden et al. (2004) point out that to the translator the word 'ambiguity' refers to words or expressions that are capable of being understood in two or more ways; while in the organizational sciences, ambiguity refers to a general vagueness or uncertainty. In writings on culture and international management, researchers identify 'tolerance of ambiguity' as a cross-cultural competence. Based on an example, Holden et al. (2004) show that contextual (and thus cultural) knowledge is critical to understanding a translation and solving problems related to its ambiguity.

In translation theory, 'interference' refers to the transfer of usages peculiar to the source language to the target language (Holden et al., 2004, pp. 130–131). This happens when words look the same in different languages, but mean something else. Also the pronunciation, grammatical structures and vocabulary of the translators own language play a role in the translation process when they are carried into the foreign language and may be perceived as 'errors' in the target language, marking the speaker as a foreigner.

In translation theory, equivalence refers to situations where translators and receivers lack corresponding words or concepts because the sender's (or translator's) language is different from the receivers' language (Holden et al., 2004, p. 131). Since translation consists of producing in the target language the closest natural equivalent of the source language message, first with respect to meaning and second with respect to style, this process will be influenced by a lack of corresponding words and concepts between the sender's and the receiver's languages.

Holden et al. (2004) now explain in more detail what characterizes human languages and what are the challenges of translating knowledge in equivalent ways from one human language to another:

> by way of considerable simplification we may say that human languages differ from each other formally in four principal ways: in their syntax (the way in which words are arranged and combined 'grammatically'), in their morphology (which refers to the study of ways in which the forms of words change according to context (e.g. walk, walked, walking; big, bigger, biggest); in their Lexis, which refers to the vocabulary items of a language; and in their phonology, which refers to the speech sounds of a language. Anyone who has studied foreign languages will be aware of the complicated ways in which these four systems deviate from each other among languages.
>
> (Holden et al., 2004, p. 132)

Referring to the American linguist, Edward Sapir (1956), Holden et al. (2004) continue:

> no two languages are ever sufficiently similar to be considered as representing the same social reality. The worlds in which different societies live are distinct worlds, not merely the same world with different labels attached". In other words, there is not only distance among languages owing to similarities and differences in the four basic systems of language, but distance as a function of language as a repository of

knowledge, experience and impressions and a device for facilitating social interaction. The challenge for the translator in finding equivalence is
not just to render the words of one language into a second one, but also to
re-express psychological and related factors with in the terms of reference
of that second language.

(Holden et al. 2004, p. 132)

Holden et al. (2004) conclude that the above-mentioned discussion draws our
attention to three important factors:

- Knowledge transfer, like translation, is a sense-making activity.
- Knowledge transfer, like translation, is literally concerned with personal
  cognition and the inter-lingual transfer of knowledge from head to head
  and into social networks.
- Knowledge transfer, like translation, is subject to constraints, which
  affect not just transfer, but rather transferability: The extent to which
  knowledge can be transmitted to others.

Holden et al. (2004) introduce Nonaka and Takeuchi's (1995) model of
knowledge transfer and explain that the process – whereby members of social
groups or teams acquire tacit knowledge through socialization, transform
tacit to explicit knowledge through externalization, combine new and old
or different types of explicit knowledge and then turn explicit knowledge
into tacit knowledge through internalization – involves sense-making and
knowledge translation (and thus transfer) from head to head and into social
networks. They thus conclude that this process is also a part of the knowledge
translation process between cross-cultural teams.

Finally, Holden et al. (2004) introduce the idea that there exist constraints
on efficiency in knowledge-sharing activities, which relates to knowledge
translatability and convertibility. Translatability is theorized as analogue to
the transferability of knowledge. Translatability concerns how the properties
of a text as well as the translator's competence and ability to make an accurate translation affect the knowledge translation process. Ideally, a translator
should be a domain expert both in terms of the languages between which
he needs to translate and in terms of the subject matter of the text being
translated. Convertibility is not just a property of the text. It also refers to its
perceived utility and the availability of domain experts/translators who will
reveal its import to the final user. A successful knowledge transfer act is the
proof that the knowledge content was transferable, and its successful implementation (and thus the collective use of the knowledge) is the measure of its
convertibility.

Holden et al. (2004) now bring together concepts from the above-
mentioned discussion and construct an extended model of knowledge transfer as translation aimed at theorizing how knowledge translation happens
between cross-cultural teams. This model is reproduced in Figure 8.1.

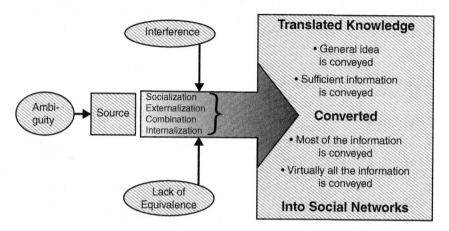

Figure 8.1 Extended model of knowledge transfer as translation.
Reproduced with permission

The model theorizes the factors that influence knowledge translation processes when knowledge moves between cross-cultural teams (see Holden et al., 2004, pp. 134–135). The first factor is the lack of cultural understanding, uncertainty and thus ambiguity related to the source of the knowledge that leaves room for interpretation by the receiving group or team. Other factors are interference and lack of equivalence; that is, the errors of translation that may occur because of differences in the use of words, grammar or pronunciation between the source and target languages and the (possible) lack of corresponding words and concepts between the languages of the sender and the receivers. Other factors that influence the knowledge translation process are given as follows:

1   The ability of the translators or receivers of new knowledge to make tacit knowledge that is necessary for the functioning of the knowledge and is acquired through socialization explicit,
2   Their ability to combine new and local explicit knowledge in relevant ways and
3   Their ability to internalize and make this new explicit knowledge tacit again.

Moreover, the knowledge translation process is influenced by the translatability and convertibility of the knowledge that is being translated. The translatability of the knowledge concerns the properties of the knowledge and whether the translator is a domain expert both in terms of the languages between which he needs to translate and in terms of the subject matter of the text/knowledge being translated. The convertibility of the knowledge will depend on whether domain experts/translators as well as other receiving team/group members find it useful and choose to implement it. Finally, when the knowledge has been through this process, the translated knowledge may be converted into social networks (the receiving teams/groups) in at least four different ways: (1) the general idea is conveyed, (2) sufficient information is conveyed, (3) most of the information is conveyed and finally (4) virtually all the information is conveyed.

References

Holden, N. J., Harald F. O., & Kortzfleisch, O. (2004). Why cross-cultural knowledge transfer is a form of translation in more ways than you think. *Knowledge and Process Management, 11*(2), 127–136.

Nonaka, I., & Takeuchi, H. (1995). *The knowledge-creating company.* New York, NY: Oxford University Press.

Pinchuk, I. (1977). *Scientific and technical translation.* London: André Deutsch.

Sapir, E. (1956). *Culture, language and personality.* Berkeley: University of California Press.

Vensin, M. (1998). Knowledge management. *CEMS Business Review, 2*(3), 205–210.

9 An instrumental theory of translation

The Norwegian researcher Kjell Arne Røvik (2016) has developed an instrumental theory of knowledge transfer as translation. He contributes to developing translation studies by analyzing, comparing and critically reflecting upon research from neo-institutional translation studies, studies of knowledge transfer and research about literary and nonliterary translation.

Røvik (2016) suggests that studies of the mediation of information between source and target units – and thus the processes whereby someone identifies practices in a field or organization, translates them to abstract ideas and concepts, and then transfers them to other organizations – have been neglected in neo-institutional translation studies. He also points out that translation studies have focused upon documenting translation processes – including how various ideas trigger complex processes involving sense-making, power plays, resistance and bargaining among local actors – but contain few examples of instrumental thinking – that is reflections on how local translated versions affect organizations' effectiveness and efficiency. Finally, Røvik criticizes the assumption of ANT researchers and Scandinavian neo-institutionalists that translation, by definition, always involves transformation of the token (the idea or knowledge) being translated and thus the argument that it is unnecessary or perhaps even impossible for researchers to compare large samples of translation processes to reveal their rules, regularities and outcomes (Røvik, 2016, p. 293).

In contrast to these types of studies, Røvik (2016, p. 293) points out that the established interdisciplinary field of literary and nonliterary translation studies conceptualizes translation as acts of mediation and communication between a source and a target, considers translation to be a rule-based activity and includes discussions of normative-instrumental issues such as debates about translator skills, what constitutes a good translation and how these normative-instrumental ideas may be expressed in various instructions to translators. Inspired by these theories, Røvik develops a translation perspective on knowledge transfer that builds on the following assumptions:

1 Knowledge transfers between organizational sources and recipients can be conceptualized as acts of translation

2   Translation of knowledge (practices and ideas) is a rule-based activity
3   Translations make a difference; the way translations are performed may explain outcomes of knowledge transfer processes

Knowledge transfer as acts of translation

According to Røvik (2016), knowledge transfer between sources and recipients involves translation that presupposes mediating actors as translators. Multiple actors with different interests, perceptions and interpretations shape translations and coordinated efforts – as for instance in knowledge transfer projects where consultants, managers, procurers and expatriates are involved and act as key boundary spanners and translators (O'Mahoney, Heusinkveld, & Wright, 2013; Sturdy & Wright, 2011; Westney, 1987).

Røvik (2016) points out that as acts of translation, knowledge transfer involves two critical phases: The first phase is decontextualization – that is translating a desired practice in a particular organizational context into an abstract representation (e.g., images, words and texts). The second phase is contextualization, which is defined as translating an abstract representation into concrete materialized practices in a recipient context.

Decontextualizing knowledge about a practice from the source context

In the decontextualization phase, the translators focus upon translating an observed practice in a certain organizational context to an abstract representation. Here, the main challenge is to ensure that the representation contains all the relevant information required to explain and understand how the practice functions in the source context. The success of this translation process is influenced by the translatability of the practice in question – that is 'the extent to which a particular practice can be translated to an abstract representation without excluding the elements required for how it functions in the source context' (Røvik, 2016, p. 294). Røvik identifies three variables that are decisive for the translatability of a desired practice: Its complexity, embeddedness and explicitness.

The complexity of a practice is related to the relationship between technology and people involved in it. The more a practice is based on a technology component with a clear-cut application, rather than on context-specific human skills, the less complex it is. And thus the easier it is to translate it into an abstract representation including the essential elements that makes it function. Practices that depend on a strong human component however and on a low or unclear technology component are more complex and therefore more difficult to translate. Moreover, the complexity of a practice is influenced by causal ambiguity. Thus, the more ambiguous and complex the relationship between observed results and underlying practices, the more difficult it is to translate it to an abstract representation that accounts for all the essentials in the source.

The translatability of knowledge about a practice is also influenced by its embeddedness – that is the extent to which the knowledge and capabilities that constitute a desired practice are anchored in its intra- and or inter-organizational contexts. Here, the challenge becomes to identify and demarcate the exact knowledge base of superior results.

Finally, the translatability of knowledge is influenced by the explicitness of a practice. Thus, according to Polanyi (1962, 1966), knowledge among the source-based actors of a desired practice can be explicit or tacit. Explicit knowledge is verbalized, codified, well articulated and easily taught, written and expressed in formulas and manuals. Tacit knowledge however refers to the non-verbalized, non-codified and non-standardized knowledge that underlies a skillful performance. The more explicit the knowledge about a practice, the easier it is to translate it into a codified and transferable abstract representation. The more tacit the knowledge about a practice, the more difficult it becomes to translate it to the recipient context. In such a situation, the tacit knowledge about a practice must first be verbalized in order to be made communicable. Then this verbalized, context-specific knowledge must be translated to a more abstract, transferable representation. Therefore, the risk of misinterpretation increases.

Contextualizing knowledge about a practice in the recipient context

Contextualization is the second phase in knowledge transfer and concerns the translation from an abstract representation of a desired practice in a source context to a concrete practice embedded in formal structures, cultures, routines and individual skills in a recipient context. Here, the translator faces two challenges. (1) He/she may miss the essentials of the desired practice in the source context. (2) Or he/she may miss the essentials of the recipient context and not make the necessary adaptions that will enable the knowledge construct and practice to fit into the new context.

New ideas and practices are introduced in contexts containing other ideas and established practices that may hinder or facilitate its implementation. Therefore, the complexity and outcome of contextualization processes may vary, depending on the degree of compatibility between new and existing ideas and practices. New ideas and practices may challenge the competence and interests of actors performing the existing practice, it may be technically challenging and depend on trial and error translation processes, or it may be only loosely coupled to old practices and thus be more easily translated. In addition, the translators' access to the recipients' current practices may vary with those practices' degree of explicitness, complexity and embeddedness. Because of the above-mentioned characteristics of contextualization processes, Røvik concludes that the translators need to know about established practices in the recipient context in order to be able to determine how the new knowledge relates to already existing practices.

Modes and rules that influence the translation

According to Røvik (2016, p. 296), translators follow rules and shape knowledge constructs while transferring them between source and target contexts. Røvik thus develops a typology of three ideal types and modes of translation, each with their own characteristic rules: (1) the reproducing mode, (2) the modifying mode and (3) the radical mode. The reproducing mode leads to low transformation of the transferred knowledge. The modifying mode results in medium transformation of the transferred knowledge. Finally, the radical mode is related to a high degree of transformation of the transferred knowledge.

The reproducing mode is used when an organization that aims for a competitive advantage deliberately and systematically adopts and replicates other organizations innovations or best practices. In this situation, the organization follows the translation rule of copying. Copying refers to actions that aim to replicate in a recipient context certain practices and/or results found in a source context.

The modifying mode is characterized by translators balancing off competing concerns of replication and adjustment. On the one hand, they need to conceptualize and include the essentials of the desired source practice in the translated version. On the other hand, they need to assure that the transferred knowledge construct (or imagined practice) is adjusted to fit into existing practices in the recipient organizational context. According to Røvik, this may be done following two translation rules. The first rule – addition – involves adding a few elements to the source version when translating it to the recipient version. Another translation rule that may be followed is omission. Omission (or partial implementation) refers to the toning down or subtraction of certain aspects of the desired source version of practices in the recipient version.

In the radical mode, translators are relatively unbound by the source context versions of a practice when creating its recipient versions. In this situation, the translators follow the translation rule of alteration. This translation rule is defined as the comprehensive transformation and mixing of one or more source versions of a practice, leading to the creation of a unique version in the recipient organization. Thus, it refers to creating something new while imitating something that already exists.

Translation competences: Handling the relationship between modes, rules and outcomes

As mentioned, Røvik thinks that the way translations of desired practices from source contexts (organizations) are performed may explain the outcomes they produce in the recipient organizations and contexts. He thus emphasizes that from a translation perspective, the flow of knowledge from the source to the recipient is not just transferred, but also a two-faced translation process of de-contextualization and contextualization (Røvik, 2016, p. 300). How translators apply translation rules when decontextualizing practices and contextualizing ideas may, according to Røvik, be just as decisive for outcomes of knowledge transfer processes as the effects of researched knowledge barriers:

> translator's application of such rules, regardless of whether they slavishly follow or deliberately choose the rules, may have considerable consequences for the outcomes of the knowledge transfer processes. The application may be decisive for whether the desired source practices are reproduced, slightly modified or radically transformed.
>
> (Røvik, 2016, p. 300)

Røvik now introduces the idea that translators must have certain translation competences to be able to translate desired practices from one organizational context to another. Røvik defines translation competences as '...the ability of translators to translate practices and ideas between organizational contexts in

Table 9.1 Features influencing translators' choice of translation rules

Key element	Features influencing the key element
The source	The translatability of source practice: – Explicitness (tacit/non-codified vs. explicit/codified) – Complexity (technological vs. human component), degree of causal ambiguity, embeddedness (is knowledge base concentrated or dispersed in intra- and inter-organizational networks?)
The knowledge construct	The transformability of the knowledge construct: – Depends on translators' freedom to interpret, change and make their own version of the construct – If construct depends on technology with clear-cut application in order to function it is less transformable – The more authorities regulate the transfer process the less transformable the transferred construct is
The relation between recipient and source	The degree of similarity and difference between recipient and source context: – The greater the difference the more difficult it is to arrive at proper translations

Table 9.2 When do different translation rules apply?

Translation rule	Hypothesis
Copying: To replicate, with great exactitude, a desired source practice	1 The more explicit, less complex and less embedded a desired source practice, the more appropriate copying will be as a translation rule in knowledge transfer 2 The less transformable the transferred knowledge, the more appropriate copying will be as a translation rule 3 The more similar recipient and source contexts are on critical variables, the more appropriate copying will be as a translation rule
Addition: Adding a few elements to the source version when translating it to the recipient version	4 The more non-explicit aspects of a desired source practice are important for its functioning, the more addition, in the version of explicitation, becomes an appropriate translation rule 5 Medium transformability of the transferred knowledge facilitates a modifying translation mode, and inter alia, the application of addition as a translation rule
Omission: The toning down or subtraction of certain aspects of the desired source version of practices in the recipient version	6 Medium dissimilarity between the recipient and source context facilitates a modifying translation mode, and inter alia, the application of omission and addition as translation rules
Alteration: The comprehensive transformation and mixing of knowledge constructs	7 The more tacit, complex and embedded a desired source practice, the more alteration becomes an appropriate translation rule 8 The more transformable the transferred knowledge, the more likely that alteration will be used as a translation rule 9 The more dissimilar recipient and source contexts are on critical variables, the more appropriate alteration will be as a translation rule

ways that increase the probability of achieving organizational ends' (Røvik, 2007, 2016). He points out that an important prerequisite for translation competence is contextual bilingualism, which means that the translators should have thorough knowledge of both the source and the recipient contexts. He moreover points out that a critical feature of translation competence in knowledge transfer is the translators' knowledge about translation rules and about how various rules relate to and can be applied in various conditions (Røvik, 2016, p. 300).

In order to identify which translation rules apply in which types of situations, Røvik (2016) first identifies the key elements of the knowledge transfer process. These are the source, the transferred knowledge construct, and the recipient and its relationship to the source. Røvik then claims that specific features of each of these three elements represent important conditions for translators who, in various settings, search for the most appropriate among the four main translation rules identified by Røvik. The features that influence the translators' choice of translation rules are summed up in Table 9.1.

Røvik now analyzes the complex relations between conditions (the three key conditional variables: Translatability, transformability and similarity) and the translation rules that apply in different situations. The outcome of Røvik's analysis is a number of hypotheses about when certain translation rules apply or may be used by a translator. The results of his analysis are reproduced in Table 9.2.

References

Røvik, K. A. (2007). *Trender og Translasjoner: Ideer som former det 21.Århundrets organisasjon.* Oslo: Universitetsforlaget.

Røvik, K. A. (2016). Knowledge transfer as translation: Review and elements of an instrumental theory. *International Journal of Management Reviews, 18*(3), 290–310.

Polanyi, M. (1966). *The tacit dimension.* London: Routledge & Kegan Paul.

Polanyi, M. (1962). *Personal knowledge.* London: Routledge & Kegan Paul.

O'Mahoney, J., Heusinkveld, S., & Wright, C. (2013). Commodifying the commodifiers: the impact of procurement on management knowledge. *Journal of Management Studies, 50*, 204–235.

Sturdy, A., & Wright, C. (2011). The active client: the boundary-spanning roles of internal consultants as gatekeepers, brokers and partners of their external counterparts. *Management Learning, 42*, 485–503.

Westney, D. E. (1987). *Imitation and innovation: The transfer of western organizational patterns to Meiji Japan.* Cambridge, MA: Harvard University Press.

10 Translating strategy

The strategy researcher Søren Obed Madsen (2013) has studied what leaders do with strategy documents when they move from one context to another. He suggests that the great challenge in strategy work unfolds in the meeting between plans and processes and particularly in the interaction between strategy documents and the actors who translate them. His analysis of the strategy, leadership, organization and translation research literature shows that how leaders relate to and translate strategy documents to their own contexts have not received sufficient academic attention. Therefore, he asks the following research question: How do leaders translate strategy documents? Leaders are identified as top managers, middle managers or employees with formal positions and authority in organizations. They have different areas of responsibility that include decision-making, communicating information and functioning as a liaison between parts of the organization (Madsen, 2013, p. 31).

Studying strategy translation as translation of texts

Inspired by Røvik (2007), Madsen (2013) suggests that translating strategy texts is similar to translating literary texts because it concerns translating a text from one context to another. He points out that a translator's task reminds of what actors, like leaders, do with strategy documents and therefore literary translation theory may contribute to the strategy literature. Madsen (2013) explains that textual translation is a research field that focuses upon the translation process, the role of the translator, the relationship between texts and actors, as well as the relationship between texts (Baker, 2006, 2009; Gentzler, 1993; Gile, 2009; Nord, 1997; Pym, 2004; Schulte & Biguenet, 1992; Tymoczko & Getzler, 2002). The study of translations has spread from literary to other research fields and is today considered a cross-disciplinary research field that covers areas such as literature, philosophy, discourse theory, history and organization theory (Madsen, 2013, p. 40; Munday, 2009). The field may be divided into four theoretical perspectives on translation of texts that reflect the fields' historical development and the accumulation of all the approaches that you find with translation theory that works with language, culture, meaning, relations between the actors, the translators power, the power of the texts and social factors (Baker, 2010; Munday, 2008; Schnell-Hornby, 2006; Venuti, 1995) (Madsen, 2013, p. 40). Referring to Munday (2008) and Pym (2010), Madsen (2013) identifies these four main perspectives as the linguistic, the cultural, the functional and the ideological perspectives on translation.

Madsen (2013) conducts an analysis of former research studying strategy as texts. Pälli, Vaara and Sorsa (2009) have a normative view and suggest that it is not possible to distinguish between the strategy text and its social use. Giraudeau (2008) suggests that strategy documents function as cognitive support rather than as a plan and that there is therefore not necessarily a relation between an author's intention with the strategy document and how it is used. Swales and Rogers' (1995) rhetorical analysis suggests that strategy texts about mission statements function as a means to persuade employees to like the strategy texts and that they are carriers of culture, ethos and ideologies and a particular type of language. Connell and Galasinski (1998) suggest that mission statements are socially negotiated. Williams (2008) emphasizes that the function of mission statements is to build up an organizational identity. According to Vaara et al. (2010), a strategy consists of a text that represents certain ideas and uses a certain terminology that supports creation of consensus, gives itself authority and creates discursive innovation as well as uses words and an imperative grammar that refers to the future and how it is realized. Finally, Nord (1997) suggests that a plan is only a plan as long as the actors involved ascribe this function to the strategy text. Madsen (2013) notes that as a consequence it is an empirical question how the receivers of strategy plans react to and use such a text. Based on the literature review, Madsen (2013) concludes that strategy documents have been studied as texts before but not in a way that distinguishes between the characteristics of the text, how it is used socially and the author's intentions.

Developing a view on translation of strategy text

Madsen's (2013) own view on leader's translation of strategy documents is developed and based on his analysis of the strategy, leadership, organization and translation research literature. Through his analysis, he develops a view on strategy as texts that distinguish it from the planning and process perspectives on strategy. He sums up these differences in Table 10.1.

Madsen (2013) explains the basic assumptions, concepts and ideas on which his view on literary translation of texts and thus translation of strategy documents is based.

Table 10.1 Strategy as plan, process and text

Strategy is a	plan	process	text
Function	The strategy document tells the receiver, what needs to be done and reduce the actors' possibilities for actions	The strategy document offers a number of possibilities that participants need to relate to, including relations, negotiations and power games	The strategy document offers a number of possibilities th the translator may choose t use or not use. The strateg is something that is created on the basis of an original
Success	When goals are achieved	When processes have been completed and their success criteria have been achieved	Will vary depending on the translators model of translation
Assumptions	Methodological individualism. The world stands still. The strategy is stable and depends on the environment. High degree of predictability	Methodological collectivism. The world moves. The strategy is unstable and is adapted to the environment. High degree of unpredictability	Pragmatic methodological individualism. The world moves and stands still at the same time. The strategy has stable and unstable elements. The strategy is both adapted an influences the environmer at the same time
Leaders' role	Has a certain knowledge that makes it possible for them to describe what is needed to succeed with the strategy. Leaders make things happen and follow up on strategy	Is in a negotiation situation with others and needs to be updated about what goes on internally and externally. The group makes things happen	May be an author, a translator or a receiver. The translators can speak with the authors, but will often be alone with the translation task. What happens depends on the interplay between actors and groups
View on the organization	Is hierarchical and univocal. Characterized by harmoni where everyone is pursuing the same goals. Uni-culture and language	Multi-vocal arena for negotiation of common goals. Characterized by conflicts of interests between actors. Differences exist between cultures and languages	Is both a network and hierarchical. Is univocal depending on the context There are one or more authors. The translators' responsibility is to transla the text so that it is understood by the receive Differentiated cultures and languages that need the translator in order to understand each other. Tl translator is subordinate t the initiator of strategy

Language

According to Madsen (2013) languages belong to certain language groups (Danish, German, Indo-European, Roman, etc.) and there may be different dialects. They are characterized by particular signs that have different meanings and the grammar decides the right way to combine and change the signs (Gleason, 1961). A language is dynamical and changes over time. Words disappear, new words emerge and the meaning they express can change over time. A language also results in certain ways of thinking, values and perspectives and plays a role in relation to the feeling of identity of groups (Rombach & Zapata, 2010). A language can also be specific for certain groups – for instance, professionals like doctors, economists, IT experts and leaders (Rombach & Zapata, 2010). A language makes communication possible and includes those who understand the language but excludes those who do not (Ricoeur, 2006). When translating texts from one language to another and across groups, you may make the receiver start thinking differently.

Translation

Madsen (2013, p. 42) starts with citing David Bellos (2011, p. 37) who defines translation as follows:

> Translations are substitutes for original texts. You use them in the place of a work written in a language you cannot read with ease.

He then refers to two levels of translation identified by Ricoeur (2006). The first level is the linguistic level, which is about the relationship between words and meaning within a language and how texts are translated from texts to texts, from word to word, from word to text or text to word. The second ontological level refers to how humans translate something to himself/herself and others. The first level is applied when doing text analysis. The second level is applied when you analyze how the translator influences the translation or tries to identify what the influence of translators and texts is on social relationships. Translations include translation from text to text, from text to talk, from talk to text and from talk to talk (Baker & Saldanha, 2009; Munday, 2009; Ricoeur, 2006).

Referring to Ricoeur (2006), Madsen (2013) points out that a translator is both a receiver and an author of that which is translated. The translator is a receiver when he/she receives and tries to understand that/the text which he/she is about to translate. This is the case because the precondition for translating something is that you yourself understand it. When the translator starts translating the text, however, he/she becomes an author. Therefore, a translator may be loyal to the original text or betray it when he/she translates it. Finally, a translator may be the one who sets the translation process in motion. Madsen (2013) concludes that the many ways a translator may influence a text means that translation is an indeterministic process where it is not possible to construct general rules for what a translator should do when he/she translates a text. He/she could however reflect upon whom or what (for instance top management and the original strategy document) the translator can, must or should be loyal to.

The translation task

A translation task may be defined as making a text available for other people who cannot understand the language in which it is written. It concerns overcoming the boundaries and barriers for understanding that are set up by language and culture (Friedrich, 1992; Madsen, 2013, p. 44). This process may be divided into two steps: The translator first needs to decode the meaning in the original language; and, second, to reproduce this meaning in the new language (Munday, 2009). According to Madsen (2013), this view has however been criticized which has led some authors (Duff, 1981) to define the task of translation as being about applying a 'third language' which lies between the source and target languages.

Madsen (2013) concludes that the translator's task is to decode a text and to translate it while taking into consideration how words, culture, function and ideology as well as the translator him/herself influences the translation.

The translatability of texts

In literary translation theory, the concept of translatability refers to an evaluation of how difficult it is to translate a text between two languages and cultures (Benjamin, 1968; Jakobson, 1959; Madsen, 2013; Rubel & Rosman, 2003). Some texts are easy to translate others are not. This has resulted in an awareness of how translators' competences may influence a translation process. Referring to Røvik (2007), Madsen (2013) thus points out that the translatability of a strategy text is influenced not just by the translatability of the strategy text itself and characteristics of language and culture but also by the translators' competences' and translation difficulties. Madsen (2013) thinks this is interesting in relation to strategy documents because it suggests that a translator can evaluate and estimate which parts of a strategy document are difficult or easier to translate as well as make translators reflect on which translation competences may be needed in order to succeed with the translation.

Translators' competences

Like Røvik (2007), Madsen (2013) suggests that translators' competences may influence the translation process. Literary translation theory deepens our understanding of translation competences and suggests that in-depth knowledge about rhetoric, grammar, culture, history, ideologies and text functions is necessary for solving translation tasks. The competence needed of the translator is to be able to produce different translations of an original text and then select the text that fits best (Pym, 1990). Which translation/text that fits best depends on what the translator prioritizes to take into account. And what he/she takes into account refers back to the four perspectives that have been developed within literary translation theory: the linguistic, the cultural, the functional and the ideological perspectives (Madsen, 2013, p. 46).

The intertextuality of texts

Madsen (2013) points out that texts have relations to other texts (Allen, 2001; Bakhtin, 1986; Fairclough, 1992; Schnell-Hornby, Pöchhacker, & Kaindl, 1994). A translator thus has supplementary texts that help with making the purpose of the original text more clear, answers questions raised by the original text and helps qualifying the choices that are made to make the best translation possible. Such texts may for instance be lexica, wordbooks, historical texts or other texts.

The four perspectives on literary translation

Madsen (2013) now presents the four perspectives that have been developed within literary translation studies: the linguistic, the cultural, the functional and the ideological perspectives on translation. He suggests that the four perspectives together describe the considerations and choices that a translator has when translating a text and that a translator may shift between the different models as he/she translates the same text. During the process, the translator must decide who and what to be loyal to.

The linguistic perspective

Madsen (2013) refers to Catford's (1965, p. 1) definition of the linguistic perspective:

> Translation is an operation performed on languages: a process of substituting a text in one language for a text in another.

Linguistic translation focuses on the translation of words from one language to words that means the same thing in another language (Munday, 2008). In this type of translation, the loyalty of the translator lies with the original text that the translator tries to reproduce as correctly as possible in another language. A weakness with this form of translation may be that words that exist in one language may not exist in another or may be used differently in that language.

The cultural perspective

Madsen (2013) refers to Katan (2009) and Bassnett and Lefevere (1990, p. 8) who suggest:

> Neither the word, nor the text, but the culture becomes the operational 'unit' of translation.

The cultural perspective focuses on how the meaning of words varies and changes depending on the cultural context. It focuses on rewriting the text in a way that makes it more accessible to others. Translator's reflections about similarities and differences between the cultural context of the original text and the cultural context of the target audience for the translated text may therefore result in major changes of the text. For instance, if the translator(s) judge that it will make the translation better for the receivers.

The functional perspective

Madsen (2013) refers to Nord's definition of the functional perspective (Nord, 1997, p. 29):

> Skopos of a particular translation task may require a "free" or a "faithful" translation, or anything between these two extremes, depending on the purpose for which the translation is needed.

In this perspective, the translators' loyalty shifts from being loyal to the language or culture to being loyal to the intention the author had with his/her text. What is focused upon is to make the text function for the receiver in the way the author intended (Nord, 1997; Reiss, 2000; Vermeer, 1989). Linguistic and cultural aspects need to be considered but supplemented with reflections about the purpose of the text. As a consequence, it may be considered to ask the author or initiator of a text to give the translator a translation guide to the translation of his/her text.

The ideological perspective

Here, Madsen (2013) cites Venuti (1995):

> Translation is, of course, a rewriting of an original text. All rewritings, whatever their intention, reflect a certain ideology and a poetics and as such manipulate literature to function in a given society in a given way.

In this perspective, the translator is assumed to be a political actor who exercises power by influencing or manipulating the way people perceive the world or by communicating information that helps an actor with obtaining power over another actor (Madsen, 2013, p. 54). The source culture is assumed to influence the target culture, which results in a mix of these two (Bhabha, 2004). The perspective focuses on the problems of loyalty related to the translator and the translator as a potential traitor. It emphasizes that the translator functions as a mediator between two persons or worlds that do not understand each other. In such a situation, the target audience of a translation must rely on the translator to translate and not change the text or what is said in a way that changes the content. You cannot however always trust that translators do so (Madsen, 2013; Venuti, 1998). A translator may himself/herself have interests and a certain ideology or represent someone who has.

Translating strategy texts – A model

Madsen (2013) sums up his analysis of the literary translation literature in a model that explains how translators, like leaders, in organizations translate strategy documents. This model is reproduced in Figures 10.1 and 10.2.

The model suggests that a translator in an organization may reflect about the following things when he/she works with translating a strategy (or other) text:

- Language: How are the words translated so that the meaning of the text/talk is communicated?
- Function: How do you translate text/talk in a way that makes the text work as intended?
- Cultural: How do you translate the text/talk so that it is understood in another culture?
- Ideological: How is the translation affected by the interests and ideology of the translator?

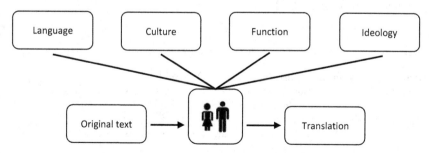

Figure 10.1 What a translator needs to attend to
Source: Madsen, 2013, p. 55. Reproduced with permission.

Table 10.2 The four perspectives of translation theory

Perspective	Linguistic	Cultural	Functional	Ideological
Focus	How can words be translated from one language to another?	How can culture influence the meaning of words?	How can the intention of the author be translated so that the text maintains its wished-for function?	How do texts influence receivers and how can the translator manipulate with the text?
Key concept	Equivalence	Rewriting	Functionality	Power
The translators' role	To decode the source language and find equivalent words in the target language	To rewrite the source text so that it fits with the target culture	To be loyal to the authors' intention with the text	To find out what interests he or she wants to support
Assumptions	The meaning of the text is in the words	The meaning with the text is an interaction between words and culture	It is possible to identify the authors' intention with the text	The translator can manipulate others through texts

Source: Madsen, 2013, p. 56. Reproduced with permission.

Madsen (2013) emphasizes that this also implies that a translator may be loyal to the content, the intention, the context or an ideology/certain interests when he/she translates a text/talk. Alternatively, he/she may be loyal to a combination of these. A translator does thereby not stand outside the process and neutrally move a text from one place to another. He/she may be influenced by the text, culture and political interests and ideology as he/she moves the text. It is thus not the strategy text that is translated in an organization but the translators translated its version. Madsen (2013) sums up the focus, translator's role in and assumptions of the four perspectives on translation of (strategy) texts in Table 10.2.

References

Allen, G. (2001). *Intertextuality*. New York, NY: Routledge.
Baker, M. (2006). *Translation and conflict-A narrative account*. New York, NY: Routledge.
Baker, M., Saldanha, G. (2009) *Routledge encyclopedia of translation studies* (2nd ed.). London: Routledge.
Baker, M. (2010). Interpreters and translators in the war zone: Narrated and narrators. *The Translator, 16*(2), 197.

Baker, M., & Saldanha, G. (2009). *Routledge encyclopedia of translation studies* (2nd ed.). London: Routledge.

Bakhtin, M. M. (1986). *Speech genres and other essays.* V. Mcgee (Trans.); M. Holquist & C. Emerson (Eds.). Austin: University of Texas Press.

Bassnett, S., & Lefevere, A. (1990). *Translation, history and culture.* London: Pinter.

Bellos, D. (2011). *Is that a fish in your ear: Translation and the meaning of everything.* London: Particular books.

Benjamin, W. (1968) The Task of the Translator in Benjamin, W. (1968) Illuminations, New York: Harcourt, Brace and World.

Bhabha, H. (2004) The Location of Culture, London: Routledge.

Catford, J. C. (1965). *A linguistic theory of translation.* Oxford: Oxford University Press.

Connell, I., & Galasinski, D. (1998). Academic mission statements: An exercise in negotiation. *Discourse & Society, 9*(4), 457–479.

Duff, A. (1981). *The third language.* New York, NY: Pergamon Press.

Fairclough, N. (1992). Discourse and text: Linguistic and intertextual analysis within discourse analysis. *Discourse Society, 3*(2), 193.

Friedrich, H. (1992). On the art of translation. In R. Schulte & J. Biguenet (Eds.), *Theories of translation: An anthology of essays from Dryden to Derrida.* Chicago, IL: University of Chicago Press.

Gentzler, E. (1993). *Contemporary translation theories.* London: Routledge.

Gile, D. (2009). *Basic concepts and models for interpreter and translator training.* Philadelphia, PA: John Benjamins Pub. Company.

Giraudeau, M. (2008). The drafts of strategy: Opening up plans and their uses. *Long Range Planning, 41*(3), 291.

Gleason Jr, H. A. (1961). *An introduction to descriptive linguistics.* New York: Holt, Rinehart and Winston.

Jakobson, R. (1959). On linguistic aspects of translation. *On Translation, 3,* 30–39.

Katan, D. (2009). Translation as intercultural communication. In J. Munday (Ed.), *Introducing translation studies theories and applications* (2nd ed.). London: Routledge.

Madsen, S. O. (2013). *The Leader as a Translator – A translation perspective on strategy work.* PhD dissertation, Copenhagen Business School.

Munday, J. (2008). *Introducing translation studies: Theories and applications.* New York: Routledge.

Munday, J. (2009). *The Routledge companion to translation studies.* London: Routledge.

Nord, C. (1997). *Translating as a purposeful activity.* Manchester: St. Jerome Pub.

Pälli, P., Vaara, E., & Sorsa, V. (2009). Strategy as text and discursive practice: A genre-based approach to strategizing in city administration. *Discourse & Communication, 3*(3), 303–318.

Pym, A. (1990). *A definition of translational competence, applied to the teaching of translation.* Paper presented to the 12th world congress of the FIT, Belgrade. Unpublished manuscript.

Pym, A. (2004). *The moving text, localization, translation, and distribution.* Philadelphia, PA: J. Benjamins.

Pym, A. (2010). *Exploring translation theories.* London: Routledge.

Reiss, K. (2000). *Translation criticism, the potentials and limitations: Categories and criteria for translation quality assessment.* Manchester: American Bible Society: St. Jerome Pub.

Ricoeur, P. (2006). *On translation.* London: Routledge.

Rombach, B., & Zapata, P. (2010). *The rise of management-speak.* Stockholm: Santérus Academic Press, Sweden.

Røvik, K. A. (2007). *Trends and translations. Ideas that forms the organisations of the 21th Century.* Oslo: Universitetsforlaget.

Rubel, P. G., & Rosman, A. (2003). *Translating cultures: Perspectives on translation and anthropology.* Berg Publishers.

Schnell-Hornby, M. (2006). *The turns of translation studies: New paradigms or shifting viewpoints?* Amsterdam: John Benjamins Publishing Company, The Netherlands.

Schnell-Hornby, M., Pöchhacker, F., & Kaindl, K. (1994). *Translation studies: An interdiscipline.* Selected papers from the translation studies congress, Vienna, pp. 9–12, September 1992. John Benjamins Publishing Company.

Schulte, R., & Biguenet, J. (1992). *Theories of translation: A anthology of essays from Dryden to Derrida.* Chicago, IL: University of Chicago press.

Swales, J. M., & Rogers, P. S. (1995). Discourse and the projection of corporate culture: The mission statement. *Discourse & Society, 6*(2), 223–242.

Tymoczko, M., & Getzler, E. (2002). *Translation and power.* Amherst: University of Massachusetts Press.

Vaara, E., Sorsa, V., & Pälli, P. (2010). On the force potential of strategy texts: A critical discourse analysis of a strategic plan and its power effects in a city organization. *Organization, 17*(6), 685–702.

Venuti, L. (1995). *The translator's invisibility – A history of translation.* London: Routledge.

Venuti, L. (1998). *The scandals of translation towards an ethics of difference.* New York, NY: Routledge.

Vermeer, H. J. (1989). Skopos and commission in translational action. In A. Chesterman (Ed.), *Readings in translation theory* (pp. 173–187). Helsinki: Oy Finn Lectura Ab.

Williams, L. S. (2008). The mission statement. A corporate reporting tool with a past, present, and future. *Journal of Business Communication, 45*(2), 94–119.

11 Policy translation

Researchers in policy and public administration studies have started studying the movement of policy ideas from a translation perspective (Clarke & Bainton, 2015; Johnson & Hagström, 2005; Mukhtarov, 2014; Stone, 2012, 2017). The perspective has been offered as an alternative to other perspectives on the movement of policy ideas as the policy diffusion and policy transfer perspectives (Johnson & Hagström, 2005; Stone, 2017).

From policy diffusion to translation

Johnson and Hagström (2005) relate the policy transfer and policy diffusion perspectives (Berry, 1994; Berry & Berry, 1999; Dolowitz & Marsh, 1996, 2000; Rogers, 1995; Rose, 1993) with a traditional understanding of communication as a transfer of messages (Fiske 1990). Shannon and Weaver's model of communication (Shannon & Weaver, 1949) explains how messages are transported or transmitted between a transmitter and a receiver through the use of certain media. The model focuses upon the content that the sender puts into the message and how the intentions that the sender had with the message may be realized among the receivers. The model suggests that the communication process may be influenced by noise and problems in the transmission process that may hinder that the original message reaches the receivers and have the intended effects. The model thus implies that it may be possible for a receiver to decode the senders' message as it was intended by him/her.

Building on Latour (1986), Johnson and Hagström (2005) relate the translation model with the semiotic communication model (Fiske, 1990). According to this model, humans are continuously engaged in meaning production. We interpret everything we get in contact with. And these interpretations are influenced by certain socio-cultural contexts and environments as well as our experiences from our daily lives. Instead of focusing on transmission of messages, the semiotic communication model focuses on the locally situated work with producing and exchanging views on the meaning of the message or messages that have been received. According to this view, it is the meaning that the culturally embedded receiver ascribes to a message that is important rather than the content that the sender has put into the message or the intentions he/she had with it. In the semiotic communication model, the communication thus fails if the receivers of a (policy) message are not able to ascribe meaning to and make sense of the content of the message.

Drawing on the above-mentioned points and Latour's (1986) critique of the diffusion perspective, Johnson and Hagström (2005) point out that policy ideas do not move by themselves but are in the hands of and constructed by people as suggested by the translation perspective. They conclude that the idea that policy ideas and messages are stable across contexts is problematic because it will always be possible for the receivers to interpret them in different ways and it will never be possible to ascribe a certain final content or intention to them. Policies/policy ideas must instead be interpreted as carriers and producers of meaning. And it is the underlying thoughts and ideas of the policies as perceived by the receivers that are spread (Johnson & Hagström, 2005, p. 370). Moreover, ideas do not force themselves on organizations, which then have to adopt them as suggested by the diffusion perspective. Rather, 'the impetus for imitation must come from the imitators themselves, from their conception of the situation, self-identity and others' identity, as well as from analogical reasoning by which these conceptions are combined' (Johnson & Hagström, 2005, p. 371; Sevón, 1996, p. 51).

Based on the discussion, Johnson and Hagström (2005) redefine policy diffusion in the view of a constructivist translation perspective:

> ...it is now possible tentatively to define policy diffusion as an imitation process where meaning is constructed by temporally and spatially disembedding policy ideas from their previous context and using them as a model for altered political structures in a new context.
>
> (Johnson & Hagström, 2005, p. 370)

Johnson and Hagström (2005, pp. 370–373) now identify the most important theoretical implications of the policy translation perspective as follows:

1   It is always the underlying thoughts and ideas of policies that are spread
2   These ideas are not innovations as supposed in the diffusion perspective because there will always be a number of organizational ideas in circulation, disembedded from their original contexts (Czarniawska and Joerges, 1996). As a consequence, very few ideas are actually new
3   The translation of policy ideas is personal. The spread in time and space of anything –claims, orders, artifacts, goods – is in the hands of people; each of these people may act in many different ways (Latour, 1986, p. 267) by adding or taking away particular elements and reshaping or merging others. Local actors must therefore be prepared to take policy ideas as a starting point, transport them into their organizations and, once there, translate them into action (Johnson & Hagström, 2005, p. 371)
4   The more people participating in the translation of policy ideas the more powerful it gets because 'the force is not a property inherent in the idea, but rather a consequence of it being championed by a great number of

people' (Latour, 1986). Power is moreover performed through the dispositions, maneuvers, tactics, techniques and functionings that are used by translators to gain support from other actors (Foucault, 1991, p. 26)

5   Because it is the local receiver and imitator of a policy idea that decides how the sender's message is interpreted, ascribed meaning and imitated the translation processes are always anchored in local contexts. What the implications of global or local political, economic, social, cultural and historical conditions are for the translation of a specific policy idea are therefore always locally interpreted and decided and thus specific to the translation process in focus. It is a glocalization process rather than a localization process (Beck, 2000, p. 49)

6   Finally, the policy translation process must be seen as an open-ended, unfinished process where policy ideas are continuously interpreted and re-interpreted

Studying translation of policy ideas across countries and political jurisdictions

While Johnson and Hagström (2005) studied the introduction of a methadone treatment program in Sweden, other researchers in policy studies have utilized the translation perspective to study the travel of policy ideas across countries and political jurisdictions as well as international organizations (Mukhtarov, 2014; Stone, 2012, 2017).

Actors, ideas and scale in policy translation

Mukhtarov (2014) studies conventional approaches to the study of the travel of ideas in policy studies such as 'policy transfer', 'policy diffusion', 'lesson-drawing' and 'institutional isomorphism', and criticizes them for assuming perfect rationality of actors, the stability of governance scales and the immutability of policy ideas in their travel. Based on his analysis of the policy transfer and policy translation perspectives, he sums up the main difference between them in Table 11.1.

Mukhtarov (2014) defines policy translation as the process of modification of policy ideas and creation of new meanings and designs in the process of the cross-jurisdictional travel of policy ideas. He advocates a narrow use of policy translation to focus on key policy actors in their struggle to engage with the travel of ideas across countries or political jurisdictions by framing, reframing and modifying the meaning of ideas that travel; and engaging in constructing problems and solutions as pertinent to certain scales (Mukhtarov, 2014, p. 76). He offers the translation perspective as a solution to the problems related to the three problematic assumptions identified in the policy transfer, diffusion, 'lesson-drawing' and 'institutional isomorphism' literature. He thus points out that the translation perspective may contribute to another view on the actor, the stability of governance scales and the immutability of policy ideas as they travel:

Table 11.1 Comparison of policy transfer and policy translation approaches

Approaches	Policy transfer	Policy translation
Who transfers/ translates?	Initially only government officials and policy elites; later broadened to include non-state actors	All types of actors engaged in policymaking; tailored to study informal networks that pervade levels of governance
What is transferred/ translated?	Policies, institutions, ideas; the more complex a policy is, the less 'transferable' it is	Policies, institutions, ideas; the notion of 'transferability' is rejected as the outcome of this process cannot be reduced to only qualities of the policy at hand
How does transfer/ translation happen?	Mechanistic and linear with prescriptive guidelines	Highly contingent; no guidelines are available
What enables and constrains transfer/ translation?	Characteristics of a policy idea, path dependency, ideology of the country where the policy idea is introduced, bureaucracy, size and efficiency	Constraints and opportunities for translation are socially and politically constructed and are meaningful only in the context
Rationale for analysis	Instrumental: Looking for a 'fit' between a policy and the context	'Unfit to fit': Looking to understand how policy ideas are translated to construct a temporary 'fit'

Source: Muchtarov, 2014, p. 78. Reproduced with permission

- Instead of being a rational actor, the translation perspective assumes that translators of policies socially construct their views on policy problems and solutions
- What they think and mean about policy ideas is not stable but contingent and modified as policy ideas move across contexts. As a consequence, policy ideas are not immutable
- Instead of applying multilevel approaches studying policy transfer across global, national and local time-space contexts, the translation perspective emphasizes the importance of focusing on how local translators socially construct such time-space relationships (and thus such 'politics of scale') (Lebel, Daniel, Badenoch, Garden, & Imamura, 2008, p. 129)

International organizations as intermediaries of translation between states

Diane Stone (Stone, 2012) has studied translation of policy ideas across international organizations. She analyzes the diffusion, transfer, convergence (institutional) and translation perspectives on the travel of policy ideas. She points out that the emergence of concepts such as divergence, hybridization, adaption and mutation of policy ideas in the literature has increased the interest of researchers in the idea of policy 'translation' (Prince, 2009, p. 173) and 'variation' (Newburn, 2010; Stone, 2012, p. 487). Stone (2012) cites Lendvai and Stubbs (2007, p. 175) who define translation as

> a series of interesting, and sometimes even surprising, disturbances that can occur in the spaces between the "creation", the "transmission" and the "interpretation" or "reception" of policy meanings.

She describes translation of policy ideas as a 'collaborative performance in the co-evolution of politics' (Stone, 2012, p. 496). Building on Dunlop and Radealli (2012), she relates learning in policy translation processes to two types of learning:

1 Reflexive learning where new knowledge from elsewhere is influencing the cognition of policy problems and their solutions, potentially informing/destabilizing the fundamental beliefs of decision-makers who thus become attuned to opportunities for transfer
2 Political competition, bargaining and social interaction through which the participants come to better appreciate and understand alternative policy ideas/routes and help promote an 'international policy culture' and commonly accepted norms

Stone (2012) suggests that the translation perspective is particularly well suited to study inter-governmental organizations because:

- They depend on 'client' states for implementation
- They depend on persuasion rather than sanctions
- Policy ideas are distorted, transformed and modified (Lendvai & Stubbs, 2007, p. 176) in the dialogues and negotiations within and between international organizations
- Translations occur in a complex web with a considerable overlap and joint enterprises between states, international organizations and relevant non-state bodies

Diane Stone (2012) states:

> not only do these collective processes of policy transfer or diffusion create new cycles and circuits of interpretation, it also contributes to new architectures of transnational governance. Translation and meaning-making becomes the very workings of power.
>
> (Stone, 2012, p. 491)

Explaining policy failure

In another contribution, Diane Stone (2017) offers the translation perspective as a way of understanding the failure of policy ideas that travel (Czarniawska & Joerges, 1996). She defines policy failure as follows:

> Failure is the mirror image of success: A policy fails if it does not achieve the goals that proponents set out to achieve and opposition is great and/or support is virtually non-existent.
>
> (McConnell, 2010, p. 356)

She re-assesses the literature on policy transfer and diffusion between countries and their governments in light of what constitutes failure or limited success and presents policy translation as an alternative view on why policies fail. She assumes that the movement of policy ideas, instruments or practices from jurisdiction A to B or from one innovating organization or political community to the next is not a linear process but characterized by the following:

- Diffusion and transfer of policy ideas, instruments or practices involves a large number of people/proponents and intermediaries reflecting different interests and discordant views on what may amount to success
- The process is characterized by assemblage (Lendvai & Stubbs, 2009) and bricolage (De Jong, 2013) – that is, creation from a diverse range of available things
- Learning through trial and error
- Interpretation (or misinterpretation), mutation and revision on route
- Localization – that is, the local adaption, indigenization and modification of policy in new formats (McCann & Ward, 2012)

Policy translation is therefore defined as:

> multiple and variable processes incorporating (i) diffusion/transfer; (ii) assemblage/bricolage; (iii) mobilities/mutation; (iv) interpretation/localization; and (v) trial and error.
>
> (Stone, 2017, p. 56)

Stone (2017) suggests that policy translation is a better conceptual framework for comprehending the learning and policy innovations that come with the trial and error inherent in policymaking. According to her, asking if policy transfer fails (or is 'inappropriate' or a poor 'fit') is in many respects the wrong question for the phenomenon. Instead, the translation perspective suggests that divergence is expected: policy translation – characterized by fluid multi-actor processes of interpretation, mutation and assemblage – is the constant reality.

> (Stone, 2017, p. 67)

Other studies

Sausman, Osborn and Barrett (2016) seek to explain how national policies in the United Kingdom undergo translation from general policy guidelines to implementation in practice at the local level. It is shown that policy guidelines are iteratively transformed through multiple distributed agencies including local actors, infrastructure, data sets and organizational practices. Sausman et al. (2016) suggest that as policy implementation is defined and enacted, meaning is negotiated by local and central actors. In this way, adaptation occurs in order to account for local realities, and these adaptations can in turn reshape the policy content (Sausman et al., 2016, p. 581). She refers to Brunsson, Rasche and Seidl (2012) who describe the process as a 'two-way process of translation and adjustment'.

Park, Wilding and Chung (2014) draw on the policy transfer and translation literature as well as public relations theory to investigate the impact of communication types on the modification of policies. Their study suggests that two-way communication processes lead to greater modification of policy to contexts, which makes it likely that policy 'success' is increased.

Mcdermont (2013) shows that voluntary sector advice agencies in the United Kingdom bring the rights, responsibilities and grievances of the individual into dialogue with formal legal structures and thus contribute to translating personal grievances into matters-of-public-concern.

According to Clarke and Bainton (2015), critical policy analysis may be informed by actor-network theory. Their aim is to 'expand the analytical repertoire of critical policy studies by borrowing and deploying concepts from beyond policy studies and from beyond the established lines of critical policy studies' (Clarke & Bainton, 2015, p. 34). They point out that – according to Richard Freeman (2004, 2009) – the concept of translation highlights the constructed and communicative character of policy – policy exists and acts through language; and, second, translation identifies policy as emerging through processes of representation and association (Clarke & Bainton, 2015, p. 37). They cite Freeman (2004, p. 7) who states:

> we call translation, or the replacing of terms in one language with those in another, is also a substitution of one set of relationships or associations with another. These may be similar to the original but can never be identical. To translate, therefore, is to make new associations, to reassociate or perhaps to reassign.

Policy is thus not just expressed in words; it is literally 'constructed through the language in which it is described' (Fischer, 2003, p. 543). The language constructs relations of symbolic power through which relations of force between the speakers and their respective groups are actualized in a transfigured form (Bourdieu & Wacquant, 1992, pp. 142–143). Clarke and Bainton (2015) emphasize the importance of the articulation and association processes related to the translation of policies. The concept of articulation originates from cultural studies (Slack, 1996) and brings multiple senses of connections into play: Articulation as association (connecting X and Y to make something new), articulation as bringing to voice (articulating a position or point of view) and articulation as mobilization (connecting social agents into alliances, blocs or political projects) (Clarke & Bainton, 2015, p. 38). As a consequence, Clarke and Bainton (2015, p. 38) sum up their view on policy translation as follows:

> Translation, then, speaks simultaneously to the content, movement and contexts of policy. The concept opens up the content of policy, inviting us to study the processes of its making and remaking through language, through the practices of association and articulation.

References

Beck, U. (2000). *What is globalization?* Cambridge: Polity Press.

Berry, F. (1994). Sizing up state policy innovation research. *Policy Studies Journal, 22*(3), 442–456.

Berry, F., & Berry, W. (1999). Innovation and diffusion models in policy research. In P. Sabatier (Ed.), *Theories of the policy process.* Boulder, CO: Westview Press.

Bourdieu, P., & Wacquant, L. (1992). *An invitation to reflexive sociology.* Chicago, IL: Polity Press

Brunsson, N., Rasche, A., & Seidl, D. (2012). The dynamics of standardization: Three perspectives on standards in organization studies. *Organisation Studies, 33*(5–6), 613–632.

Clarke, J., & Bainton, D. (2015). *Making policy move: Towards a politics of translation and Assemblage.* Cambridge: Polity Press.

Czarniawska, B., & Joerges, B. (1996). Travels of ideas. In B. Czarniawska & G. Sevón (Eds.), *Translating organizational change.* Berlin: Walter de Gruyter.

De Jong, M. (2013). China's art of institutional bricolage: Selectiveness and gradualism in the policy transfer style of a nation. *Policy and Society, 32*(2), 89–101.

Dolowitz, D., & Marsh, D. (1996). Who learns what from whom: A review of the policy transfer literature. *Political Studies, 44*(2), 343–357.

Dolowitz, D., & Marsh, D. (2000). Learning from abroad: The role of policy transfer in contemporary policy making. *Governance, 13*(1), 5–24.

Dunlop, C. A., & Radealli, C. M. (2012). Systematizing policy learning: From monoliths to dimensions. *Political Studies, 61*, 599–619.

Fischer, F. (2003). *Reframing policy analysis: Discursive politics and deliberative practices.* Oxford: Oxford University Press.

Fiske, J. (1990). *Introduction to communication Studies.* London: Routledge.

Foucault, M. (1991). *Discipline and punish.* Harmondsworth: Penguin.

Freeman, R. (2004). Research, practice and the idea of translation, consultation paper. Previously retrieved from www.pol.ed.ac.uk/freeman.

Freeman, R. (2009). What is translation? *Evidence and Policy, 5*(4), 429–447.

Johnson, B., & Hagström, B. (2005). The translation perspective as an alternative to the policy diffusion paradigm: The case of the Swedish methadone maintenance treatment. *Journal of Social Policy, 34*(3), 365–388.

Latour, B. (1986). The powers of association. In J. Law (Ed.), *Power, action and belief – A new sociology of knowledge?* London: Routledge & Kegan Paul.

Lebel, L., Daniel, R., Badenoch, N., Garden, P., & Imamura, M. (2008). A multi-level perspective on conserving with communities: Experience from upper tributary watersheds in montane mainland Southeast Asia. *International Journal of Commons, 2*(1), 127–154.

Lendvai, N., & Stubbs, P. (2007). Policies as translation: Situating transnational social policies. In S. Hodgson & Z. Irving (Eds.), *Policy reconsidered: Meanings, politics and practices* (pp. 173–190). Bristol: The Policy Press.

Lendvai, N., & Stubbs, P. (2009). Assemblages, translation and intermediaries in South East Europe. *European Societies, 11*(5), 673–695.

McCann, E., & Ward, K. (2012). Policy assemblages, mobilities and mutations: Toward a multidisciplinary conversation. *Political Studies Review, 10*(3), 325–332.

McConnell, A. (2010). Policy success, policy failure and grey areas in-between. *Journal of Public Policy, 30*(3), 345–362.

Mcdermont, M. (2013). Acts of translation UK advice agencies and the creation of matters-of-public-concern. *Critical Social Policy, 33*(2), 218–242.

Mukhtarov, F. (2014). Rethinking the travel of ideas: Policy translation in the water sector. *Policy & Politics, 42*(1), 71–88.

Newburn, T. (2010). Diffusion, differentiation and resistance in comparative penality. *Criminology and Criminal Justice, 10*(4), 341–353.

Park, C., Wilding, M., & Chung, C. (2014). The importance of feedback: Policy transfer, translation and the role of communication. *Policy, Studies, London, 35*(4), 397–412.

Prince, R. (2009). Policy transfer as policy assemblage: Making policy for the creative industries in New Zealand. *Environment and Planning A, 42,* 169–186.

Rogers, E. (1995). *The diffusion of innovations.* New York, NY: Free Press.

Rose, R. (1993). *Lesson-drawing in public policy.* Chatham, NJ: Chatham House Publishers.

Sausman, C., Osborn, E., & Barrett, M. (2016). Policy translation through localization: Implementing national policy in the UK. *Policy and Politics, London, 44*(4), 563–589.

Sevón, G. (1996). Organizational imitation in identity transformation. In B. Czarniawska & G. Sevón (Eds.), *Translating organizational change.* Berlin: Walter de Gruyter.

Shannon, C., & Weaver, W. (1949). *The mathematical theory of communication.* Illinois: University of Illinois Press.

Slack, J. (1996). The theory and method of articulation in cultural studies. In D. Morley & K. H. Chen (Eds.), *Stuart K.H. Hall: Critical dialogues in cultural studies.* London: Routledge.

Stone, D. (2012). Transfer and translation of policy. *Policy Studies, 33*(6), 483–499.

Stone, D. (2017). Understanding the transfer of policy failure: Bricolage, experimentalism and translation. *Policy & Politics, 45*(1), 55–70.

12 Knowledge translation in healthcare

When we go to the hospital we, the patients, want to be treated by doctors who base their treatments upon the latest evidence-based knowledge. The healthcare sector has organizations such as the Cochrane Collaboration that promotes evidence-informed health decision-making by producing high-quality, relevant, accessible systematic reviews and other synthesized research evidence. The knowledge production process in healthcare consists of knowledge creation (i.e., primary research), knowledge distillation (i.e., the creation of systematic reviews and guidelines) and knowledge dissemination (i.e., appearances in journals and presentations).[1] Research has shown however that these activities on their own do not ensure the use of research-based knowledge in the decision-making of politicians, administrators and healthcare professionals such as doctors (Grimshaw, Eccles, Lavis, Hill, & Squires, 2012). This means that patients are denied treatment of proven benefit because the time it takes for research to become incorporated into practice is unacceptably long (Graham et al., 2006). Consequently, knowledge translation research focuses upon how you may ensure that evidence-based knowledge about treatment of patients is actually used in the decision-making processes of the above-mentioned groups. Straus, Tetroe and Graham (2013) shortly define knowledge translation as the methods for closing the gaps from knowledge to practice (Straus et al, 2013, p. 4). Formally, however, knowledge translation is defined by the Canadian Institutes of Health Research as following:

> a dynamic and iterative process that includes the synthesis, dissemination, exchange and ethically sound application of knowledge to improve health, provide more effective health services and products, and strengthen the health care system.
>
> (Straus et al. 2013, p. 4)

The Knowledge-to-action framework

Straus et al. (2013) point out that many proposed theories and frameworks exist for the practice of knowledge translation and that this is confusing.

They adopt however a conceptual framework developed by Graham and colleagues (Graham et al., 2006), termed the knowledge-to-action cycle. The framework builds on a combination of insights from a review of planned action theories and supplements it with a process of knowledge creation. The framework has been adopted by the Canadian Institute of Health Research as the accepted model for promoting the application of research and for the process of knowledge translation. The framework is shown in Figure 12.1.

The framework shows and combines the activities of researchers and the people who use the research-based knowledge that has been produced by the researchers. The activities are thus divided into a knowledge creation cycle that is managed by researchers and an action cycle where the evidence-based knowledge produced by the researchers is connected to problems and used in decision-making processes of practitioners such as politicians, administrators and healthcare professionals/doctors.

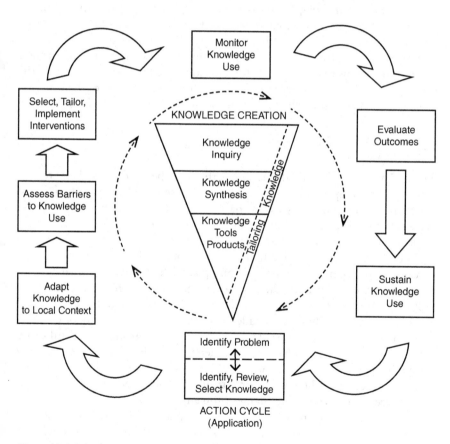

Figure 12.1 The knowledge to action process
Source: Graham et al., 2006, p. 19. Reproduced with permission.

The knowledge creation cycle

Graham et al. (2006) describe the knowledge creation process in healthcare as a knowledge funnel consisting of three generations of knowledge. As knowledge moves through the funnel, it becomes more distilled and refined and thus more useful to stakeholders. The first-generation labeled 'knowledge enquiry' is described as 'the un-manageable multitude of primary studies or information of variable quality that is out there and that may or may not be easily assessed'. The second-generation 'knowledge synthesis' represents the aggregation of existing knowledge. The process involves the application of explicit and reproducible methods to the identification, appraisal and synthesis of studies or information relevant to specific questions. This knowledge often takes the form of systematic reviews, including meta-analysis and meta-synthesis. Finally, the third generation of knowledge consists of products such as practice guidelines, decision aids and rules and care pathways. The purpose of these tools is to present knowledge in clear, concise and user-friendly formats, and ideally to provide explicit recommendations with the intent of influencing what stakeholders do and to meet the stakeholders' knowledge or informational needs, thereby facilitating the uptake and application of knowledge. Graham et al. (2006) point out that researchers can tailor their research questions to address the problems identified by users. And when the results are available, they can tailor or customize the message for the different intended users including the public, practitioners and policymakers.

The action cycle

The action cycle describes the activities that may be needed and leads to implementation or application of knowledge. These activities are dynamic and can influence each other as well as be influenced by the knowledge creation process (Straus et al., 2013). The first phase involves a group or individual who identifies that there is a problem or issue that deserves attention, that search for knowledge or research that might address the problem and critically assess its validity and usefulness. In the second phase, the knowledge is adapted to the local context. An individual or group makes decisions about the value, usefulness and appropriateness of the particular knowledge to their setting and circumstances. This also includes activities aimed at tailoring or customizing the knowledge to the particular situation of the group. The third phase consists of assessing the barriers to knowledge use. The uptake of knowledge can be influenced by issues related to the knowledge to be adopted, the potential adopters, and the context or setting in which the knowledge is to be used. Here, those who want change (implementers or change agents) assess the potential areas that may impede or limit uptake of the knowledge so that these variables may be targeted and overcome or diminished through the use of intervention strategies. The barrier assessments should also identify supports or facilitators that can be taken advantage of. In the next phase, the implementer or change agent selects, tailors and implements interventions to make the target group use the evidence-based knowledge. This involves selecting and tailoring interventions to the identified barriers and audiences. In the following phase, the use or application of the knowledge is monitored. The phase consists of defining what constitutes knowledge use so that it can be measured. Graham et al. (2006) distinguish between three types of knowledge use: (1) conceptual use of knowledge consists of changes in levels of knowledge, understanding or attitudes; (2) instrumental use consists of changes in behavior or practice; and (3) strategic use relates to stakeholders manipulation of knowledge to attain specific power or profit goals. In the following phase, the outcomes of the knowledge translation process are evaluated and it is decided whether the application of the knowledge has made a difference in relation to wished-for health, practitioner and system outcomes. The last phase of the knowledge translation process consists of sustaining knowledge use. Graham et al. (2006) suggest that a feedback loop that cycles through the action phases should be set in motion. In the sustainability phase, change agents/implementers should thus assess barriers to knowledge sustainability, tailor interventions to handle these barriers, monitor ongoing knowledge use, and evaluate the impacts of individual use and sustained use of the knowledge.

Barriers, facilitators and intervention strategies

Knowledge translation researchers agree that planned knowledge translation for healthcare professionals is more likely to be successful if the choice of knowledge translation strategy or intervention is informed by an assessment of the likely barriers and facilitators to change (Grimshaw et al. 2012; Straus, Tetroe, & Graham 2009; Straus et al. 2013). They have therefore produced much research aimed at identifying the barriers and facilitators to change in healthcare organizations as well as at producing research-based evidence of the likely effectiveness of different strategies or interventions aimed at overcoming barriers to change. Some barriers to change relate to the knowledge creation cycle, others to the action cycle.

According to Grimshaw et al. (2012), the barriers related to the knowledge creation cycle include issues related to knowledge management, such as the volume of research evidence being produced, access to research evidence sources (for instance systematic reviews and clinical practice guidelines), time to read evidence sources, and skills to appraise and understand research evidence. Such barriers are handled through the development and use of better approaches and tools to knowledge management.

The barriers related to the action cycle include structural barriers (e.g., financial disincentives), organizational barriers (e.g., inappropriate skill mix, lack of facilities or equipment), peer group barriers (e.g., local standards of care not in line with desired practice), professional barriers (e.g. knowledge, attitudes and skills) and professional-patient interaction barriers (e.g., communication and information processing issues) (Grimshaw et al., 2012). Handling such barriers depends on implementers'/change agents' research-based knowledge about the likely effectiveness of different strategies and interventions aimed at overcoming barriers to change.

Grimshaw et al. (2012) suggest that the intervention used is chosen using the following process:

> Individuals involved in knowledge translation need to: identify modifiable and non-modifiable barriers relating to behavior; identify potential adopters and practice environments; and prioritize which barriers to target based upon consideration of "mission-critical" barriers. Furthermore, the potential for addressing these barriers through knowledge translation activities (based upon consideration of the likely mechanisms of action of interventions) and the resources available for knowledge translation activities also needs to be addressed
>
> (Grimshaw et al. 2012, p. 5)

Both Grimshaw et al. (2012) and Straus et al. (2013) refer to and build upon the systematic reviews that the Cochrane Effective Practice and Organization of Care (EPOC) group have made of the effectiveness of different professional behavior change strategies and interventions. Grol and Grimshaw (2003) made an overview of the evidence for the effectiveness of different knowledge translation/implementation strategies (see Table 12.1) in 2003.

The overview demonstrates the types of change strategies or types of interventions that the knowledge translation researchers (still) consider when they make systematic reviews of which interventions are most effective in producing behavior change among healthcare professionals. It thereby also demonstrates the types of interventions that are investigated when translation researchers try to find out which interventions are most effective in making healthcare professionals' use and make decisions based on the evidence-based knowledge that is communicated to them.

Table 12.1 Overview of strategies for implementation of evidence and conclusions of reviews

Strategy	Number of reviews*	Number of studies	Conclusions
Educational materials	9	3–37	Mixed effects
Conferences, courses	4	3–17	Mixed effects
Interactive small group meetings	4	2–6	Mostly effective, but limited numbers of studies
Educational outreach visits	8	2–8	Especially effective for prescribing/prevention
Use of opinion leaders	3	3–6	Mixed effects
Education with different educational strategies	8	5–63	Mixed effects, dependent on combination of strategies

Strategy	Number of reviews*	Number of studies	Conclusions
Feedback on performance	16	3–37	Mixed effects, most effective for test ordering
Reminders	14	4–68	Mostly effective, particularly for prevention
Computerized decision support	5	11–98	Mostly effective for drug dosing and prevention
Introduction of computers in practice	2	19–30	Mostly effective
Substitution of tasks	6	2–14	Pharmacist: Effect on prescribing Nurse: Mixed effects
Multiprofessional collaboration	5	2–22	Effective for a range of different chronic conditions
Mass media campaigns	1	22	Mostly effective
Total quality management/ continuous quality improvement	1	55	Limited effects, mostly single-site non-controlled studies
Financial interventions	6	3–89	Fundholding and budgets effective, mainly on prescribing
Patient-mediated interventions	8	2–14	Mixed effects; reminding by patients is effective in prevention
Combined interventions	16	2–39	Most reviews: More effective than single interventions; not confirmed in recent reviews

*Number of reviews that included studies addressing the interventions.
Source: Grol and Grimshaw, 2003, p. 1227. Reproduced with permission.

Note

1 https://www.cochrane.org/about-us

References

Graham, I. D., Logan, J., Harrison, M. b., Straus, S. E., Tetroe, J., Caswell, W., & Robinson, N. (2006). Lost in knowledge translation: Time for a map? *The Journal of Continuing Education in the Health Professions, 26*(1), Winter, 13–24.

Grimshaw, J. M., Eccles, M. P., Lavis, J. N., Hill, S. J., & Squires, J. E. (2012). Knowledge translation of research findings. *Implementation Science*, no. 7, Article number: 50.

Grol, R., & Grimshaw, J. (2003). From best evidence to best practice: Effective implementation of change in patients' care. *The Lancet, 362*, 1225–1230.

Straus, S. E., Tetroe, J., & Graham, I. (2009). Defining knowledge translation. *Canadian Medical Association*, August 4, 165–168.

Straus, S. E., Tetroe, J., & Graham, I. D. (2013). *Knowledge translation in health care – Moving from evidence to practice*. Hoboken, NJ: Wiley Blackwell, BMJ Books.

13 Translation through design

Secundo, Del Vecchio, Simeone and Schiuma (2020) explain that open innovation occurs when knowledge flows beyond the boundaries of a single organization (Chesbrough, 2003) and a high degree of cross-border organizational collaborations takes place, allowing the intersection of reciprocal relationships across academia, government and industry (Audretsch, Lehmann, & Warning, 2005; Drechsler & Natter, 2012; West & Bogers, 2014). They define open innovation as 'the use of purposive inflows and outflows of knowledge to accelerate internal innovation, and expand the markets for external use of innovation, respectively' (Chesbrough, 2006, p. 1).

The authors show how researchers studying open innovation processes have become increasingly aware of the importance of involving stakeholders in collaborative and participatory processes aimed at knowledge transfer and co-creation of new products and services. They also show how creativity in open innovation processes is related to interactions between stakeholders and the combination of knowledge, ideas and information that these interactions make possible (Andersson, 1985). Here, individual's capacity to combine and integrate knowledge from different contexts to create new knowledge is considered important (Amabile, Conti, Coon, Lazenby, & Herron, 1996). Moreover, social interactions among the actors/stakeholders involved in an open innovation process are considered important because participation in such interactions allows individuals (with certain types of knowledge) to be exposed to new information and knowledge from other individuals or groups of individuals allowing different forms of information and knowledge to be shared and combined (Westlund, Andersson, & Karlsson, 2014). The authors point out that knowledge is however not just transferred but also translated during the above-mentioned processes:

> When knowledge is transferred across very diverse contexts (e.g. from academia to industry), knowledge needs to be translated to still be interesting and relevant (Graham et al., 2006). Translating knowledge involves processing new knowledge, interpreting it according to the needs and interests of the different actors involved, and transforming it

into forms that are more suitable for the specific organizational context of the application (Albino et al., 1998).

(Secundo et al., 2020, p. 3)

Secundo et al. (2020) set out to investigate the role of design as a knowledge translation mechanism in technology-intensive enterprises because 'little attention has been paid to the analysis of the interplay between design (as a translation mechanism) and creativity in open innovation processes, in which generally different stakeholders interact in the process of value creation' (Secundo et al., 2019, p. 3). In their case study, they focus on how design can be used to connect and combine the contributions of creativity resulting from multiple stakeholders, including entrepreneurs, university students and academics, in a process in which knowledge is openly shared and transferred across the boundaries of companies' R&D laboratories, a university and other institutions. Especially, the role of design artifacts as a means to support the translation of stakeholders' creativity and knowledge into new formats to nurture open innovation is looked into in this connection.

According to the authors, design has the following characteristics:

- Design is a multifaceted activity, including creating visual representations to conceiving, prototyping and deploying a product or service
- It builds on involvement of stakeholders including users, customers, suppliers, etc. through participatory and service design processes
- It includes the use of design tools, methods, techniques and activities: Hackathons, design jams and other forms of participatory processes. Research, user participation and testing, rapid and frequent prototyping, development and visualization/materialization techniques support divergent as well as convergent thinking
- It includes the use of design artifacts (sketches, visualizations, animation videos, etc.) to ease the communication among different stakeholders speaking different 'languages'

The authors suggest that design processes may be understood as a knowledge translation mechanism in the following ways:

- Participation in design is tied to 'problems of interpretation and translation of varying user and expert perspectives' (Reich, Konda, Monarch, Levy, & Subrahmanian, 1996)
- Translation is seen as a complex process riddled with negotiations (Cooper, Bruce, Wootton, Hands, & Daly, 2003; Tomes, Oates, & Armstrong, 1998) in which

  - The designer acts as 'intermediary' between disparate ideas, viewpoints and goals where being able to translate in this manner is an essential precondition for being able to integrate many things (Boyer, Cook, & Steinberg, 2011). And where designers use;

- Design artifacts such as sketches, visualizations and more or less refined versions of prototypes to ease the communication among different stakeholders (Ito, 2016; Leonard and Rayport, 1997; Rust, 2004, 2007).

Based on their case study, the authors conclude:

> different stakeholders are generally participating in and looking at projects from their own perspectives and regarding their own specialized knowledge. As a result, enterprises are much more expert in processes of commercial exploitation, but may know very little about the scientific advancements in the technological innovation. Academic partners are quite expert in advancement in technologies required by the innovation projects, but not so much aware of business strategy. University students are more conscious of scientific and business knowledge, but do not know how to translate this into innovation outputs. In a project that relies on open innovation dynamics and, consequently, on a quiet high number of potential external stakeholders, design as a translation mechanism can support the overcoming of all these obstacles (Chesbrough, 2003) and ignite and sustain mental and social creativity.
>
> (Secundo et al., 2020, p. 7)

They moreover conclude:

> In all the open innovation phases, design is detected as a translation mechanism for the different forms of knowledge and competencies that were fundamental for combining ideas, knowledge and competencies of entrepreneurs, students and institutions. This shows that stakeholders are becoming increasingly empowered, interconnected and willing to share their knowledge and ideas with firms (through the design process, JDS).
>
> (Secundo et al., 2020, p. 7)

Finally, Secundo et al. (2020, p. 8) explain that design artifacts (sketches, prototypes, diagrams, graphics, etc.) were used throughout the innovation process and that they may be used strategically to stimulate and manage the interplay of different stakeholders across phases of divergent and convergent thinking. They moreover helped with translating and combining ideas, knowledge and competencies (creativity) from different actors speaking different languages and who had different interests into new formats that could be more easily understood and appreciated by other actors.

References

Albino, V., Garvelli, C., & Schiuma, G. (1998). Document knowledge transfer and interfirm relationships in industrial districts: The role of the leader firm. *Technovation, 19*(1), 53–63.

Amabile, T. M., Conti, R., Coon, H., Lazenby, J., & Herron, M. (1996). Assessing the work environment for creativity. *Academy of Management Journal, 39*(5), 1154–1184.

Andersson, Å. E. (1985). Creativity and regional development. *Paper in Regional Science, 56*(1), 5–20.

Audretsch, D., Lehmann, E., & Warning, S. (2005). University spillovers and new firms location. *Research Policy, 34*(7), 1113–1122.

Boyer, B., Cook, J. W., & Steinberg, M. (2011). *Recipes for systemic change.* Helsinki (Finland): Sitra/Helsinki Design Lab.

Chesbrough, H. (2003). *Open innovation. The new imperative for creating and profiting from technology.* Boston, MA: Harvard Business School Press.

Chesbrough, H. (2006). *Open business models: How to thrive in a new innovation landscape.* Boston, MA: Harvard Business School Press.

Cooper, R., Bruce, M., Wootton, A., Hands, D., & Daly, L. (2003). Managing design in the extended enterprise. *Building Research and Information, 1*(5), 367–378.

Drechsler, W., & Natter, M. (2012). Understanding a firm's openness decisions in innovation. *Journal of Business Research, 65*(3), 438–445.

Graham, I. D., Logan, J., Harrison, M. B., Straus, S. E., Tetroe, J., Caswell, W., & Robinson, N. (2006). Lost in knowledge translation: Time for a map? *Journal of Continuing Education in the Health Professions, 26*(1), 13–24.

Ito, J. (2016). Design and science. *Journal of Design Science* [Online]. Retrieved from http://jods.mitpress.mit.edu/pub/designandscience.

Leonard, D., & Rayport, J. F. (1997). Spark innovation through empathic design. *Harvard Business Review, 75*(6), 102–113.

Reich, Y., Konda, S. L., Monarch, I. A., Levy, S. N., & Subrahmanian, E. (1996). Varieties and issues of participation and design. *Design Studies, 17*(2), 165–180.

Rust, C. (2004). Design enquiry: Tacit knowledge and invention in science. *Design Issues, 20*(4), 76–85.

Rust, C. (2007). Unstated contributions: How artistic inquiry can inform interdisciplinary research. *International Journal of Design, 1*(3), 69–76.

Secundo, G., Del Vecchio, P., Simeone, L., & Schiuma, G. (2020) Creativity and stakeholder's engagement in open innovation: Design for knowledge translation in technology-intensive enterprises. *Journal of Business Research*, Vol.119, 272–282.

Tomes, A., Oates, C., & Armstrong, P. (1998). Talking design: Negotiating the verbal–visual translation. *Design Studies, 19*, 127–142.

West, J., & Bogers, M. (2014). Leveraging external sources of innovation: A review of research on open innovation. *Journal of Product Innovation Management, 31*(4), 814–831.

Westlund, H., Andersson, M., & Karlsson, C. (2014). Creativity as an integral element of social capital and its role for economic performance. In R. Sternberg & G. Krauss (Eds.), *Handbook of research on entrepreneurship and creativity* (pp. 60–96). Cheltenham, UK, Northampton, MA: Edward Elgar Publishing.

14 The middle manager as translator

Middle managers may be defined as

> a position in organizational hierarchies between the operating core and the apex whose occupants are responsible for a particular business unit at this intermediate level of the corporate hierarchy that comprises all those below the top-level strategic management and above first-level supervision.
>
> (Raidelli & Sitton-Kent, 2016, p. 312)

The intermediate position represents a defining feature of middle managers, because it triggers one property that separates them from other, i.e., they are 'at once controller, controlled, resister and resisted' (Harding, Lee, & Ford, 2014, p. 1231).

Raidelli and Sitton-Kent (2016) define a new idea as 'knowledge, practices, strategies, rules and technologies that are "new" to the context of translation, and that are translated because they carry the potential for significant changes in established routines, practices and products /services' (Raidelli & Sitton-Kent, 2016, p. 313). They define translation as 'the effort to embed in a given work context (e.g., in an organization, team or unit) ideas that have been originated elsewhere' (Raidelli & Sitton-Kent, 2016, p. 312). They point out that studies that focus on the role of translating actors are few and lack cumulative impact. Past research has thus emphasized that actors play a central role in translation theory, because as pointed out by Bruno Latour (1986) 'the spread in time and space of anything – claims, orders, artefacts, goods – is in the hands of people' (Latour, 1986, p. 267). But only a few studies have moved from local and context-specific descriptions of individual behaviors to theories on the role that specific cadres of actors in organizations have during the translation of ideas (Raidelli & Sitton-Kent, 2016, p. 312). Raidelli and Sitton-Kent (2016) therefore review the literature on middle managers' translation of new ideas. They follow middle managers throughout the translation process from the acquisition of the new ideas to its stabilization. And they:

> identify the micro-practices pursued by middle managers to affect the travel of the new idea within the organization, and the contingencies that

explain when and how middle managers engage in specific translation stages.

(Raidelli & Sitton-Kent, 2016, p. 311)

The micro-practices of middle managers

Building on Rouleau (2005), Raidelli and Sitton-Kent define micro-practices as 'individual activities that have been abstracted from their specific context/ time of application' (Raidelli & Sitton-Kent, 2016, p. 314). Their study is based on a comprehensive review of 116 relevant articles in top-tier journals from 2005 to 2015 and identifies: (1) the micro-practices that are reported in studies where middle managers introduce new ideas in their organizations/ units, (2) the themes (or types of activities performed by middle managers) they relate to, and (3) how these themes relate to six theoretical stages derived from the translation studies literature (including studies by Doorewaard & van Bijsterveld, 2001; Gherardi & Perrotta, 2011; Orlikowski, 2000; Phillips, Sewell, & Jaynes, 2008; Cornelissen, Holt, & Zundel, 2011; Czarniawska & Joerges, 1996). As a result, middle managers work with introducing new ideas in their organizations/units are empirically and theoretically identified as consisting of seven translation stages:

1 Idea acquisition
2 Appropriation of translation role
3 Legitimization of role
4 Enrollment of actors in networks
5 Idea variation
6 Alignment of actors
7 Idea stabilization

Each of these theoretical stages and the themes and micro-practices reported in studies of middle managers related to them are summed up in Table 14.1.

In the idea acquisition phase, the middle manager exploits his/her intermediate position to access ideas from a wide pool of knowledge, and work to differentiate and integrate diverse types of knowledge by differentiating and merging typologies of knowledge, sources of information and typologies of enquiry.

Appropriation is the process through which actors embed the role of 'translator of new ideas' as part of their identity. At this stage, middle managers decide whether they support or resist the new idea and how much effort they will devote and how explicitly they will manifest their involvement to others. This happens through a process where MMs first try to make sense of an idea and the organizational context in which it is to be introduced, then re-interpret and negotiate the translators own as well as the organization's understanding of its own identity. The phase is influenced by a number of contingencies that relate to the translator's individual features, his/her organizational role and relationship with top managers. Moreover, turf protection

Table 14.1 The micro-practices of middle managers

Theoretical concept	Theme	Micro-practice/action
1 Idea acquisition	Differentiate and merge typologies of knowledge	Collect knowledge from science, operations, strategy, best practice
	Differentiate and merge sources of information	Connect to top and bottom of organization, middle managers and external stakeholders
	Differentiate and merge typologies of enquiry	Use inquiries, formal consultations, informal chats, experiments and procedural methods
2 Appropriation of translation role	Make sense of idea	Judge outcomes, consequences controllability and values of idea
	Make sense of context	Interpret top management, the market, actors and socio-cultural system(s)
	Build translation identity	Assess personal interests and engage in dialogue, interpret and explain actors and socio-cultural system(s)
3 Legitimization of role	Exploit embeddedness	Manage up to top managers and implant information and cues
	Exploit ancillary roles	Perform clerical roles to be close to top management and fix problems to grow confidence
	Frame role as claims-maker	Claim responsibility from top management, minimize exposure and risks, incorporate others frames, reinforce identity
	Delegitimize opponents as claims-makers	Deny their skills, use data and analysis, divide into us and them, undermine authority
4 Enrollment of actors in network	Identify and connect allies in durable coalitions	Handpick allies, separate from opponents, attribute responsibility and identity, use ad hoc meetings
	Stage the involvement	Use rhetoric, create change atmosphere, balance emotions, frame action
	Develop conversation about involvement	Justify change, make proselytes, highlight non-financial incentives

Theoretical concept	Theme	Micro-practice/action
5 Idea variation	No evidence	No evidence
6 Alignment of actors	Sell own version of translation	Package it in appropriate media, translate to recipients, prove the value, encourage trying
	Mediate other versions of translation	Undermine moral foundation, cause-effect claims, effects on middle managers' identity, delegitimize, use roadblocks + time as buffer, pay lip service to change
	Align goals and agendas	Bridge goals to common agenda. Amplify, extend, transform MMs goals to include others agendas. Adjust measurement systems
	Align meanings and interpretations	Develop common interpretation, change MMs meaning so it resonates with and includes others interpretation, facilitate collective meaning
7 Idea stabilization	Fit new way into established system	Adopt definition of new practice, review positions, align with new practice, formalize new practice

Source: Further developed by the author on the basis of Raidelli and Sitton-Kent, 2016, pp. 5–6.

from peers and expert resistance from frontline employees may influence this phase.

This phase is followed by MMs effort to gain others' acceptance of their involvement in translation. This happens through processes where MMs first exploit their embeddedness and ancillary roles in the organization to get close to top management, gain top management's confidence in their skills and show them that they can fix problems. Second, it happens through a process where the translator frames his/her role as claims-maker by 'talking up' responsibility, resources and autonomy, talking down exposure and risks, incorporating others' frames and influencing their understanding of their identities. The MM/translator moreover uses different tactics to delegitimize opponents as claims-makers during this phase.

Enrollment concerns the development and preservation of a social network of actors who pursue the translation of the idea in question. Enrollment is

crucial 'because all translations are social processes in which proponents/resist-
ers of change involve others to embed their idea in practice' (Czarniawska &
Sevon, 1996; Raidelli & Sitton-Kent, 2016). The work that MMs do to succeed with this includes identifying and connecting allies in durable coali-
tions, staging the involvement – including setting the frame for following
actions – and developing conversations about involvement.

Raidelli and Sitton-Kent (2016) now introduce a theoretical stage found
in the translation literature which they have however found no or very sparse
evidence for in their review of the middle management literature – namely,
the stage of idea variation. They point out that idea variation is central to
translation theories and that ideas vary because stakeholders adapt ideas to
specific interests and needs (Ansari, Fiss, & Zajac, 2010; Czarniawska &
Sevon, 1996). As pointed out by Røvik (1996), ideas may thus be copied,
added to, omitted or altered when they are translated.

Alignment refers to the efforts made by MMs to reach a shared course
of action in the translation network. In this phase, middle managers make
efforts to sell their version of the translation, mediate other versions (including make efforts to undermine, delegitimize and block other versions), align
goals and agendas of the network actors, and align meanings and interpretations of network actors. The phase may be influenced by contingencies
related to individual features of the translators, their organizational role and
relationship with top managers. It may moreover be influenced by turf protection from peers and expert resistance from frontline employees.

Idea stabilization is the final translation process, in which MMs consoli-
date the idea within established routines and structures. The phase includes
translator's adoption of a consistent definition of new practices, a review of
whether positions should change as a consequence of these new practices and
a formalization of the scope of new practices and responsibilities by making
related job descriptions. Moreover, the alignment of the meaning of the new
routines, positions and jobs may be important.

References

Ansari, S. M., Fiss, P. C., & Zajac, E. J. (2010). Made to fit: How practices vary as
   they diffuse. *Academy of Management Review, 35*, 67–92.
Cornelissen, J. P., Holt, R., & Zundel, M. (2011). The role of analogy and metaphor
   in the framing and legitimization of strategic change. *Organization Studies, 32*,
   1701–1716.
Czarniawska, B., & Joerges, B. (1996). Travel of ideas. In B. Czarniawska & G. Sevôn
   (Eds.), *Translating organizational change* (pp. 13–48). Berlin: Walter de Gruyter.
Czarniawska, B., & Sevon, G. (1996). *Translating organizational change*. Berlin: Walter
   de Gruyter.
Doorewaard, H., & Van Bijsterveld, M. (2001). The osmosis of ideas: An analysis of
   the integrated approach to IT management from a translation theory perspective.
   Organization, 8, 55–76.

Gherardi, S., & Perrotta, M. (2011). Egg dates sperm: A tale of a practice change and its stabilization. *Organization, 18,* 595–614.

Harding, N., Lee, H., & Ford, J. (2014). Who is the middle manager? *Human Relations, 67,* 1213–1237.

Latour, B. (1986). The powers of association. In J. Law (Ed.), *Power, action and belief.* London: Routledge.

Orlikowski, W. J. (2000). Using technology and constituting structures: A practice lens for studying technology in organizations. *Organization Science, 11,* 404–428.

Phillips, N., Sewell, G., & Jaynes, S. (2008) Applying critical discourse analysis in strategic management research. *Organizational Research Methods, 11,* 770–789.

Raidelli, G., & Sitton-Kent, L. (2016). Middle managers and the translation of new ideas in organizations: A review of micro-practices and contingencies. *International Journal of Management Reviews, 18*(3), 311–332.

Rouleau, L. (2005). Micro-practices of strategic sensemaking and sensegiving: How middle managers interpret and sell change every day. *Journal of Management Studies, 48,* 953–983.

Røvik, K. A. (1996). Deinstitutionalization and the logic of fashion. In B. Czarniawska & G. Sevôn (Eds.), *Translating organizational change* (pp. 139–172). Berlin: Walter de Gruyter.

15 The consultant as translator

Some postmodernist and social constructivist researchers in organization studies have embraced ideas originating from 'the linguistic turn' in philosophy (Clegg, Kornberger, & Rhodes, 2004). According to these ideas, language is a cultural artifact that enables humans to coordinate their conceptions, engage in joint action, and construct and reconstruct the realities they see (Krippendorff, 2006, p. 20). These researchers suggest that language actively configures entities and events in the world in the very act of representing. Thus, in their use of language researchers as well as practitioners do not just write about their objects/subjects of analysis, but bring these objects into existence through representational acts of writing (Chia, 1996, p. 37). Consequently, knowledge in this type of research is seen as socially constructed narrative knowledge that arises from what actors (researchers or practitioners) think and say about the world as well as from how they critically reflect upon it. As suggested by Ludwig Wittgenstein (1953), the meaning of words and utterances is not found in what they represent but in how they are used. And use can be recognized in what utterances accomplish in 'language games', conversations, dialogues and discourses. Words are thus assumed to 'do things', create artifact, and change worlds. Accordingly, Clegg et al. (2004, p. 34) define an organization as

> a combination of both order and disorder   a mixture of different texts, potentially conflicting, produced from the varied perspectives and uses of language of those who comprise and interact with it (Rhodes, 2001), each pregnant with new possibilities for organizing and disorganizing.

As a consequence of this view,

> consulting, as an intentional intervention in an organization, need not be seen as just organizing in the sense of the creation of a new order, but also as a disruption of order, an exploration and exploitation of the spaces in between present order and potential, future order.
>
> (Clegg et al., 2004, p. 35)

Thus, where management consultants are traditionally assumed to contribute to simplify, stabilize and arrest the flux and constant transformation of organizations and to help organize them, Clegg et al. (2004) suggest that their role may rather be to bring chaos, noise and disorder into order. And this because:

> the inability of people in organizations to tolerate equivocal processing may well be one of the most important reasons why they have trouble. It is the unwillingness to disrupt order, ironically, that makes it impossible for the organization to create order.
>
> (Weick, 1979, p. 189)

Clegg et al. (2004) point out that talking, listening, reading and writing are what consultants do. They use new language games and new concepts to make people/organizations see, perceive and think differently. Consulting practice thus produces and introduces new language, deconstructs and disturbs established orders of discourse, and translates and mediates between new and old languages and metaphors. Clegg et al. (2004, p. 37) conclude:

> Consulting may be conceived as a process of tension, oscillating between order and disorder and de- and reconstruction. It can deconstruct organisational routines and taken for granted convictions in order to open up a space to the other voices, different perspectives, and differing opinions that operate within it-producing dissensus, searching for instabilities, gaps and divisions, building creative dissonance into practice, even if it challenges the core values of the organisation.

Therefore, Clegg et al. (2004) view the consultant as a parasite – as that which brings noise into the heart of a system, disturbs and disrupts it so that a new order may be created. The consultant translates language games, produces noise through introducing new metaphors and mediates through translation. Consultants as parasites 'mediate between two or more systems, they are in between, neither here nor there but in the middle, 'crossed by a network of relations" (Clegg et al., 2004, p. 39; Serres, 1982, p. 39). And translation circumscribes the productive and creative process: It is a displacement, invention, mediation and creation of a new link, which did not exist before and modifies in part the two agents: It comprises what exists and what is created (Clegg et al., 2004, p. 39; Czarniawska and Joerges, 1996, p. 182). Consultants' translation work is thus an intervention. It is at the same time however also an invention because during the unfolding of a translation both the sender's language and the receiver's language are modified and changed through improvisational processes (Weick, 1998, p. 548). Clegg et al. (2004, p. 40) now sum up their view on what they label 'parasitic consulting' like this:

> to sum up: the task of the consultant as translator consists in finding an effect on the language into which he or she is translating that produces an

echo of the original (Benjamin, 1982, p. 75). Further, rather than transporting a clear-cut message from one point to another, such translation creates a bridge between differing language games that shape organisational reality, deferring both of them. Translation is not about turning the language of theory into management's language; it is not about simulating the foreign in order to make it the same.... Concentrating on a foreign language, we deepen the understanding of our own language and enrich its vocabulary – it is here one can find the possibility to create alternative realities.

By introducing the concept of parasitic consulting, the authors attempt to contribute to making organizational systems more self-reflexive. The concept does not contribute to improving the organization of production but analyses the production of organization such that new productions might be possible. Neither does it increase the knowledge of the organization but questions the organization of knowledge in it.

References

Benjamin, W. (1982). The task of the translator. An introduction to the translation of Baudelaire's Tableaux Parisiens'. In W. Benjamin (Ed.), *Illuminations*. London: Fontana/Collins.

Chia, R. (1996). The problem of reflexivity in organizational research: Towards a postmodern science of organization. *Organization, 3*(1), 31–59.

Clegg, S. R., Kornberger, M., & Rhodes, C. (2004). Noise, parasites and translation – Theory and practice in management consulting. *Management Learning, 35*(1), 31–44.

Czarniawska, B., & Joerges, B. (1996) Travels of ideas. In B. Czarniawska & G. Sevon (Eds.), *Translating organizational change* (pp. 13–48). Berlin: de Gruyter.

Krippendorff, K. (2006). *The semantic turn – A new foundation for design*. Boca Raton, FL, London, New York: Taylor & Francis Group.

Rhodes, C. (2001). *Writing organization: (Re)presentation and control in narratives at work*. Amsterdam/Philadelphia, PA: John Benjamin.

Serres, M. (1982) The Parasite. Baltimore: Johns Hopkins University Press.

Weick, K. (1998). Improvisation as a mindset for organizational analysis. *Organization Science, 9*, 543–555.

Weick, K. (1979). *The social psychology of organizing*. Reading, MA: Addison Wesley.

Wittgenstein, L. (1953). *Philosophical investigations*. Oxford: Blackwell.

16 The knowledge translation value chain

Thorpe, Eden, Bessant and Ellwood (2011) conceptualize management scholarship as a knowledge translation value chain. The aim of introducing the model of the knowledge translation value chain is explained as follows:

> What this paper sets out to achieve, through the introduction of a knowledge translation (KT) value-chain, is to identify how an individual academic's interests and interactions might play out over time and be recognized when assessing the contribution of a business school.
>
> (Thorpe et al., 2011, p. 421)

The authors propose that to maximize relevance knowledge must be reconfigured in multiple contexts. As a consequence, they also reflect upon what skills researchers need to engage with other stakeholders across the knowledge translation value chain.

They explain that the knowledge translation value chain model provides another perspective on the delivery of relevant research compared to the one represented by for instance the UK Research Excellence Framework and the UK RAE system with its focus upon researcher's production of 'four-star' research papers of 'world-leading' quality. The model has a longitudinal view on business school researchers and understands a researcher's (and through him a business school's or university's) relevance and impact as something that plays out over a long period of time and as something that is socially constructed by the researcher as well as by the different users of the research. Thorpe et al. (2011) explain the idea with the model as follows:

> In advancing this value-chain, we do not intend to downplay the importance of rigorous scientific enquiry in our discipline; the value-chain clearly acknowledges the foundational position that such work must occupy in an environment demanding new insight. Our emphasis is rather on creating and recreating relevant knowledge through an individual management researcher engaging with users in various ways. Through such interactions, knowledge becomes reconfigured in a process that depends as much on the tacit knowledge of the management researcher as it

does on the formal findings of the research. Similarly, the success of the academic is influenced by the institutional context within which they work.

(Thorpe et al., 2011, p. 421)

The knowledge translation value chain thus describes how research (or a researcher) contributes to theory and practice over time through an interactive process including researchers as well as users of the research. The knowledge translation (KT) value chain includes the following types of activities and outputs:

1   KT through theory development resulting in
2   Output 1: Reporting of basic research in journals, research books, etc.
3   KT through theory-to-practice thought experiments by academics aimed at constructing meaning for practice and reflecting on strategies for engagement with practitioners resulting in
4   Output 2: Practitioner-oriented research outputs like journal articles that link research to practice, publications in academic or practitioner journals, collaboration with users in the form of joint publications
5   KT through engagement with users: Evidence of explicit engagement with users, use of knowledge transfer partnerships, case award studentships, etc.
6   Output 3: Texts and evidence designed to engage a greater number of practitioners – green papers, evidence of organizational changes resulting from interaction, savings achieved, case studies and reports
7   KT through widespread dissemination and involvement of user groups. Ongoing collaboration and interaction through innovation laboratories, use of web pages, education of academics and practitioners, transfer of knowledge onto the curriculum at universities, etc.
8   Output 4: Sector reports addressed to whole industry services and support written by for example journalists making the information widely available to the public and stakeholder groups including through web pages
9   Output 5: Directly usable outputs including teaching materials, textbooks tools, web publications, software, etc.

According to Thorpe et al. (2011), the process may be theorized as an interactive process where knowledge translation activities are performed and boundary objects in the form of outputs are produced that are then later translated and turned into other forms of knowledge and outputs by other translators:

The chain is built from combinations of specific KT activities and their associated assessable outputs (OPs), with the OPs from one KT episode providing input to the next, or feedback to earlier KTs. Rather than simply being end points in themselves, OPs are seen as 'boundary objects' that allow new organizational knowledge to be developed in more specific and possibly narrower terms (Carlile, 2002). Through this chain, knowledge is created and accumulated by a process of translation between actors engaged with a particular challenge and, with the encouragement and support of the institution.

(Thorpe et al., 2011, p. 425)

The implications of the model are given as follows:

- Research knowledge/the original idea is adapted, modified and configured during the processes of development and diffusion among multiple partners
- Impact of research/ideas is created through these multiple types of interactions and user engagements
- During the process research, findings are only one input among others to the process of translation
- User's experience, conceptual perspectives and challenges means that the knowledge is reconfigured and becomes expressed in different languages and formats
- Research institutions (and researchers) may focus their activities on parts of or the whole knowledge translation value chain
- Measurement of a researchers or an institutions impact should include measurements of impact across the whole knowledge translation value chain

Finally, the model implies that the points that academics (and doctoral students) need to learn to create an impact of their research include the following:

- Better understanding of how the individual researcher contributes to both theory and practice and makes an impact
- Understanding of different types of engagement with users and how you may develop long-term relationships with individuals in organizations who can provide access and knowledge
- Ability to create research and not research-related links to practitioners and intermediaries in different contexts
- Knowledge about how to design projects in collaboration with policy-makers and/or organizations dealing with significant challenges
- Ability to produce tools that may be used by practitioners
- Educate practitioners in how research outputs may be understood and used
- Behavior and communication skills that make the individual researcher able to explain how his/her research contribute by helping us all 'to live, to live well, to live better'

References

Carlile, P. R. (2002). A pragmatic view of knowledge and boundaries: boundary objects in new product development. *Organization Science, 13*, 442–455.

Thorpe, R., Eden, C., Bessant, J., & Ellwood, P. (2011). Rigour, relevance and reward: Introducing the knowledge translation value-chain. *British Journal of Management, 22*, 420–431.

17 Translation studies – focus points, research themes, research questions and gabs

Focus points in organizational translation studies

Table 2.1 gives an overview of the different theories and models of organizational translation that have been developed in organization studies according to this book's literature review. As demonstrated by this overview, researchers in translation studies share an interest in and try to theorize how tokens (including ideas, knowledge, texts) are moved between people and groups of people. They moreover characterize the process through which movement happens as a translation process. How the concept of translation is defined and integrated in theories and models describing how translation unfold as a process differ however. In order to answer the question 'what is organizational translation studies about?', it is relevant to ask what are the focus points and themes of translation studies in organization studies. What types of empirical processes do researchers in organizational translation studies focus upon and what types of theories and models have they developed about them that have raised certain types of research questions and themes that have resulted in focus points that distinguish translation studies from other types of research? Figure 17.1 gives an overview of and an answer to this question.

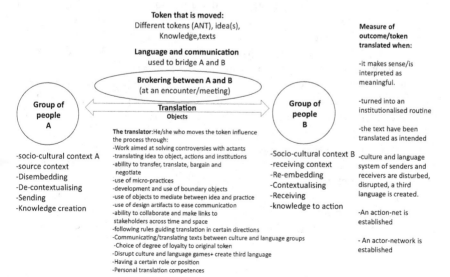

Figure 17.1 Focus points of organizational translation studies.

The token

Researchers in organizational translation studies focus upon the movement of tokens. In actor-network theory, tokens may be anything that move: Claims, orders, artifacts, goods, ideas, etc. (Latour in Law, 1986, p. 267). In Scandinavian institutionalism (the idea model and the theory of action nets) and in studies of policy translation and middle managers, it is ideas that are moved (Czarniawska, 2014; Czarniawska & Joerges, 1996; Johnson & Hagström, 2005; Mukhtarov, 2014; Raidelli & Sitton-Kent, 2016; Stone, 2012). In yet another group of theories/models, it is knowledge that is moved (Carlile, 2002, 2004; Graham et al., 2006; Røvik, 2016; Star & Griesemer, 1989; Thorpe, Eden, Bessant, & Ellwood, 2011; Yanov, 2004). Finally, some researchers suggest that it is texts (written and as talk) that are moved (Clegg, Kornberger, & Rhodes, 2004; Holden, Harald, & Kortzfleisch, 2004; Madsen, 2013).

Language and communication

Researchers in organizational translation studies emphasize that language and communication are important to create a bridge or connection between people in groups A and B when tokens are translated. Language and communication are either implied as important indirectly by the researchers (Callon, 1986; Carlile, 2002/2004; Czarniawska, 2014; Czarniawska & Joerges, 1996; Johnson & Hagström, 2005; Latour, 1986; Star & Griesemer, 1989; Stone, 2017) or turned into a main theme of organizational translation studies by them (Clarke & Bainton, 2015; Clegg et al., 2004; Holden et al., 2004; Madsen, 2013).

Group A and group B

Moreover, researchers in organizational translation studies emphasize that the tokens that are moved move between groups of people belonging to/ embedded in different socio-cultural contexts and 'language groups' (Carlile, 2002, 2004; Clegg et al., 2004; Johnson & Hagström, 2005; Holden et al., 2004; Madsen, 2013; Star & Griesemer, 1989; Yanov, 2004), or between a source context and a receiving context (Røvik, 2016). Different vocabularies are used to describe how tokens enter/arrive in or leave groups A and B: Disembedding and re-embedding (Czarniawska & Joerges, 1996), decontextualizing and contextualizing (Røvik, 2016), sending and receiving (Johnson & Hagström, 2005), knowledge creation and knowledge to action (Graham et al., 2006). Some researchers focus primarily on the source group A of a token or the target group B that receives it (Clegg et al., 2004; Czarniawska & Joerges, 1996; Graham et al., 2006; Røvik, 2016). Other researchers focus on the brokering that happens in the meeting or encounter between representatives of groups A and B as the token is translated (Carlile, 2004; Secundo,

Del Vecchio, Simeone, & Schiuma, 2020; Star & Griesemer, 1989; Yanov, 2004). Yet other researchers accentuate translators brokering between groups through their use of particular practices (Raidelli & Sitton-Kent, 2016) or work with translating texts (talk and written) (Holden et al., 2004; Madsen, 2013). Actor-network researchers emphasize the movement of tokens and suggest that it is 'in the hands of people' (Latour, 1986, p. 267). They, however, downplay the role of the different groups that tokens move between. They instead emphasize that the movement of tokens from A to B does not just involve mobilizing humans but also nonhumans to succeed. It is thus the (rhizomatic) expansion of the actor-network of humans and nonhumans who do work that realizes the token that may/or may not make a token move between groups A and B.

Translation

The authors in translation studies label the process through which tokens move as translation. They define the concept differently however. Translation is thus defined as follows:

- A spread in time and space of anything (tokens) that is in the hands of people: Each of whom may act in many different ways, letting the token drop, modifying it, deflecting it, betraying it, adding to it or appropriating it (Latour, 1986; also adopted by Czarniawska & Joerges, 1996; Czarniawska, 2014)
- A process that involves (1) problematization, (2) interessement, (3) enrollment, and (4) mobilization (Callon, 1986, also partly adopted by Star & Griesemer, 1989, Raidelli & Sitton-Kent, 2016)
- Part of a process involving transfer of information, translation (including sharing and interpretation of meanings) and political and interest-related negotiations at the boundary between groups of people (Carlile, 2004)
- A de-contextualization and contextualization process (Røvik, 2016)
- A language-based, functional, cultural and ideological translation of a (strategy) text (Madsen, 2013)
- An imitation process where meaning (of policy ideas) is constructed by temporally and spatially disembedding policy ideas from their previous contexts and using them as a model for altered political structures in a new context (Johnson & Hagström, 2005)
- The process of modification of policy ideas and creation of new meanings and designs in the process of the cross-jurisdictional travel of policy ideas (Mukhtarov, 2014)
- 'A series of interesting, and sometimes even surprising, disturbances that can occur in the spaces between the 'creation', the 'transmission' and the 'interpretation' or 'reception' of policy meanings' (Lendvai & Stubbs, 2007; Stone, 2012)

- The multiple and variable processes incorporating (i) diffusion/transfer, (ii) assemblage/bricolage, (iii) mobilities/mutation, (iv) interpretation/localization and (v) trial and error when moving policy ideas (Stone, 2017)
- The replacing of terms in one language with those in another. It is also a substitution of one set of relationships or associations with another. These may be similar to the original but can never be identical. To translate, therefore, is to make new associations, to reassociate or perhaps to reassign (Freeman, 2004) (adopted by Clark, 2015)
- To translate is to convert knowledge from one domain/cross-cultural team and language group to another (Holden et al., 2004)
- Translating knowledge involves processing new knowledge, interpreting it according to the needs and interests of the different actors involved and transforming it into forms that are more suitable for the specific organizational context of the application (Albino, Garvelli, & Schiuma, 1998; Secundo et al., 2020)
- A dynamic and iterative process that includes the synthesis, dissemination, exchange and ethically sound application of knowledge to improve health, provide more effective health services and products, and strengthen the healthcare system (Straus, Tetroe, & Graham, 2013)
- A displacement, invention, mediation and creation of a new link that did not exist before (Clegg et al., 2004)
- An interactive process where knowledge translation activities are performed and boundary objects in the form of outputs are produced that are then later translated and turned into other forms of knowledge and outputs by others/the following translators (Thorpe et al., 2011)

Objects

The translation researchers also have different views on the role of objects in the translation process. Actor-network researchers perceive nonhumans (material objects) as actors who 'act' and play an equally important role as humans in the construction of performative actor-networks and thus the materialization (Czarniawska & Joerges, 1996) of phenomena in the world (including in the 'materialization' of ideas, organizations, strategies, policies, technology etc.) (Callon, 1986; Latour, 1986). Scandinavian institutionalists and symbolic interactionists view objects as things that may be used by human actors to facilitate translation processes in different ways – either as intermediate objects supporting the translation between an abstract idea and an institutionalized routine, or as boundary objects facilitating the creation of meaning and collaboration between groups A and B (Czarniawska & Joerges, 1996; Star & Griesemer, 1989; Thorpe et al., 2011). In the theory of action nets, Czarniawska (2014) identifies a wide range of objects hypothesized to be involved in the establishment of the action nets of which the organization is constructed: Texts that are translated, edited and inscribed by managers; budgets that translate actions into numbers; machines used to manage people; and people who manage machines by using codes, writing and translating codes (for instance the law), written norms about machine behavior (A4 in the printer, 220 V in Europe, etc.) and regulating environmental issues (limits to pollution of air, water, etc.). For linguistic and strategy translation researchers (Holden et al., 2004; Madsen, 2013), it is the translation of texts as objects (written and spoken) that are primarily focused upon. In a design, view objects may be used to facilitate communication between stakeholders in open innovation processes (Secundo et al., 2020). Røvik (2016) reflects very briefly on what objects 'do' during decontextualizing and contextualizing processes. He identifies them as 'abstract representations' of ideas and practices. He also reflects upon how a strong or weak human component compared to a technological component may influence the translation process. But further reflections about the role of objects during translation processes are missing. Other translation studies researchers focusing on translation as symbolic interpretative processes or practices do not include objects in their theorizing or modeling of organizational translation processes (Clegg et al., 2004; Johnson & Hagström, 2005; Mukhtarov, 2014; Raidelli & Sitton-Kent, 2016; Stone, 2012, 2017).

The translator

In organizational translation studies, the translator plays a key role in the movement of ideas. As suggested in Latour's definition of translation, the movement of tokens is in the hands of people (Latour, 1986, p. 267). He/she who moves the token is assumed to do different things as they translate it by different researchers however. For actor-network researchers, the main task of translators is to perform different types of work aimed at associating and solving controversies with actants that are needed in the actor-network that realizes/performs a given token (Callon, 1986; Callon & Latour, 1981; Latour, 1986). The work includes all the 'negotiations, intrigues, calculations, acts of persuasion and violence', etc. (Callon & Latour, 1981, p. 279) needed to create connections between and associate 'token relevant' human and non-human actants. Scandinavian institutionalists like Czarniawska and Joerges (1996) and Czarniawska (2014) adopt Latour's definition of translation but 'build it into' a social constructivist model of translation where the translation work involves translating an idea into an object, and then into actions, which then become institutions if they are repeated and typified (Berger & Luckmann, 1966) in a similar manner over time. For other researchers, translators need to transfer, translate, bargain and negotiate when they move ideas or knowledge from one group of human actors to another (Carlile, 2004; Stone, 2017). For yet other researchers, it is the use of particular micro-practices that makes translation happen (Raidelli & Sitton-Kent, 2016). For researchers like Star and Griesemer (1989), it is the ability of translators to develop and use boundary objects that assures that tokens/knowledge makes sense and supports collaborative work that is emphasized. Researchers studying design as a translation mechanism on their part emphasize the importance of using design artifacts to ease communication between stakeholders (Secundo et al., 2020). Thorpe et al. (2011) highlight the importance of researchers' ability to support translation of their research findings through their ability to collaborate with and make links to stakeholders across space and time along the knowledge translation value chain. For Røvik (2016), it is the following of appropriate translation rules when ideas are decontextualized and contextualized that is important. The linguistically influenced translation researchers emphasize the importance of the translator being able to translate and communicate texts between culture and language groups A and B that are different (Holden et al., 2004). Madsen (2013) emphasizes the degree of language-related, functional, cultural and ideological and interest-related loyalty that a translator practices when translating an original token (text). Finally, Clegg et al. (2004) think that the translators being able to disturb and disrupt taken-for-granted cultures and language games in groups A and B and to create a third language (game) are the most important tasks of the translator. Yet other researchers suggest that translators having a certain role as for instance being a middle manager or a consultant may have an influence on the translation process (Clegg et al., 2004; Raidelli & Sitton-Kent, 2016). The translator may also influence the translation process through his/her translation competences (Røvik, 2016) which include whether the translator is bilingual and has thorough knowledge about the source as well as the recipient context of ideas/practices. Yet another competence mentioned by Røvik is his/her knowledge about translation rules and how various translation rules can relate to and be applied under various conditions.

Outcomes

The measure of the outcome of the translation process and the way to decide whether a token has been translated do also vary in organizational translation studies. Some researchers assume that the token has been translated when it makes sense and is interpreted as meaningful by the receivers of the token (Carlile, 2002/2004; Johnson & Hagström, 2005; Mukhtarov, 2014; Star & Griesemer, 1989; Stone, 2012; Thorpe et al., 2011; Yanov, 2004). For Czarniawska and Joerges (1996), an idea has been translated and it produces an outcome when it has been translated into an institutionalized routine (habitualized actions that are typified in the same way over time by the group of actors receiving the token (Berger & Luckmann, 1966)). For the researchers influenced by linguistic translation theory, the positive outcome of a translation process occurs if and when the translator succeeds with translating the text from one cultural and language group to another as intended (Holden et al., 2004; Madsen, 2013). For Clegg et al. (2004), a translation process is successful if it disturbs and interrupts the culture and language systems of both the senders and receivers of a token and results in the formation of a third type of language (game) and thus a new type of cultural understanding. In her contribution from 2014, Czarniawska connects the translation process identified in the idea model (Czarniawska & Joerges, 1996) with establishment of all the different types of action nets that produce and re-produce organizations as phenomena (including actions of investing, constructing, producing, buying, selling, transporting, collaborating). The 'organizing' outcome of translation processes is thus supposed to be all these different types of action nets. Finally, in actor-network theory a successful translation depends on the establishment of a performative actor-network whose actants (human and nonhuman) do the work necessary to realize and materialize (Czarniawska & Joerges, 1996) a given token. As we will discuss in Chapter 23, the above-mentioned views on how you may measure whether the translation of a token has produced an outcome and been translated differ. The reason is the different philosophies of the social sciences and ontological assumptions on which the different theories and models of translation are based.

What influence translation processes?

Having identified the focus points and 'elements' influencing translation processes according to organizational translation studies researchers, it is relevant to ask how each of these elements influences the translation process. Table 17.1 gives an overview of this.

The token

According to actor-network theory, a token may influence the translation process by creating a connection and relation that was not there before (Callon, 1986; Callon & Latour, 1981; Latour, 1986). According to Scandinavian institutionalists, a token (an idea) may influence the ongoing translation processes in organizations if it creates attention and is perceived as fashionable (Czarniawska & Joerges, 1996). In Clegg et al.'s (2004) view, a token may influence the translation process through disturbing and disrupting the cultural order and language systems of both senders and receivers of the token. Holden et al. (2004) think it is the lack of cultural understanding, uncertainty, and ambiguity related to the source of the token (knowledge) that leaves room for interpretation by the receiving group or team. Røvik (2016) points out that the translatability of the source practice related to a token (i.e., its explicitness, embeddedness and complexity) may influence the translation process. He moreover points out that the transformability of the knowledge construct related to a token (including translators' freedom to interpret and change it and its dependence on a certain use of technology) may also influence the translation process. Holden et al. (2004) suggest that the translatability and convertibility of tokens (as texts) influence the translation process. Holden et al.'s (2004) view on translatability is different from Røviks' (2016) and

Table 17.1 What influence translation processes?

Focus point	May influence the translation process through/because	Authors
The token	• Creating a connection and relation that was not there before • It creates attention and/or is perceived as fashionable • Disturbing and disrupting language and cultural order • Its degree of translatability, transformability and convertibility • Lack of cultural understanding, uncertainty and ambiguity of the source knowledge • It has been socially authorized, theorized, made into a product, timed, harmonized, dramatized and individualized	Latour/Callon (1986) Czarniawska and Joerges (1996) Clegg et al. (2004) Carlile (2002, 2004) Røvik (2016) Holden et al. (2004) Røvik (1998)
Language and communication	• Language is a means to transfer, translate, communicate meaning, mediate, negotiate, bargain, learn about, integrate and co-construct phenomena (tokens) • Language-related errors, lack of equivalent words and concepts • Making tacit knowledge explicit, combine new and local explicit knowledge and contribute to internalize and make new knowledge tacit again • Degree to which token is generally, sufficiently, mostly or fully conveyed to the receivers (the degree to which it is explained in a contextualizing or decontextualizing manner) • Creating noise, disturbing and disrupting cultural order and subgroups language games • Creating a third language (game) that did not belong to neither the senders' nor receivers' original language systems	Latour/Callon (1986) Czarniawska and Joerges (1996) Star and Griesemer (1989) Carlile (2002, 2004) Stone (2012, 2017) Madsen (2013) Holden et al. (2004) Røvik (2016) Clegg et al. (2004)
Characteristics of and differences between groups A and B	• Humans/persons/groups (actants) who act and become 'carriers' of characteristics and similarities and differences during the co-construction of the actor-network • Degree of similarity and difference between recipient and source context • Social and cultural similarities and differences • Political and interest-related similarities and differences • Differences related to languages • Differences in knowledge of translators distributed along knowledge translation value chain • Barriers to knowledge and action cycles	Latour/Callon (1986) Røvik (2016) Star and Griesemer (1989) Carlile (2002, 2004) Stone (2012, 2017) Clegg et al. (2004) Thorpe et al. (2011) Graham et al. (2006)

Focus point	May influence the translation process through/because	Authors
The way tokens: Leave a group Arrive in a group Are brokered between groups	• Disembedding: The process through which a token (an idea) becomes a quasi-object, transgresses the barriers of local time and enters a translocal path • Decontextualizing: The way a token (practice) is translated into an abstract representation. Depends on its translatability: Its complexity, embeddedness and explicitness • Sending: The nature of the content that the sender encodes into a message and the intention he/she had with it • Knowledge creation: Process of (1) knowledge enquiry, (2) knowledge synthesis, (3) production of knowledge tools (guidelines, decision aids, rules, pathways, etc.) that are communicated to users • Re-embedding: The process through which a token 'lands' in a new locality, become materialized in actions and institutions • Re-contextualizing: The way an abstract representation of token (a practice) is translated into a concrete local practice embedded in formal structures, cultures, routines and individual skills. Depends on understanding the essentials of source and recipient contexts and on the making of suitable adjustments of the practice • The way it is received: The receivers culturally embedded and influenced decoding of a senders message. If receivers cannot ascribe meaning to and make sense of the message communication fails • Knowledge to action activities: (1) group identify problem and search knowledge, (2) knowledge is adapted to local context, (3) barriers and facilitators to change are assessed and interventions are chosen, (4) knowledge use is monitored, (5) Evaluation of outcome compared to goals, (6) sustaining the knowledge use • The token (knowledge) is expressed through different languages, transferred, translated, bargained, negotiated and learned about through interaction and communication between representatives from groups A and B • The micro-practices that are used • The translation of tokens as text (talk or written) needs to be translated as effectively as possible given the source and recipient contexts of the text	Czarniawska and Joerges (1996) Røvik (2016) Johnson and Hagström (2005) Graham et al. (2006) Czarniawska and Joerges (1996) Røvik (2016) Johnson and Hagström (2005) Graham et al. (2006) Carlile (2002, 2004) Star and Griesemer (1989) Stone (2012, 2017) Secundo et al. (2020) Clegg et al. (2004) Raidelli and Sitton-Kent (2016) Holden et al. (2004) Madsen (2013)

(*Continued*)

Focus point	May influence the translation process through/because	Authors
The translator	• What translators choose to attend to and translate into objects and actions • Work aimed at creating links between and solving controversies with actants • Ability to transfer, translate, bargain, negotiate and learn • Use of micro-practices • Development and use of boundary objects • Use of objects as intermediaries to mediate between idea and practice • Use of design artifacts to ease communication • Ability to collaborate with and make links to stakeholders across time and space • Personal translation competences and insight in appropriate translation rules • His/her choice of degree of loyalty to original token (text) • Having a certain role or position (manager or consultant) • Ability to create and disturb language systems through introducing a third language	Czarniawska and Joerges (1996) Latour/Callon (1986) Carlile (2002, 2004) Stone (2012, 2017) Raidelli and Sitton-Kent (2016) Star and Griesemer (1989) Secundo et al. (2020) Thorpe et al. (2011) Røvik (2016) Madsen (2013) Clegg et al. (2004)
Objects	• Acting (as actants) during the co-construction of the actor-network • Mediating/facilitating the translation between abstract tokens/ideas and institutionalized routines/action nets • Facilitating translation and creation of meaning between groups that try to coordinate and/or collaborate across boundaries • They are texts (talk and written) that need to be translated from one language and cultural group to another • Design objects used to facilitate communication between stakeholders	Latour/Callon (1986) Czarniawska and Joerges (1996) Star and Griesemer (1989) Carlile (2004) Madsen (2013) Secundo et al. (2020)
The outcome	• That which was translated was perceived/not perceived as meaningful • The text was/was not translated as intended and/or according to appropriate rules • The language and cultural systems of groups A and B was/was not disturbed (or disrupted) and a third language and cultural system was/was not established • An institutionalized routine or action-net was/was not established • An actor-network was/was not established	Star and Griesemer (1989) Carlile (2002, 2004) Holden et al. (2004) Madsen (2013) Clegg et al. (2004) Czarniawska (2014) Latour/Callon (1986)

concerns how the properties of a text as well as the translator's competence and ability to make an accurate translation of it affect the translation process. The convertibility of tokens (as texts) depends on the degree to which the translator is a domain expert in the languages in groups A and B and subject matters related to the token as well on the perceived utility of the token for its receivers.

In an earlier contribution, Røvik (1998, p. 152) reflected upon what made tokens (ideas/recipes) travel far and fast in organizational fields. Here, he suggested that a token (an idea) that was socially authorized, theorized, productivated, timed, harmonized, dramatized and individualized would travel further and faster than other ideas. Social authorization happens when an idea/recipe (like for instance the management idea: LEAN) is developed, communicated by or associated with an entity that is perceived as an authoritative center by other organizations. Theorization happens when an idea/a recipe is communicated as a universal solution to certain problems that will produce positive results in all types of companies because they work in accordance with universal cause-effect relationships so that correct installation will assure positive results independently of contexts. Productivation means that the idea/recipe is presented in a way that makes it easy to communicate and makes it look like a user-friendly commodity on a market. Timing concerns defining the idea/recipe as a modern answer to changes in the environment and as a new, future-oriented and better idea/recipe than older ones. Harmonization is about designing the idea/recipe in a way that does not favor or conflict with certain group interests within the organization. Dramatizing is the communication of the idea/recipe through dramatic stories about how the idea/recipe was developed and obtained support. Finally, individualization concerns designing the idea/recipe in a way so that it present itself as an offer that may contribute to development, growth, career and empowerment of the individual member of the organization.

Language and communication

According to organizational translation studies, researcher's language and communication influence translation processes because they are means to transfer, translate, communicate meaning, mediate, negotiate, bargain, learn about, integrate and co-construct phenomena (tokens) (Callon, 1986; Carlile, 2004; Clegg et al, 2004; Czarniawska, 2014; Czarniawska & Joerges, 1996; Holden et al., 2004; Latour, 1986; Madsen, 2013; Star & Griesemer, 1989; Stone, 2012, 2017). The degree to which a token is generally, sufficiently, mostly or fully conveyed to the receivers may influence the translation process (Holden et al., 2004). Drawing on Røviks' (2016) view, you may also say that language and communication affect translation processes through the way the token is explained in either a contextualizing or decontextualizing manner. That is in a manner where particulars related to the functioning of the token in its original context are either communicated or not in detail when explained to the receivers. It is language and communication that allow humans to make tacit knowledge explicit, combine new and local explicit knowledge, and internalize and make new knowledge tacit again (Holden et al., 2004). Language-related errors and lack of equivalent words and concepts are another factor that may influence the translation process (Holden et al., 2004). Finally, Clegg et al. (2004) point out that language and communication affect translation processes by creating noise, and disturbing and disrupting cultural order and subgroups language systems/games. Language and communication thus influence translation processes when translators (as for instance consultants) succeed with creating a third language (game) that did not belong to neither the senders' nor receivers' original cultures and language systems.

Characteristics of and differences between groups A and B

Researchers of organizational translation studies agree that the characteristics of and differences between people in groups A and B may influence the translation process. For actor-network researchers, what influences the translation process is an empirical question that may not be decided a priori. Humans, persons and groups of people, may (or may not) act and may be shown to be 'carriers' of characteristics, similarities and differences, that influence the translation process and thus the co-construction of the (however always heterogeneous) actor-network that performs a given token (Callon, 1986; Callon & Latour, 1981; Latour, 1986). Other researchers think that the degree of similarity and difference between the recipient and the source context influences the translation process (Clegg et al., 2004; Holden et al., 2004; Johnson & Hagström, 2005; Madsen, 2013; Røvik, 2016). Just as social, cultural and political/interest-related similarities and differences between groups A and B are also assumed to influence the translation process (Carlile, 2004; Clegg et al., 2004; Johnson & Hagström, 2005; Secundo et al., 2020; Star & Griesemer, 1989; Stone, 2017; Yanov, 2004). For Thorpe et al. (2011), differences in knowledge of translators distributed along the knowledge translation value chain may also influence the translation process. Graham et al. (2006) distinguish between the knowledge creation cycle (inquiry, synthesis and production of tools/knowledge products) and the action cycle (identifying and using knowledge/knowledge products (including tools) to solve problems). Group A is related to the knowledge creation cycle and includes the researchers (doctors) producing 'scientific evidence'. Group B is related to the action cycle and consists of the users (doctors) using the evidence. The barriers related to group A may influence the translation process through the volume of and access to research, lack of time and skills of group A members to read and appraise the current research evidence. The barriers related to group B and thus the action cycle may be structural, organizational, related to the peer group, professional, patient-related, etc.

The way tokens arrive in, leave groups or are negotiated between them

As mentioned above, researchers in organizational translation studies have different views on how tokens leave, arrive in or are brokered between groups of people.

According to Czarniawska and Joerges (1996), disembedding is the process through which a token (an idea) becomes a quasi-object, transgresses the barriers of local time and enters a translocal path, and which influences the translation process because it makes it possible for tokens (ideas) to travel between groups that are separated in time and space in organizational fields. Fashion is suggested to play a role in that connection. The token (idea) will moreover influence the translation process through the way it is re-embedded, when it 'lands' in a new locality, and becomes materialized in actions and institutions. Røvik (2016) on his part emphasizes that tokens (practices) are de-contextualized when they leave the source group. The contextual information related to what makes a token work is to a certain extent stripped away in the process. Whether the process is successful therefore depends on the translatability of the token including: Its complexity, its embeddedness in a specific intra- and/or inter-organizational context and the degree to which it is based on explicit or tacit knowledge (Polanyi, 1962, 1966). When the token (practice) arrives in the recipient group, the translation process is influenced by the way translators chose to re-contextualize the token. The success of the process depends on the translator's understanding of the essentials of the source and recipient contexts that may be relevant in relation to the functioning of the token and are needed to make suitable adjustments to the token to make it 'fit' the recipient context. It moreover depends on whether the translator succeeds with using this knowledge or insight so that the abstract representation of the token may eventually be translated into concrete new practices that are embedded in formal structures, cultures, routines and individual skills. Johnson and Hagström (2005) contrast Shannon and Weawer (1949) traditional communication model with the semiotic communication model. The first model explains how messages (about for instance policy ideas) are transmitted between a transmitter and a receiver through the use of certain media. The second model – which is related to the translation perspective – suggests that it is the meaning that the culturally embedded receiver ascribes to a message that is important rather than the content that the sender puts into the message or the intentions he/she had with it. The encoding of messages into tokens by a sender is thus part of the process but less important than the decoding of the token performed by its receivers. For Graham et al. (2006), the translation of tokens (knowledge) depends on the knowledge creation process, including knowledge inquiry, knowledge synthesis, and production of knowledge tools performed by a group of researchers producing these things and communicating them to the users (doctors). And it depends on the users (doctors) who receive and use the token (knowledge). The process where users receive the token (knowledge) unfolds in a way where users (1) identify a problem and search for knowledge about it, (2) adapt knowledge to the local context, (3) assess barriers and facilitators to change and chose appropriate interventions, (4) monitor the knowledge use, (5) evaluate the outcomes of the translation compared to goals, and then (6) sustain the knowledge use. A third group of researchers focuses upon how the brokering between groups (A and B) unfolds in the encounter or meeting between representatives from groups A and B. They focus upon how a token (knowledge) is transferred, translated, bargained, negotiated and learned about as well as (socially) constructed through interaction and communication between the representatives from groups A and B (Carlile, 2004; Clegg et al., 2004; Secundo et al., 2020; Star & Griesemer, 1989; Stone, 2017); or is brokered through the use of micro-practices (Raidelli & Sitton-Kent, 2016) or translation of texts (Holden et al., 2004; Madsen, 2013). In the latter case, tokens are considered to be texts (talk or written) that need to be translated as effectively as possible given their specific source and recipient contexts.

The translator

According to Czarniawska and Joerges (1996), translators influence translation processes through what they choose to attend to. Thus, it is only when a token (a management idea) becomes the center of a translator's attention and is selected, it may be translated into an object, actions and institutions. In the theory of action nets, Czarniawska (2014) points out that translators need to translate many things in order to establish the different action nets of which the organization consists (which performs actions such as investing, buying, selling, producing, transporting, etc.) – including translating ideas into narrative forms; managing texts by translating, editing and inscribing them; translating actions into numbers and the opposite way round through budgets; constructing machines; writing codes and creating norms. In actor-network theory, translators influence translation processes through their work by creating links between and solving controversies with human and nonhuman actants needed in the actor-networks that realize (or materialize) tokens (Callon, 1986; Callon & Latour, 1981; Latour, 1986). Other researchers emphasize the importance of translators' ability to transfer, translate, bargain, negotiate and learn as they move tokens between groups A and B (Carlile, 2004; Johnson & Hagström, 2005; Secundo et al., 2020; Star & Griesemer, 1989; Stone, 2017; Yanov, 2004); or translators' ability to use micro-practices (Raidelli & Sitton-Kent, 2016). Yet other researchers point out the importance of the translators ability to develop and use boundary objects when he/she tries to make group A collaborate or coordinate their actions with group B (Star & Griesemer, 1989). According to Czarniawska and Joerges (1996), the translators' ability to use objects as intermediaries to mediate between idea and practice is important while Secundo et al. (2020) suggest that translators may facilitate the translation process if they are able to use design artifacts to ease communication between stakeholders having different perspectives, ideas, viewpoints, goals and interests. Thorpe et al. (2011) on their part find that the ability of a translator to collaborate with and make links to stakeholders situated differently in time and space across the knowledge translation-value-chain is important for researchers who want to make an impact with his/her research. Røvik (2016) emphasizes that a critical feature of a translator's translation competence is to know about different translation rules and about how various rules relate to and can be applied under various conditions – including knowing under which conditions a knowledge construct should be copied, added to or altered. Madsen (2013) on his part points out that the degree of loyalty that a translator has toward the content, the intention, the context and the ideology/interests of the original token (strategy text) when he/she translates it will influence the translation process. Finally, some researchers point out that having a certain role or position in the organization may influence the translation process. Middle managers may play a particular important role as translators in organizations because they are situated between top management and the employees (Raidelli & Sitton-Kent, 2016). They are both controllers, controlled, and resisters, as well as resisted (Harding, Lee, & Ford, 2014). Clegg et al. (2004) point out that consultants play an important role as translators since they do not – as normally suggested – contribute to simplify, stabilize and arrest the flux and constant transformation of organizations and to help organize them; but rather influence them through introducing chaos, noise, disorder and a new (third type of) language (game) different from the senders' and receivers' original culture and language systems resulting in a transformation of the organizations' cultural system.

Objects

Objects are assumed to influence translation processes in different ways by translation studies researchers. In actor-network theory, objects (nonhumans) may be said to 'act' during translation processes in the same way as humans may be ascribed being the source of actions. How they may act is an open and empirical question (Callon, 1986; Latour, 1986, 1996). Scandinavian institutionalists think that objects influence the translation process through mediating or facilitating the translation between abstract tokens/ideas and institutionalized routines and action nets (Czarniawska, 2014; Czarniawska & Joerges, 1996). Symbolic interactionist researchers emphasize that objects influence translation processes when they are used as boundary objects to facilitate translation and the creation of meaning between groups that try to coordinate or collaborate across boundaries (Star & Griesemer, 1989). For linguistically influenced translation researchers, it is texts (talk and written) as objects that are in focus and need to be translated from one language and cultural group to another; while researchers studying design as a translation mechanism emphasize that design objects may be used to facilitate communication between stakeholders with different perspectives, ideas, viewpoints, goals and interests.

The outcome

Finally, building on different philosophies of the social sciences, translation studies researchers have different views on how the outcomes of translation processes are identified, evaluated and assumed to influence the translation processes that follow. Some researchers suggest that the translation processes that follow will be influenced in different ways (be successful or unsuccessful), depending on whether that which was translated was perceived or not as meaningful by the receivers of a token (knowledge) (Carlile, 2004; Johnson & Hagström, 2005; Star & Griesemer, 1989; Stone, 2017; Yanov, 2004); or as useful (Thorpe et al., 2011). Researchers influenced by linguistics emphasize the importance of translating an 'original' source text (talk or written) from one language and cultural group to another language/cultural group as faithfully and/or effectively as possible. The translation process is influenced by whether the text was translated or not as intended or as suggested by translation rules (Holden et al., 2004; Madsen, 2013; Røvik, 2016). For Clegg et al. (2004), change occurs when the senders' and receivers' cultures and language systems have been disturbed and disrupted and a new third type of language (game) and culture has been introduced that was not there before. In the idea model and the theory of action nets, the outcome of the translation process and further translations are influenced by whether a translation process results in or does not result in an institutionalized routine or action-net being established (Czarniawska, 2014; Czarniawska & Joerges, 1996). Finally, in actor-network theory the outcome of the translation process depends on whether an actor-network that 'performs' the token was established or not during the translation process (Callon, 1986; Callon & Latour, 1981; Latour, 1986).

Moving translation studies research forward

Translation processes: similar or different?

When compared it may be noted that the different theories about translation focus upon translation processes related to different types of empirical phenomena. Examples include the Scandinavian institutionalists who focus upon the movement of different types of management ideas. The symbolic interactionists and the translation in healthcare perspectives where researchers study the movement of knowledge. While researchers using actor-network theory are interested in how all kinds of tokens including ideas (and claims, orders, artifacts, goods, knowledge, etc.) are moved through translation and assembled into performative actor-networks that perform work realizing tokens (phenomena) in the world.

Researchers in translation studies share an interest in and try to theorize how ideas and tokens are moved between people and groups of people. Whether a fashionable management idea is adopted or translated, whether valuable knowledge is utilized in companies or public organizations, whether evidence-based knowledge about how to provide healthcare services or a performative actor-network or action-net is built up are all considered important questions to answer. It may be noted however that – as demonstrated above – researchers in translation studies define the concept of translation as well as theorize the translation process differently. The knowledge about similarities and differences and systematic discussions of how translation should be defined and how translation processes should be theorized across research streams have been missing (O'Mahoney, 2016, Wæraas & Nielsen, 2016).

One question that may be asked is: Whether the process through which humans move ideas (or tokens) between people and groups of people is generally similar or different? And how differences between the token (for instance an idea), the participants, the objects involved and the situation and context influence the translation process? When researchers like O'Mahoney (2016) in translation studies suggest that critical realism provides a basis for interdisciplinary dialogue between translation study researchers from different research streams and provides a common basis on which different types of translation might be studied, it seems to be implied that translation processes through which ideas are moved may be similar. That is, that translation processes follow a pattern and unfold as a more generic process than formerly recognized by researchers in organizational translation studies.

So are translation processes similar or do they unfold differently depending on characteristics of the idea, humans, objects and situation/context involved? Are they always different or are they similar within larger assemblies of groups (like nation states), sectors (healthcare, the car industry, the building industry, agriculture, etc.), individual organizations or subgroups or teams with different sub-cultures? Or put differently, does it not make sense to generalize about what characterizes translation processes because they are always different? Or does it only make sense to develop translation theories about context-specific translation processes (for instance related to movement of management ideas, knowledge translation in companies and healthcare)? Or is it possible to formulate a general and 'unified' theory about translation processes involved in people's movement of ideas (and other tokens) when they try to organize and make changes in organizations?

It is beyond the scope of this book to answer these questions. It does not mean, however, that such questions should not be asked and discussed by researchers from the different research streams in translation studies.

Need to challenge assumptions and learn from differences

The researchers and theories about translation that have been presented in this book have been used and referred to by many other researchers in each of their individual research streams. Instead of questioning and challenging the basic assumptions of translation and about how translation processes unfold, the researchers in each silo have to a large extent taken their own ways of theorizing translation processes for granted. The literature review conducted in relation to producing this book as well as the literature reviews presented in the appendices (O'Mahoney, 2016; Wæraas & Nielsen, 2016) has thus shown that researchers in each silo refer back to and use the conceptualizations and theories about translation developed by a limited number of researchers developed within their own research silo without questioning the ontological and epistemological assumptions on which these theories are based. Conceptualizations and theories about translation processes within each silo have thus primarily been used as conceptual frameworks to study the movement of ideas (and other tokens) within these silos but not been discussed or challenged by other silo internal and external researchers. Consequently, important research questions about what characterizes translation processes have not been researched and discussed to a sufficient degree.

As suggested by Spyridonidis, Currie, Heusinkveld, Strauss and Sturdy (2016), there is a need to map 'how, if at all, can varying theoretical traditions be combined'. At the same time, the editors of the special issue about translation studies published in the *International Journal of Management Review* in 2016 are skeptical. They conclude that no single or dominant conceptual framework has emerged to guide translation research. Research in translation studies is characterized by a multitude of perspectives. Reflecting upon the different perspectives may lead to conceptual integration. However, since different perspectives have different strengths and weaknesses a separation of them should remain. They thus question whether integration of the different translation perspectives is at all possible (Spyridonidis et al., 2016).

Different but complementary views

Wæraas and Nielsen (2016) point out the lack of cross-references between the three perspectives of translation they identify in their literature review and that there are ontological differences between the perspectives. They point out that these issues might suggest that the approaches focus on three different phenomena, or are separate or incompatible research traditions altogether. The authors however conclude that they do not believe that this is the case. They instead suggest that the perspectives focus on different aspects of translation processes, and do so with different emphasis and terminology. The authors thus view the perspectives as complementary and as trying to say something about the same phenomenon: How an object changes from one state to another within and across organizational settings. They explain that their analysis points to a variety of outcomes following the travel of translation theory into different organizational research communities, how the conceptualizations of translation differ and how they are similar.

Wæraas and Nielsen (2016) further emphasize that they do not think their literature review gives reason to encourage the development of one single theory of translation in organizational research because such an objective would in itself be in disagreement with the notion that local variants emerge as a result of the movement in time and space of objects, ideas and practices. Rather, they encourage other researchers to maintain some degree of distinctiveness within each approach while at the same time learning from the contributions of other perspectives. And they suggest that no approach should develop in ignorance of the others.

In another in-depth literature review focusing on differences in the philosophies of social sciences of the three different translation perspectives identified, O'Mahoney (2016) suggests critical realism as a method to investigate and sort out the differences among them. And that even though this would mean that other researchers building their understandings of translation on other types of philosophies of the social sciences (like ANT and Scandinavian institutionalist researchers) would then have to accept the realist ontology and epistemology suggested by such a perspective.

Focus points and themes in organizational translation studies

The comparative analysis of theories and models in organizational translation studies above identified a number of focus points and themes that translation studies researchers in organizational studies share and 'look into' in their research. These included a focus on the token that is translated; the role of language and communication in the movement of tokens; a focus on the movement of tokens from a group of people A to another group of people B; the way tokens arrive in, leave groups or are negotiated between them; the role of translators, humans and objects in that connection; and how outcomes of translation processes are measured, evaluated and assumed to influence further translation processes. The comparative analysis also identified how these different focus points or elements related to translation processes were assumed to influence the translation process.

The result of the comparative analysis and its identification of shared focus points and themes in organizational translation studies suggest that Wæraas and Nielsen (2016) were right when they suggested that the different translation perspectives are complementary and try to say something about the same phenomenon: How an object changes from one state to another within and across organizational settings. They were also right when they suggested that the different translation perspectives focus on different aspects of translation processes, and do so with different emphasis and terminology. And that – as shown by O'Mahoney (2016) – while taking their point of departure in different philosophies of the social sciences. The analysis has thereby contributed to identifying key issues and themes across different theories and perspectives in organizational translation studies and created a basis for further discussions among organizational translation studies researchers of 'how, if at all, can varying theoretical traditions be combined' (Spyridonidis et al., 2016, p. 246).

The comparative analysis shows that theories and models of organizational translation are similar in their choice of focus points and themes but different in the way they theorize and model translation processes within these areas. The analysis moreover shows that the main reason for these differences is that each of the different theories/models or groups of theories/models builds on different modes of research and philosophies of the social sciences (see Chapter 23 that discusses these differences).

Research questions and knowledge gabs

The comparative analysis makes it possible to identify knowledge gabs across perspectives and raise research questions in a new and more systematic way in organizational translation studies. Some of the basic research questions, relevant research themes and knowledge gabs in organizational translation studies that the analysis has identified include the following:

1 What token is moved?
2 If the token is subject to translation, who is translating what, how and for what purposes (Spyridonidis et al., 2016)?
3 Does characteristics of the token influence the translation process?
4 What is the role of language and communication in the movement of tokens?
5 How does characteristics of and differences between people and groups of people – including language-, cultural- and interest-related differences – influence the translation process?
6 Who are the translators?
7 What are the different types of work done and roles played by translators, humans and nonhumans (objects) in organizational translation processes?
8 What influences the direction, content, speed and outcome of the translation of tokens? Do characteristics of tokens play a role (Røvik, 1998)? Are or may certain translation rules (Røvik, 2016) be applied? Do patterns of attention, fashion (Czarniawska & Joerges, 1996), objects or other things play a role?
9 Do translators have or need to have certain translation competences (Røvik, 2016)?
10 If how tokens arrive in, leave or is negotiated between groups of people is studied by organizational translation researchers; then what happens during and characterizes these 'moments' in the movement of tokens through space and time?
11 How are outcomes of translation processes identified, measured and evaluated?
12 In what way does this outcome influence translation processes that follow?
13 What are the strengths and weaknesses of the different translation perspectives and their different philosophies of the social sciences when trying to understand organizational translation processes as a phenomenon?

14 To what degree may the different translation perspectives cross-fertilize each other and/or be combined (Spyridonidis et al., 2016; Wæraas & Nielsen, 2016)?

15 How may translation processes be researched using different theoretical perspectives, methods and different and perhaps shared data sets (Spyridonidis et al., 2016)?

16 What approaches to translation are more effective and for whom (Spyridonidis et al., 2016)?

17 Is formulating an 'instrumental' theory of translation (Røvik, 2016) possible? And if so how may it look like?

18 (A) Is it possible to formulate a unified theory of organizational translation? (B) Should theories/models of organizational translation be developed and adjusted to specific contexts (travel of management ideas, movement of healthcare or research-related knowledge, strategy translation in firms or policy translation in public organizations, etc.)? (C) Or does it not make sense to try to theorize or model what happens during translation processes because they are all unique?

19 What are the similarities and differences between an organizational translation view on the movement of tokens and other research-based views that have a similar research interest? For instance, the similarities and differences between an organizational translation view and other views, including views on the flow of management ideas, implementation science in healthcare, strategy and policy implementation studies, diffusion and knowledge transfer studies, etc.

References

Albino, V., Garvelli, C., & Schiuma, G. (1998). Document knowledge transfer and interfirm relationships in industrial districts: The role of the leader firm. *Technovation, 19*(1), 53–63.

Berger, P., & Luckmann, T. (1966). *The social construction of reality.* New York, NY: Doubleday.

Callon, M. (1986). Some elements of a sociology of translation: Domestication of the scallops and the fishermen of St. Brieuc Bay. In J. Law (Ed.), *Power, action and belief – A new sociology of knowledge?* London: Routledge & Kegan Paul.

Callon, M., & Latour, B. (1981). Unscrewing the big Leviathan: How actors macrostructure reality and how sociologists help them to do so. In K. Knorr-Cetina & A. V. Cicourel (Eds.), *Advances in social theory and methodology, toward an integration of micro and macro-sociologies.* Boston, MA: Routledge & Kegan Paul.

Carlile, P. R. (2002). A pragmatic view of knowledge and boundaries: Boundary objects in new product development. *Organization Science, 13*, 442–455.

Carlile, P. R. (2004). Transferring, translating, and transforming: An integrative framework for managing knowledge across boundaries. *Organization Science, 15*(5), 555–568.

Clarke, J., & Bainton, D. (2015). *Making policy move: Towards a politics of translation and assemblage.* Bristol: Policy Press.

Clegg, S. R., Kornberger, M., & Rhodes, C. (2004). Noise, parasites and translation – Theory and practice in management consulting. *Management Learning, 35*(1), 31–44.

Czarniawska, B. (2014). *A theory of organizing* (2nd ed.). Edward Elgar Publishing, Cheltenham, UK, Northampton, MA, USA.

Czarniawska, B., & Joerges, B. (1996). Travel of ideas. In B. Czarniawska & G. Sevón (Eds.), *Translating organizational change* (pp. 13–48). Berlin: Walter de Gruyter.

Freeman, R. (2004). Research, practice and the idea of translation, consultation paper. Previously retrieved from www.pol.ed.ac.uk/freeman.

Graham, I. D., Logan, J., Harrison, M. b., Straus, S. E., Tetroe, J., Caswell, W., & Robinson, N. (2006). Lost in knowledge translation: Time for a map? *The Journal of Continuing Education in the Health Professions, 26*(1), Winter, 13–24.

Harding, N., Lee, H., & Ford, J. (2014). Who is the middle manager? *Human Relations, 67*, 1213–1237.

Holden, N. J., Harald, F. O., & Kortzfleisch, O. (2004). Why cross-cultural knowledge transfer is a form of translation in more ways than you think. *Knowledge and Process Management, 11*(2), 127–136.

Johnson, B., & Hagström, B. (2005). The translation perspective as an alternative to the policy diffusion paradigm: The case of the Swedish methadone maintenance treatment. *Journal of Social Policy, 34*, 365–388.

Latour, B. (1996). On actor-network theory A few clarifications. *Soziale Welt, 47* Jahrg., H.4, 369–381.

Latour, B. (1986). The powers of association. In J. Law (Eds.), *Power, action and belief* (pp. 261–277). London: Routledge and Kegan Paul.

Law, J. (1986). Power, action and belief – a new sociology of knowledge? London: Routledge & Kegan Paul.

Lendvai, N., & Stubbs, P. (2007). Policies as translation: situating transnational social policies. In: S. Hodgson & Z. Irving (Eds.), *Policy reconsidered: meanings, politics and practices* (pp. 173–190). Bristol: The Policy Press.

Madsen, S. O. (2013). *The leader as a translator – A translation perspective on strategy work.* PhD dissertation, Copenhagen Business School.

Mukhtarov, F. (2014). Rethinking the travel of ideas: Policy translation in the water sector. *Policy & Politics, 42*(1), 71–88.

O'Mahoney, J. (2016). Archetypes of translation: Recommendations for dialogue. *International Journal of Management Reviews, 18*(3), 333–350.

Polanyi, M. (1966). *The tacit dimension.* London: Routledge & Kegan Paul.

Polanyi, M. (1962). *Personal knowledge.* London: Routledge & Kegan Paul.

Raidelli, G., & Sitton-Kent, L. (2016). Middle managers and the translation of new ideas in organizations: A review of micro-practices and contingencies. *International Journal of Management Reviews, 18*(3), 311–332.

Røvik, K. A. (1998). Modern organizations – Trends in organizational thinking at the millennium shift, Fagbokforlaget.

Røvik, K. A. (2016). Knowledge transfer as translation: Review and elements of an instrumental theory. *International Journal of Management Reviews, 18*(3), 290–310.

Secundo, G., Del Vecchio, P., Simeone, L., & Schiuma, G. (2020). Creativity and stakeholder's engagement in open innovation: Design for knowledge translation in technology-intensive enterprises. *Journal of Business Research*, 272–282.

Secundo, G., Del Vecchio, P., Simeone, L., Schiuma, G. (2020) Creativity and stakeholder's engagement in open innovation: Design for knowledge translation in technology-intensive enterprises, *Journal of Business Research, 119*, 272–282.

Shannon, C., & Weawer, W. (1949). *The mathematical theory of communications.* Urbana: University of Illinois Press.

Spyridonidis, D., Currie, G., Heusinkveld, S., Strauss, K., & Sturdy, A. (2016). The translation of management knowledge: Challenges, contributions and new directions. *International Journal of Management Reviews, 18,* 231–235.

Star, S. L., & Griesemer, J. (1989). Institutional ecology, 'translations', and boundary objects: Amateurs and professionals on Berkeley's museum of vertebrate zoology. *Social Studies of Science, 19,* 387–420.

Stone, D. (2012). Transfer and translation of policy. *Policy Studies, 33*(6), 483–499.

Stone, D. (2017). Understanding the transfer of policy failure: Bricolage, experimentalism and translation. *Policy & Politics, 45*(1), 55–70.

Straus, S. E., Tetroe, J., & Graham, I. D. (2013). *Knowledge translation in health care – Moving from evidence to practice.* Wiley Blackwell, BMJ Books.

Thorpe, R., Eden, C., Bessant, J., & Ellwood, P. (2011). Rigour, relevance and reward: Introducing the knowledge translation value-chain. *British Journal of Management, 22,* 420–431.

Wæraas, A., & Nielsen, J. A. (2016). Translation theory 'translated': Three perspectives on translation in organizational research. *International Journal of Management Reviews, 18*(3), 236–270.

Yanov, D. (2004). Translating local knowledge at organizational peripheries. *British Journal of Management, 15,* 9–25.

18 Part 2

Conclusion

The literature review identified 13 theories and models of organizational translation excluding the diffusion perspective (which is not a translation perspective) and the idea-practice-translation model, which is developed in Part 3 of the book. Table 2.1 sums up the main characteristics of these models and the analysis conducted in this section has answered the first two research questions of the book: (1) what different theories of organizational translation exist? (2) How do they define, theorize and/or model the translation process?

As demonstrated in Table 2.1, the different theories and models of organizational translation confirm actor-network researchers' assumption that tokens including the idea of 'translation' as a way of theorizing and model the movement of tokens in organizations are translated by researchers in organization studies. In this sense, the idea of 'translation' is not different from what happens to other tokens (ideas, knowledge, texts, etc.) that move. When analyzed in detail, the theories thus focus on the movement of different types of tokens (ideas, knowledge and texts), theorize and model how the token is moved differently, and suggest different types of factors that influence the translation process. Moreover, key actors are identified as translators, humans (of different types), nonhumans (objects of different types), and texts. Just as different vocabularies and key concepts have been developed and used when describing the translation process. Finally, as will be shown in Chapter 23, the theories and models may be grouped around four different modes of doing research in organizational translation processes: A scientific mode, an actualist mode, a humanistic mode and a design mode.

The analysis of the different theories and models of translation in organization studies was followed by a comparative analysis aimed at identifying key focus points, research themes and key research questions of organizational translation theories/models across theories and models; and finding out what influences translation processes according to these theories/models. Moreover the aim was to explore similarities and differences in the theories/models view on organizational translation processes (research questions 3, 4 and 5).

The comparative analysis of theories and models in organizational translation studies above identified a number of focus points and themes that translation studies researchers in organizational studies to some degree share and 'look into' in their research. These included a focus on the token that is translated; the role of language and communication in the movement of tokens; a focus on the movement of tokens from a group of people A to another group of people B; the way tokens arrive in, leave groups or are negotiated between them; the role of translators, humans and objects in that connection; and how outcomes of translation processes are measured, evaluated and assumed to influence further translation processes. For each focus point and theme, an overview of how theories and models suggested that each element influenced the translation process was constructed (see Table 17.1). Moreover, a list of key research questions and knowledge gabs across theories and models in organizational translation studies were identified (questions 1–19 above).

The comparative analysis has thus shown that theories and models of organizational translation are often similar in their choice of focus points and research themes but often different in the way they theorize and model translation processes within these areas. Each of the theories and models that have been analyzed in the previous chapters have covered and looked into some but not all of the above-mentioned focus points, research themes and questions, and have prioritized some of them over others. Some of them have come up with similar answers to some of the questions. Others have suggested different types of answers to them – often because of differences in the philosophies of social sciences (modes of doing research) on which the theories and models are based (see Chapter 23 for its analysis). The analysis shows that authors in organizational translation studies have most often provided answers to the key research questions in ignorance of the existence of (sometimes similar sometimes different) answers provided by other research streams, perspectives, theories and models in organizational translation studies. This study thus confirms similar conclusions concerning this issue found in other discussions and reviews of the translation research literature in organization studies (O'Mahoney, 2016; Spyridonidis, Currie, Heusinkveld, Strauss, & Sturdy, 2016; Wæraas & Nielsen, 2016).

The comparative analysis thus contributes to organizational translation studies by presenting the focus points, key themes and issues as well as the main research questions and knowledge gabs across perspectives in organizational translation studies in a systematic manner. It thereby creates a basis for further research and development of organizational translation studies, dialogue between researchers and answering research questions as those identified above that have until now only been answered in a preliminary manner.

References

O'Mahoney, J. (2016). Archetypes of translation: Recommendations for dialogue. *International Journal of Management Reviews, 18*(3), 333–350.

Spyridonidis, D., Currie, G., Heusinkveld, S., Strauss, K., & Sturdy, A. (2016). The translation of management knowledge: Challenges, contributions and new directions. *International Journal of Management Reviews, 18*, 231–235.

Wæraas, A., & Nielsen, J. A. (2016) Translation theory 'translated': Three perspectives on translation in organizational research. *International Journal of Management Reviews, 18*(3), 236–270.

Part 3

Translation in the meeting between idea and practice

19 Why develop the idea-practice translation model?

The idea-practice-translation model that is developed in this part of the book focuses on, theorizes and models in more detail how translators materialize (Czarniawska & Joerges, 1996) tokens in organizations. It thus 'zooms in' and takes a closer look at how you may understand how tokens are received (Johnson & Hagström, 2005), re-embedded (Czarniawska & Joerges, 1996) or contextualized (Røvik, 2016) in local practice in organizations. It does so however by developing another view on this process than other researchers in organizational translation studies. In order to do so the chapter uses former research in different areas to systematically develop a number of basic assumptions about the characteristics of translation processes and the way translators co-construct phenomena including organizations through such processes. This view builds on insights coming from as diverse areas of research as actor-network theory (Callon, 1986; Latour, 1986), ventriloquist communication theory (Cooren, 2010), design theory (Love, 2002), theories about learning (Jarvis, 2006; Säljö, 2003), routines in organizations (Feldman & Pentland, 2005), sociology (Murdoch, 2001) and studies in information technology (Schmid et al., 2017).

Assumptions and values

As a researcher you are always asked to explain what kind of research gab legitimizes the need for developing new theories and/or models of organizational phenomena. A good place to start is to make clear what kinds of basic assumptions and values a specific researcher has vis-à-vis the phenomenon, which is in focus of his/her research interest. The assumptions and values of the author of this book are the following:

- Since so many groups in society work with and depend on translation processes to produce wished-for changes in organizations (improve treatments, and introduce innovative ideas, strategies, policies, new types of knowledge, etc.), it is important to understand how such processes unfold and influence the ability of change agents (translators) to achieve such aims

- On a more basic level, translation processes have to do with how humans interact with and learn from the environment(s) in which they are embedded when they try to introduce tokens and change. Consequently, a more elaborate understanding of that relationship in general as well as in organizations is needed
- Humans (including translators) are multi-dimensional beings. They behave based on more complex impulses than often assumed in existing theories and models of organizational translation (and the social sciences). They have both an 'inner life' and consciousness on the basis of which they interpret the world and they interact with and build on their experiences with the world as they try to change it
- They are moreover embedded in a wide number of complex relationships with humans and objects of different kinds in the world that influence their change efforts. And these may not be reduced to general 'evidence-based' rules or principles that may influence the 'knowledge to action cycle' (Graham et al., 2006), relationships between actors' interpretations of discourses and texts among other discourses and texts (different language games) (Clegg et al., 2004). Or be reduced to (only) interpretative relationships and constructions of 'meaning' and habitualized and similar typified actions that human actors have or may develop and share with other human actors (Carlile, 2002, 2004; Czarniawska, 2014; Czarniawska & Joerges, 1996; Star and Griesemer, 1989)
- Humans (including translators) are different from nonhumans (objects). Actor-network researchers may thus offer their theory as a semiotic vocabulary, perspective and methodology (or artificial 'trick') that may be used to make an 'unbiased' symmetric analysis of how humans' and nonhumans' work contribute to perform phenomena as organizations. They may however not offer this theory as a general ontology of phenomena (including organizations) in the world without an adjustment of the assumption that humans and nonhumans should be considered alike

The critique of existing theories and models

Taking the above-mentioned assumptions and values as a starting point, one may suggest that: Even though it is important to understand how tokens (ideas and others) are translated and materialized (Czarniawska & Joerges, 1996) locally, existing theories and models of translation in organizations have not theorized and modeled this process in a sufficient way.

In Latour's definition of translation, we are told that

> the spread in time and space of anything claims, orders, artefact, goods – is in the hands of people: each of these people may act in many ways, letting the toke drop, or modifying it or deflecting it, or betraying it, or adding to it, or appropriating it.
>
> (Latour, 1986, p. 267)

Nonhumans are not assumed able to perform the same kind of work. At the same time however we are asked to assume that humans are not different from nonhumans when we as researchers do our symmetric analysis of the work done by humans and nonhumans in the actor-networks that perform the organization (and many other phenomena in the world) (see for instance rules of method, Latour, 1987). Michel Callon's (1986) analysis of the introduction of a Japanese method for growing scallops in St. Brieuc Bay in France illustrates the same point. He describes the process through which the innovative method (token) was introduced as: (1) creating an obligatory passage point, (2) interessement, (3) enrollment and (4) mobilization. The analysis and model thus described how translators interacted with and tried to construct new types of relationships between human and nonhuman actors seen from 'the outside' by the researcher (Michel Callon). What types of interpretations and reasons humans like the three marine biologists and fishermen may have had for what they were doing is however carefully avoided. The result is a reductionist position where all phenomena in the world are reduced to outcomes of only their relational attributes and not (also) potentially inherent characteristics that may characterize humans or nonhumans themselves. Humans (including translators) are thus not assumed to have inner lives and experiences from which actants may appear that may also influence the translation process and produce relational effects. And nonhumans are not assumed to have characteristics that influence their 'work'. Rather, this work may only be observed through nonhumans relational effects.

In their 'travel of idea' model, Czarniawska and Joerges (1996) suggest that translation unfolds through a process where: (1) an idea is selected and attended to in a moment/place A, (2) that it is translated into an object (a text, picture or prototype) and translated into (3) actions that are then translated, repeated and stabilized into (4) an institution. Here, the key process is the 'materializing' of an idea (Czarniawska & Joerges, 1996). Thus, when an idea has been translated into an image, text or sound, it can be materialized as objects or actions which then result in change. Unknown new objects may be created and appear, known objects change their appearance and practices become transformed. And the way practices materialize is described as 'the cognitive process, fronted by acts of will that moves toward calibrating 'images of action' into something more like detailed 'plans of action' and then into deeds' (Czarniawska & Joerges, 1996, p. 41). Objects are assumed to mediate the translation of ideas into practices, which then – if they are institutionalized – perform the organization through these actions or action-nets. What 'performs' the organization is thereby reduced to actions (or actions organized in action-nets (Czarniawska, 2014)) that are repeated and typified in the same way. And the work of different types of nonhumans (objects) in the creation of 'order' in organizations is reduced to only playing an intermediate role in the translation of abstract ideas into action in organizations. Objects (nonhumans) may however as shown by actor-network researchers and ventriloquist communication theory (Cooren,

2010) play a much more complex and constitutive role in the construction of organizations as phenomena. The characteristics of the translator (their inner lives) that may influence the translation and materialization of a token are not explained either.

In symbolic interactionist theories of translation (Carlile, 2002, 2004; Star & Griesemer, 1989) (Yanov, 2004), humans are situated in different social worlds with different types of language and culture. And translation concerns the movement of a specific type of token: Knowledge between these groups. As suggested by symbolic interactionism, translators translate knowledge from one group to the other and learn about symbols, cultures and what is meaningful in the social interaction between these groups. Translators are thus supposed to bridge the different social worlds with their different languages and cultures as they translate a token (knowledge) from one organizational context (social world) to the other. The role objects play is reduced to how these groups make sense of them including the 'boundary objects' that need to make sense in both worlds to make translation and coordination possible. Thus, objects are reduced to things that may be interpreted and contribute to make or does not make sense for human actors as the token, organization and change are socially constructed. They are not theorized as entities that may themselves do work that may be important for the constitution of the organization (as in actor–network theory). The kind of work translators do is limited to transfer, translation, bargaining and negotiating with humans not nonhumans. Just as characteristics of translators (and their 'inner lives') that may influence the process is not described or explained.

In translation models inspired by linguistics (Holden et al., 2004; Madsen, 2013; Røvik, 2016), tokens are viewed as texts (or knowledge as text) that need to be translated from one language and cultural group to another. Here, the main object in focus is the text itself and what translators do with it in order to assure that the text is translated in a way that realizes the aims of the text. Translation work depends on adapting the text from a source context to a receiving context, having knowledge about the culture and language in the source and receiving context, having appropriate translation competences and following appropriate 'translation rules' as well as choosing whether to be loyal to the meaning, function, cultural and/or ideological features of the text. The decontextualizing process where the token (for example, knowledge about a practice) is converted into images, words and texts is influenced by the complexity, embeddedness and explicitness of the token. While the contextualizing of the token (knowledge) depends on whether the translator (like when translating texts (books)) (1) misses the essentials of what makes it work in the source context and (2) misses the essentials of what may make it work in the recipient context (Røvik, 2016). In these theories and models, the main object focused upon is 'the token as text' and what translators may do with it to make it make sense and have a wished-for effect in the receiving group; not the types of work nonhumans (objects) may more generally do when tokens (ideas or knowledge about practices, rules etc.) are translated into organizations. Some characteristics of the translator that may influence the process are however included and are identified as translators' translation competences and ability to follow appropriate translation rules.

Based on the assumptions and values and the evaluation of existing theories and models, it becomes clear what is the critique of these theories and models of translation in organizations. The process through which tokens in organizations are translated when 'received', 'embedded', 'contextualized' or 'materialized' locally is important but still not well understood and theorized/modeled by these theories and models. How humans interact with and learn from the environment(s) in which they are embedded when they try to introduce tokens and change in their local contexts needs to be specified. If humans (translators) are multi-dimensional beings, their behavior may be guided by impulses originating from their experiences and 'inner lives' as well as by impulses originating from interacting with 'body-external' humans and nonhumans (objects/materialities). Therefore, when you theorize, model and analyze that you need to include the complex types of relationships that translators have with themselves as well as other humans and nonhumans (objects) when they try to introduce tokens and change locally. And that without assuming at the outset that humans and nonhumans are similar. As demonstrated, none of the existing theories and models of organizational translation however assumed all these things.

References

Callon, M. (1986). Some elements of a sociology of translation: Domestication of the scallops and the fishermen of St. Brieuc Bay. In J. Law (Ed.), *Power, action and belief — A new sociology of knowledge?* London: Routledge & Kegan Paul.

Carlile, P. R. (2002). A pragmatic view of knowledge and boundaries: Boundary objects in new product development. *Organization Science, 13,* 442–455.

Carlile, P. R. (2004). Transferring, translating, and transforming: An integrative framework for managing knowledge across boundaries. *Organization Science, 15*(5), 555–568.

Clegg, S. R., Kornberger, M., & Rhodes, C. (2004). Noise, parasites and translation – Theory and practice in management consulting. *Management Learning, 35*(1), 31–44.

Cooren, F. (2010). *Action and agency in dialogue.* Amsterdam/Philadelphia, PA: John Benjamins Publishing Company.

Czarniawska, B. (2014). *A theory of organizing* (2nd ed.). Cheltenham: Edward Elgar Publishing Limited.

Czarniawska, B., & Joerges, B. (1996). Travels of ideas. In B. Czarniawska & G. Sevon (Eds.), *Translating organizational change* (pp. 13–48). Berlin: de Gruyter.

Feldman, M., & Pentland, B. (2005). Organizational routines and the macro-actor. In B. Czarniawska & T. Hernes (Eds.), *Actor-network theory and organizing.* Lund: Liber & Copenhagen Business School Press.

Graham, I. D., Logan, J., Harrison, M. b., traus, S. E., Tetroe, J., Caswell, W., & Robinson, N. (2006). Lost in knowledge translation: Time for a map? *The Journal of Continuing Education in the Health Professions, 26*(1), Winter, 13–24.

Holden, N. J., Harald, F. O., & Kortzfleisch, O. (2004). Why cross-cultural knowledge transfer is a form of translation in more ways than you think. *Knowledge and Process Management, 11*(2), 127–136.

Jarvis, P. (2006). *Towards a comprehensive theory of human learning*. New York: Routledge.

Johnson, B., & Hagström, B. (2005). The translation perspective as an alternative to the policy diffusion paradigm: The case of the Swedish methadone maintenance treatment. *Journal of Social Policy, 34,* 365–388.

Latour, B. (1986). The powers of association. In J. Law (Ed.), *Power, action and belief – A new sociology of knowledge?* London: Routledge & Kegan Paul.

Latour, B. (1987). *Science in action*. Cambridge, MA: Harvard University Press.

Love, T. (2002). Constructing a coherent cross-disciplinary body of theory about designing and designs: Some philosophical issues. *Design Studies, 23,* 345–361.

Madsen, S. O. (2013). *The leader as a translator – A translation perspective on strategy work.* PhD dissertation, Copenhagen Business School.

Murdoch, J. (2001). Ecologising sociology: Actor-network theory, co-construction and the problem of human exemptionalism. *Sociology, 35*(1), 111–133.

Røvik, K. A. (2016). Knowledge transfer as translation: Review and elements of an instrumental theory. *International Journal of Management Reviews, 18*(3), 290–310.

Säljö, R. (2003). *Læring I Praksis – et sociokulturelt perspektiv.* Hans Reitzels Forlag.

Schmid, A. M., Recker, J., & Brocke, J. (2017). *The socio-technical dimension of inertia in digital transformations.* Proceedings of the 50th Hawaii International Conference on System Sciences, 2017, 4796–4805.

Star, S. L., & Griesemer, J. (1989). Institutional ecology, 'translations', and boundary objects: Amateurs and professionals on Berkeley's museum of vertebrate zoology. *Social Studies of Science, 19,* 387–420.

Yanov, D. (2004). Translating local knowledge at organizational peripheries. *British Journal of Management, 15,* 9–25.

20 How are ideas materialized?

This chapter will start out with actor-network theory (ANT) and present and combine with other theories in order to build up a number of basic assumptions that together form a basis for a new ANT- and ventriloquist (Cooren, 2010)-inspired model that explains translator's role in entity construction and organizational change as ideas move. It will theorize and model in more detail how ideas are materialized (Czarniawska & Joerges, 1996) by translators in organizations. An overview of these assumptions is provided in Table 20.1.

Table 20.1 Suggestions and assumptions of the idea-practice-translation model

Suggestion	Assumptions
Ideas materialize by being translated into socio-technical systems/ actor-networks	1 Change ideas/tokens in organizations never move by themselves but depend on people who translate them. Movement and realization of change ideas only happens if they are translated
	2 Both humans and things/objects may play a role and do work in that connection
	3 The specific role humans and things/objects will play in the translation process is an open question and depends on the types of actions that are ascribed to them in the narrative produced about them during or after the translation process
	4 Effects of organizational change ideas depend on the types of relations that are established and the kind of work that is performed through the interactions between humans and things in the socio-technical system or "actor-network" that is constructed during the translation process
The organization is constituted through ventriloquist communication processes	5 Organizations may be theorized as heterogeneous assemblies of humans and nonhumans as suggested by actor-network theory
	6 Organizations (as assemblies of humans and nonhumans) are constituted on the basis of communication and are produced and reproduced through a process of ventriloquism. Ventriloquism means that humans/translators ventriloquize – that is mobilize actants (human and nonhuman) as well as are being mobilized by actants (human and nonhuman) in the interactions and dialogues through which they translate and 'constitute' the organization

(Continued)

Suggestion	Assumptions
Humans' and translators' role in translation processes are different from that of nonhumans	7 Translators are embedded in an ecology of humans and nonhumans 8 Humans' and thus translators' role in the translation process are different from nonhumans' role; translators can reflect upon their incorporation into socio-material relationships and can act upon these reflections in a way that nonhumans cannot. This happens through the use of language and communication 9 A translator may only learn about what is needed to materialize an idea in the intersection between him/her and the social and material entities (actants) in which he/she is embedded by experiencing and identifying them through communication 10 Specific characteristics of humans as well as nonhuman actants that are relevant to materializing an idea at hand may only be detected through the communication process. And that no matter whether these characteristics are specific to humans or nonhumans 11 During the communication process the translators and humans and nonhumans that are relevant to the project at hand – to introduce a certain idea or token in the organization – co-construct the organization. This happens on the basis of translators interacting with humans and nonhumans that the translators mobilize and make speak as well as on the basis of interacting with the (sometimes unexpected) human and nonhuman actants that make the translators speak 12 In the latter case the translators may voluntarily as well as involuntarily become a 'mouthpiece' for and a spokesman of specific humans but also distinct inherent characteristics of nonhumans that as expected or unexpectedly turn out to be relevant to the translation of an idea/token
The translator is a socio-material designer	13 The introduction of any idea or token in an organization will always include some types of attempts of translators to influence humans, objects (nonhumans), contexts (a local ecology of humans and nonhumans) and/or relations and interactions between them. Translators are therefore socio-technical designers 14 Translators construct designs (socio-technical systems/ actor-networks) 15 To design or designing involves (1) the intention of problem solution and (2) a tangible outcome that is realized and can be identified as the result of the design process 16 The key elements or objects of translators' design work are humans, objects (nonhumans), contexts (as defined above) and interactions between them 17 Translation/design efforts may be directed toward humans, objects, contexts or relations and interactions between them

Suggestion	Assumptions
The translator learn from interacting with body-internal and body-external actants	18 Humans learn from relating to and interacting with body-external actants such as humans and nonhumans (things) 19 They moreover learn from their relations to and interactions with body-internal actants such as reflections upon wished-for future states or past experiences, personal knowledge, history and feelings 20 As a consequence humans learning through ventriloquist processes of dialogue are not just influenced by their relations and interactions with body-external humans and nonhumans but also by body-internal actants such as feelings, mental activities and reflections that may also mobilize the translator/ventriloquist to speak 21 The construction of organizations as socio-material entities happens on the basis of translators who communicate and interact with, learn from and try to connect to body-external and body-internal human and nonhuman actants as they try to expand the number of actants that take part in and do the work that then – in practice – realize/produce the effects that we associate with the organization
Actants, relations and interactions between them need to be stabilized to 'build' the performative organization	22 Innovative organizational change ideas and other tokens have been stabilized when the communication and translation process has resulted in the ideas/tokens having been translated into assemblies (actor-networks) 23 An assembly is an outcome of the joint work done by an actor-network of people, their interactions and performances, supporting artifacts and a narrative about the assembly that explains it 24 The relationship between the above-mentioned elements of the assembly is dynamical and interdependent. If one element of the assembly changes, the whole assembly changes. As a consequence the effects of the assembly also change 25 Assemblies can be constructed, changed or dissolved through building up, changing or dissolving the relationships established between people, their interactions and performances, supporting artifacts and the narrative about the assembly 26 Assemblies may however also be characterized by dynamic stability. This happens when certain organizational relationships between people, their interactions and performances, supporting artifacts and the narratives that explain them are produced and reproduced in a similar (but not identical) way across time and space.
Assemblies may be built by using symbolic and socio-material tools	27 The actants of an assembly are co-dependent and co-produce the effects of the assembly 28 Humans use both socio-material (humans and physical artifacts) and symbolic tools (narratives, formula, etc.) when they translate and construct performative assemblies

(Continued)

Suggestion	Assumptions

29 Succeeding with translating and assembling actor-networks with wished-for effects depends on learning what socio-material and symbolic tools may help translators accomplish such an aim

30 Learning how to accomplish such an aim (an assemblage with wished-for effects) may be approached through practically experimenting with creating socio-material tools, through drawing upon or developing abstract symbolic tools (narratives, formula, etc.) or through combining these approaches

31 Knowledge (about a certain type of assemblage) stored in a symbolic and narrative form needs to be translated back to the socio-material elements that it refers to. Knowledge obtained through experiments with tools made of socio-material assemblies needs to be supplemented with a symbolic tool – a narrative that helps making sense of the type of assembly needed to accomplish the task/wished-for aim

32 Either way the success of the assembly will depend on translating back and forth between a concrete socio-material practice and an abstract symbolic and narrative knowledge of how to understand and perform such a practice (or entity)

Difficulties in entity building originates from relational inertia

33 Inertia may be present in the social and the material realm in isolation, but only in their enactment upon each other do they unfold into the socio-technical dimension. Inertia in entity building in organizations is therefore relational inertia

34 Relational inertia is defined as the accumulated and combined effect of conflicts and controversies that a translator meets and have to overcome as he/she tries to mobilize and assemble an actor-network of humans and nonhumans making it possible to perform and thus realize a given innovative change idea and its related, supposed and intended effects in an organization

35 Relational inertia thus consists of the collective forces and combined effect of all the different controversies with humans and nonhumans that holds back and hinders the forming of the wished-for performative actor-network that is needed to translate and thus realize an innovative change idea

36 The types and forms of relational inertia that may occur with humans and nonhumans during ventriloquist translation processes, are diverse and varied, and depend on how these entities relate to and enact upon each other in practice in the socio-technical dimension

37 An increase in the number of controversies with humans and nonhumans related to the translation of an idea means an increase in relational inertia. As a consequence an increase in the energy used by and the amount of translation work done by the translators is needed. A decrease in the number of controversies has the opposite effect

Assumptions about entity building (ANT)

According to ANT, any change (organizational change or other) depends on whether an innovative idea is translated or not. Bruno Latour thus explains that any tokens – including ideas about change – do not move by themselves but are only moved by humans who have also power to influence what is moved:

> ...the spread in time and space of anything – claims, orders, artefacts, goods – is in the hands of people: each of these people may act in many different ways, letting the token drop, or modifying it, or deflecting it, or betraying it, or adding to it, or appropriating it.
>
> (Latour, 1986, p. 267)

ANT researchers moreover think that translation work is a network-building activity where one or more translators mobilize and try to create new relations and interactions between humans and things and thus an actor-network, so that their joint work produces a certain new phenomenon or wished-for effect. Realizing a new idea, knowledge or effect thus depends on different forms and types of translation work aimed at mobilizing, and establishing new relations and interactions between humans and things. Translation can thus be understood as all the activities that are needed to mobilize actants and create these new relationships and types of interactions. Or as explained by Bruno Latour and Michel Callon:

> By translation we understand all the negotiations, intrigues, calculations, acts of persuasion and violence, thanks to which an actor or force takes, or causes to be conferred on itself, authority to speak or act on behalf of another actor or force.
>
> (Callon & Latour, 1981, p. 279)

Thus, if and when a translator succeeds with introducing a new innovative idea or creating a certain effect or other kind of token in an organization, it is because he/she has successfully done some work which has mobilized, and established the new types of relations and interactions between humans and things so that these wished-for effects could be produced. Then – as a consequence of this successfully completed work – a translator may now be said to have become a spokesman of and speak on behalf of all the actants – humans as well as things which in practice realize his/her/the translators' innovative idea. The translator(s) has become a spokesman of and speak on behalf of an actor-network.

And as explained earlier the actantial model suggests that both humans and nonhumans may be described as being the source of actions during such translation processes. Bruno Latour thus defines an actor as an actant:

> An "actor" in AT is a semiotic definition – an actant, that is, something that acts or to which activity is granted by others. It implies no special

motivation of human individual actors, nor of humans in general. An actant can literally be anything provided it is granted to be the source of an action.

(Latour, 1996, p. 7)

Consequently, an actor in ANT is not a human actor in a social network of other human actors. Rather, it is something, human or nonhuman, that may be described as the source of an action in a narrative about how different actors' work constructs and makes phenomena (as ideas, scientific knowledge, researchers like Pasteur, organizations, hotel keys and speed bumps (and many more) powerful and 'real' in the world.

Inspired by ANT the following assumptions about entity construction in organizations may now be suggested:

1   Change ideas/tokens in organizations never move by themselves but depend on people who translate them. Movement and realization of change ideas only happen if they are translated
2   Both humans and things/objects may play a role and do work in that connection
3   The specific role humans and things/objects will play in the translation process is an open question and depends on the types of actions that are ascribed to them in the narrative produced about them during or after the translation process
4   Effects of organizational change ideas depend on the types of relations that are established and the kind of work that is performed through the interactions between humans and things in the socio-technical system or 'actor-network' that is constructed during the translation process

Assumptions about human communication

The Montréal school of the communicative constitution of organizations' perspective builds on actor-network theory and its socio-material and relational ontology (see Cooren, 2010). It offers further insight into how translators translate and assemble socio material entities like organizations through communication and interaction processes. From a ventriloquist perspective, communication is understood as the materialization of relations through something or someone (an utterance, a force, a case, a spokesperson, a doorway, a website, etc.) (Cooren, 2018, p. 279). In this view, communication is not reduced to only human communication. People are viewed as communicating with each other but ecosystems, machines and organizations are seen as communicating too, whether to each other or to us (Cooren, 2018). According to this position, the researchers studying the 'building up of' organizations should not just consider humans who are interacting; rather, they should analyze all of the actions (human/nonhuman and/or present/

non-present) that are made present in an interaction (Clifton, 2017) through communication in the attempt to construct the organization.

Ventriloquism is a concept associated with the art of belly speaking where a performer speaks and has a conversation with a mechanical doll placed on his/her arm. The performer animates and makes the doll speak just as it seems as though the doll speaks to and animates the performer (*Encyclopedia Britannica* (Britannica.com)). François Cooren has introduced ventriloquism as a metaphor for the communication and interaction process that unfolds in and constructs (or as he puts it: constitutes) the organization (Cooren, 2010). Summarizing his view in one sentence, he says it simply consists in noticing that a variety of forms of agency are always in play in any interaction (Cooren, 2008, 2010; Cooren & Bencherki, 2010) (cited in Cooren, 2012, p. 4). Ventriloquism is thus

> understood metaphorically as the process by which interlocutors animate or make beings speak (which I propose to call figures, the word ventrilo-quists used to speak of the dummies they manipulate), beings that in turn animate these same interlocutors in interaction.
>
> (Cooren, 2010, p. 35)

As a consequence of this view, the researcher (and practitioner) needs to both identify the networks that speakers animate in their conversations and expli-cate how the speakers position themselves as being animated by the actants. This interactional approach to ANT therefore

> allows the researcher (and practitioner) to make visible the seen but un-noticed discursive resources through which humans mobilize human and nonhuman actants and present and non-present actants, which are trans-ported across time and place to be made present in the interaction and which are employed "to do things".
>
> (Clifton, 2017, p. 4)

This interactional approach to ANT thus places the emphasis on how net-works are talked into being and the actions that these networks then accom-plish. And as pointed out by Martine, Cooren, Bénel and Zacklad (2016, p. 170): 'People constantly create connections or translations between various sociomaterial elements. However, some connections or translations happen to matter more than others do. The emergence of such asymmetries is what we have to explain'.

The assumptions about human communication that may be derived from this are given as follows:

- Organizations may be theorized as heterogeneous assemblies of humans and nonhumans as suggested by actor-network theory

- Organizations (as assemblies of humans and nonhumans) are constituted on the basis of communication and are produced and reproduced through a process of ventriloquism. Ventriloquism means that humans/translators ventriloquize – that is mobilize actants (human and nonhuman) as well as are being mobilized by actants (human and nonhuman) in the interactions and dialogues through which they translate and 'constitute' the organization

Assumptions about humans as translators

Problems related to a symmetric view

Some of the problems related to theorizing the role of humans compared to nonhumans in ANT may be traced back to the origins of actor-network theory. ANT researchers have thus argued for the importance of not distinguishing between humans and nonhumans but to instead consider them to be 'actants' as suggested by Greimas; that is entities – human or nonhuman – that may be said to act or to which activity is granted by others (Latour, 1996). The idea originates from Greimas who studied fairy tales in which anything human or nonhuman might become actants – for instance the abducted princess and the prince who tries to save her, a dragon, a magic apple or a speaking kettle or dog (see Hébert, 2019). It is easy to understand that in fairy tales human and nonhuman entities – even magical ones – might be associated with each other in ways that may make sense and may seem meaningful to a reader. It is also understandable that using the same concept (actants) and a semiotic (actor-network) approach to study the construction or performance of entities in the world will assure that you are more open to and able to make sense of and tell a meaningful symmetric (research) story about which human and nonhuman entities may play a role in the construction of different phenomena in the world. If you are a practitioner in or do research about organizations instead of analyzing fairy tales however suggesting that it makes sense to assume that there are no differences between the work that humans compared to nonhumans do when constructing the organization makes less sense.

How humans are different from nonhumans

Other researchers have also criticized the symmetric view of humans and nonhumans of ANT and especially the problems related to and consequences of the analytic language that ANT researchers have offered researchers in the sociology of science (Murdoch, 2001). Actor-network researchers thus argue that it is important to not assume anything about the actor-networks and humans and nonhumans that they study a priori (see for instance Latour (1987) about the rules of method of ANT). They thus suggest to study how the phenomena being studied (like the construction of scientific knowledge or the introduction of an idea in an organization) is/or is not being realized in situ through the work done by humans and nonhumans. And that without assuming anything in advance about what are the particular characteristics of humans (for instance that they have certain 'interests' or a 'culture') and nonhumans (for instance that the material objects that influence the designing of a physical object like an instrument, IT or management information system or a building has certain inherent characteristics a priori). Therefore, according to David Bloor, we are asked to put aside all our usual assumptions about the distinctions between things and people in order to make an ANT analysis (Murdoch, 2001, p. 122). We are also asked to assume a priori that there are no differences between humans and nonhumans even though we know from former sociological and other research as well as from our daily lives that there are.

Ian Hacking has raised a similar critique. According to Murdoch (2001), he accepts that co-construction processes like the ones studied by ANT researchers happen in an ecology of humans and nonhumans. He however suggests that not all entities are equally open to processes of construction and that some entities are 'interactive' (humans) while other entities are of an 'indifferent kind' (nonhumans). Hacking uses the term 'interactive kinds' to show how forms of agency emerge that are linked to the ways in which people conceptualize themselves and how they then act upon these conceptualizations. He also claims that other entities (nonhumans) do not behave in this way and are 'indifferent'. Humans are interactive kinds because they can reflect upon their incorporation into socio-material relationships and can act upon these reflections (see also Hacking, 1986). In particular, humans can use language-based resources to assess how they are being represented (by, for instance, other humans) or how they are being acted upon (by, for instance, networks) (Murdoch, 2001, p. 124). Nonhumans however do not possess this ability and are 'indifferent' to the way we choose to construct them. They act based on their distinct characteristics regardless of what types of classifications humans choose to use about them. The interactive character of human responses thus sets them apart from the responses of nonhuman entities. Humans thus play a role in and influence the actor-network in ways that nonhumans do not:

> Hacking is quite prepared to consider the effect of complex, heterogeneous relations on the constitution of particular entities, and seems aware that being 'interactive' is dependent upon immersion in such relations; yet he clearly believes that natural and social entities will respond in different ways to their positioning within networks and these differences are attributable to some stable and immutable characteristics that are not reducible to network relations. These differences hinge on the reflective abilities of humans, abilities that derive from social relations (notably language). Therefore, (human) entities cannot always simply be thought of as potential 'allies', to be enrolled in processes of network fabrication

(as argued by Latour 1987), for they can make conscious responses to the act of enrolment and can thereby alter the whole functioning of the network.

(Murdoch, 2001, p. 124)

Summing up

Actor-network researchers have claimed that tokens (like for instance a management idea) are in the hands of people who may let the token drop, modify it, deflect it, betray it, add to it or appropriate it (Latour, 1986, p. 267). This assumption may be contrasted with the fact that no ANT researchers have suggested that nonhumans may play a similar role in the making of assemblies of humans and nonhumans that – according to this theory – make up different entities in the world (like scientific knowledge, organizations, power and electric cars). It may thus be suggested that even though actor-network researchers claim to attempt to do the opposite, human translators seem to have been theorized as 'slightly' different from nonhumans in this stream of research. Above it has been suggested that the idea that humans and nonhumans should be theorized in a symmetrical way and should be viewed as being a priori not different may have originated from Greimas idea about actants and how the concept of actants could be used to make a semiotic analysis of fairy tales that was at the same time symmetric – that is ascribed the same ability to become the source of an action to humans as to nonhumans. It has however also been shown above how this symmetric view led to critique from other researchers in the sociology of science. The minimal symmetrical ontology suggested by ANT researchers was criticized because we are asked to assume a priori that there are no differences between humans and nonhumans even though we know from former sociological and other research as well as from our daily lives that there are. The critics also showed that humans – including translators – are indeed different from nonhumans. Nonhumans act based on their distinct inherent characteristics regardless of what types of classifications humans choose to use about them. Humans however are interactive because they can reflect upon their incorporation into socio-material relationships and can act upon these reflections. In particular, humans can use language-based resources to assess how they are being represented (by, for instance, other humans) or how they are being acted upon (by, for instance, networks) (Murdoch, 2001, p. 124). This points in the direction of another way of theorizing the ontology and relations between humans and nonhumans in actor-networks than suggested by ANT researchers. This also points in the direction of another way of understanding the translator as an actor (or rather actant) who tries to co-construct the performative actor-network that makes an innovative management or other idea (or token) materialize (Czarniawska & Joerges, 1996) in organizations.

Ventriloquism as an alternative view

Francois Cooren (2010) suggests that humans – and thus translators –learn about their environments and constitute the organization through communication processes. He suggests that materiality and sociality are essential features of everything that exists: Emotions, ideas, words, but also rocks, technologies and architectures (and organizations, JDS). He also states that materiality and sociality should be considered two ways by which any being (human or nonhuman, JDS) gives itself to be experienced and identified (Cooren, 2018, p. 279). He further suggests that this way of conceiving of materiality and sociality puts communication at the forefront because communication corresponds to the materialization of relations. He thus defines communication as '...the materialization of relations through something or someone (an utterance, a force, a gaze, a spokesperson, a doorway, a website, etc.)' (Cooren & Bencherki, 2010). He thus implies that humans – including translators – are embedded in an ecology of human and nonhuman actants as they try to translate an idea into practice in organizations; and that a translator may only learn about what is needed to materialize an idea in the intersection between him/her and the social and material entities (actants) in which he/she is embedded in the world by experiencing and identifying them through communication. Specific characteristics of human as well as nonhuman actants that are relevant to materializing an idea at hand may thus (only) be detected through the communication process. And that no matter whether these characteristics are specific to humans or nonhumans.

Here, it should be noted that adopting such an ontology does not mean that the organization is socially constructed. Rather, it is co-constructed on the basis of translators interacting with humans and nonhumans that the translators mobilize and make speak as well as by them interacting with the (sometimes unexpected) human and nonhuman actants that make the translators speak. In the latter case, the translators may voluntarily as well as involuntarily become a 'mouthpiece' for and a spokesman of specific humans but also distinct inherent characteristics of nonhumans that unexpectedly turn out to be relevant to the translation of an idea/token. Translating the idea of an electronic patient record in a hospital may thus for instance turn out to depend not only on a computer system where doctors and nurses fill in data as ventriloquized and anticipated by a translator but also upon unforeseen actants that at some point make the translators speak. Wirings and computer systems that the hospitals installed before they started considering introducing this type of electronic patient record may thus cause unexpected problems and make the translators speak about how the wires cannot transmit the amount of data needed to run the system or that the computers are too old and slow to run the software related to the new electronic patient record. IT technicians coming in from the supplier may unexpectedly turn out to be incompetent and not able to construct an IT-based patient record system that works. And they will make translators talk about how incompetent these technicians are and how new technicians coming from another firm are needed. In both cases, the translators who want to materialize the idea of the electronic patient record in the hospital are unexpectedly made 'mouthpieces' for and spokesmen of these humans and nonhumans and their specific characteristics and how these characteristics cause problems in relation to the project at hand; to install the electronic patient record in the hospital.

So what assumptions may be derived from this discussion in relation to the relationships between humans, nonhumans and the translator?

- Translators are embedded in an ecology of humans and nonhumans
- Humans and thus translators' role in the translation process are different from nonhumans' role; translators can reflect upon their incorporation into socio-material relationships and can act upon these reflections in a way that nonhumans cannot. This happens through the use of language and communication
- A translator may only learn about what is needed to materialize an idea in the intersection between him/her and the social and material entities (actants) in which he/she is embedded by experiencing and identifying them through communication
- Specific characteristics of humans as well as nonhuman actants that are relevant to materializing an idea at hand may only be detected through the communication process. And that no matter whether these characteristics are specific to humans or nonhumans
- During the communication process, the translators, humans and nonhumans that are relevant to the project at hand – to introduce a certain idea or token in the organization – co-construct the organization. This happens on the basis of translators interacting with humans and nonhumans that the translators mobilize and make speak as well as on the basis of interacting with the (sometimes unexpected) human and nonhuman actants that make the translators speak
- In the latter case, the translators may voluntarily as well as involuntarily become a 'mouthpiece' for and a spokesman of specific humans and their characteristics but also of distinct characteristics of nonhumans that as expected or unexpectedly turn out to be relevant to the translation of an idea/token

The translator as a socio-material designer

According to the *Merriam-Webster* online dictionary, to design is to create, fashion, execute or construct something according to plan. Other meanings related to the word are (1) to conceive and plan in the mind, (2) to have as a purpose or (3) to device for a specific function or end. Yet other meanings related to the word are to make a drawing, pattern or sketch of something.

According to Herbert Simon, 'everyone designs who devises courses of action aimed at changing existing situations into preferred ones' (Simon, 1996, p. 111). Design is thus seen as oriented toward the future; it involves 'inquiry into systems that do not yet exist' (Romme, 2003, p. 558). What will be suggested here is that an organizational change agent or translator is a designer in the above-mentioned sense and that what he or she does is socio-technical design work.

The definition of design suggested here has been formulated by Terrence Love. Terrence Love (2002) criticizes that the word design is sometimes used as a noun, sometimes as a verb, sometimes as an adjective and sometimes as an adverb in theories of design because each of these uses is epistemologically different and points to different forms of concepts. He therefore suggests differentiating between the noun and the verb form – that is between 'a design' and 'designing' when defining design:

Design – is a noun referring to a specification or plan for making a particular artifact or for undertaking a particular activity? A distinction is drawn here between a design and an artifact:

- A design is the basis for, and precursor to, the making of an artifact while
- Designing is the human activity leading to the production of a design.

It follows from this that a 'designer' is someone who is, has been or will be designing: He, she or they are someone who create designs. Moving from the noun 'design' to the verb 'to design' implies both an intention and an emphasis on the processes of making something. To design or designing thus involves (1) the intention of problem solution and (2) a tangible outcome that is realized and can be identified as a result of the design process (Simonsen, Bærenholdt, Büscher, & Scheuer, 2010, p. 202). When a translator introduces a new management idea or other token, he/she works with design and designing in the above-mentioned sense.

According to Love (2002), the key elements of designing are humans, objects and contexts. And design work as well as theorizing about it may be directed toward design of each of them as well as their interactions. Design work may thus be directed toward designing:

- Humans
- Objects
- Contexts
- Human-to-human interaction
- Object-to-object interaction
- Human and object interaction
- Human and context interaction
- Object and context interaction and
- Interactions involving humans, objects and contexts together

Thus, according to Love (2002) the objects of designers' (and translators') design work are humans and nonhumans (objects) which are also focused upon by ANT researchers studying translation processes. The concept of context may be defined as a relational construct, which specifies what, at any given point, is considered the background for understanding a phenomena or event (Meier & Dopson, 2019, p. 13). The background/foreground relationship is continually constructed by people, as they make sense of their experiences in the socio-material worlds they are part of. Thus, even though ANT researchers reject the idea of context (see Latour, 1996) as it has been defined and used in the social sciences, the implicit background and thus context for the translation processes assumed by ANT are the ecology of pre-existing humans, nonhumans and actor-networks in the world in which translators are assumed to be socio-materially embedded. Most of them do not have anything to do with the translators' project at hand (to introduce an idea/token). But some of them do.

The reason why it is important to specify that translation work is at the same time also design work is to theorize and thus make it more clear what the translation efforts of translators are or may be directed at. The introduction of any idea or token in an organization will thus always include some types of attempts of translators to influence the relations and interactions between humans, objects (nonhumans) and contexts (defined as suggested above – that is as an ecology of humans and nonhumans). And here it should be noted that during the translation process the translators' design efforts are often not directed equally toward all these elements at the same time. Some translation/design efforts may be directed at trying to construct an object needed to realize an idea (an IT-based management information system for example). Other efforts may be directed at influencing humans who need to think or behave differently about the idea (efforts aimed at explaining managers that the introduction of the system does not mean that they will lose their jobs and that they therefore do not need to resist it). Yet other efforts may be directed toward designing how humans and nonhumans relate and interact (for instance designing the content of the management information system so that it makes sense in relation to and support managers' work practices). Finally, translation/design efforts may be directed at influencing the interaction between the object and the overall context of humans and nonhumans in which it is embedded (for instance toward aligning the data handling of the system with GDPR rules regulating management of information about individual persons in the public sector).

The assumptions that may be derived from this discussion are the following:

- The introduction of any idea or token in an organization will always include some types of attempts of translators to influence humans, objects (nonhumans), contexts (a local ecology of humans and nonhumans) and/or relations and interactions between them. Translators are therefore socio-technical designers

- Translators construct designs (socio-technical systems/actor-networks)
- To design or designing involves (1) the intention of problem solution and (2) a tangible outcome that is realized and can be identified as a result of the design process
- The key elements or objects of translators' design work are humans, objects (nonhumans), contexts (as defined above) and interactions between them
- Translation/design efforts may be directed toward humans, objects, contexts, or relations and interactions between them

How translators learn

An organizational change agent or translator needs to learn how wished-for goals may be achieved. And in accordance with ANT he/she needs to do so in a world where complex and heterogeneous entities will have to be mobilized and turned into allies acting in a way that perform wished-for ideas or effects. Peter Jarvis's theory about learning (Jarvis, 2006) will be suggested here as an appropriate theory about how human translators (and thus organizational change agents) learn in such situations. Jarvis thus states that '...learners are whole persons rather than a body or a mind; they are both material and mental' (Jarvis, 2006, p. 13) and that '...the person is in some way a combination of the material and the mental, or the non-material' (Jarvis, 2006, p. 14). Jarvis (2006) suggests that human beings learn and change as a result of hearing, seeing, smelling, tasting, touching and feeling. They change and learn by interacting with humans, things and events in certain time-space contexts and by reflecting upon these, as well as upon wished-for future states or past experiences, knowledge, and history as well as feelings, and upon what these experiences mean to one's own self and identity. Peter Jarvis thus defines learning as:

> ...the combination of processes whereby the whole person—body (genetic, physical, and biological) and mind (knowledge, skills, attitudes, values, emotions, beliefs, and senses)— experiences a social situation, the perceived content of which is then transformed cognitively, emotively, or practically (or through any combination) and integrated in the person's individual biography resulting in a changed (or more experienced) person.
>
> (Jarvis, 2006, p. 13)

According to Jarvis, there are four different relationships between the person and the world based on which individuals learn: Person-to-person; person-to-thing/event; person-to-a-future phenomenon and person-to-self (including influences from experiences and memories of the past).

Person-to-person	(the I ←→ thou relationship)
Person-to-phenomenon (thing/event)	(the I → it relationship)
Person-to-a-future-phenomenon	(the I → envisaged thou or it relationship)
Person-to-self	(the I ←→ me relationship)

In the present, people interact with their external world through relationships with other individuals (the person-to-person relation/the I-thou relation) and through an awareness of phenomena (things, events and so on: The person-to-phenomenon or 'the I-it' relation); however, individuals also have envisaged relationships with the world. They think about the future while they are still in the present; thus, they have desires, intentions and so forth (the person-to-a-future-phenomenon relation/the I envisaged-thou, or it, relation). In a similar manner, humans can think about the past, or about an idea. We can contemplate, muse and thereby relate to ourselves (the person-to-self relationship or 'I-me' relationship). This reflecting upon our past results in our own awareness of our life history and educational biography and activates what we have learned in the past as well as our own identity when we reflect upon the situation in focus.

In the first two types of relationships (the-person-to-person and the person-to-thing/event), all humans' five senses are operative and individuals may have an experience as a result of any of them, or any combination of them. Thus, humans may learn and change as a result of hearing, seeing, smelling, tasting, touching and feeling. They may however also learn and change based on mental activities as reflections upon wished-for future states or past experiences, knowledge and history. According to Jarvis (2006), transformation and learning thus occur through thought, action or emotion, or any combination of these, and occur after the experience. Thus, as pointed out by Jarvis (2006, p. 17), 'it is in the intersection of us and our world that we are presented with the opportunities to learn'.

Revisiting Peter Jarvis's theory about humans' individual learning processes, Scheuer and Simonsen (2021) show that the insights gained from this work may be combined with the ventriloquist view and translated in order to build a relational, individual as well as collective (heterogeneous) theoretical understanding of how learning processes in relation to construction of organizations as socio-material assemblies unfold. They thus show that his theory can be reinterpreted in a way that suggests that learning takes place through communication processes where human translators mobilize and learn from interacting with ventriloquized human and nonhuman actants. They moreover show that the human and nonhuman actants being ventriloquized during organizational translation processes aimed at communicatively constituting the organization may be both body-external and body-internal. The actants that may be ventriloquized during such processes may thus originate from human translators' body-external person-to-person and person-to-phenomena relationships as described by Jarvis. They may, however, also originate from human translators' relationships with body-internal actants originating from translators' personal histories, past experiences and images of imagined or wished-for futures and feelings.

This re-interpretation of Peter Jarvis's theory offers an intra-systemic view on the co-construction of organizations as socio-material entities where the actor-network expands and develops on the basis of translators who communicate and interact with, learn from and try to connect to body-external and body-internal human and nonhuman actants as they try to expand the number of actants that take part in and do the work that then – in practice – realizes/produces the effects that we associate with the organization.

The assumptions that may be derived from this are the following:

- Humans (including translators) learn from relating to and interacting with body-external actants such as humans and nonhumans (things)
- They moreover learn from their relations to and interactions with body-internal actants such as reflections upon wished-for future states or past experiences, personal knowledge and history and feelings
- As a consequence, humans (translators) learning through ventriloquist processes of dialogue are not just influenced by their relations and interactions with body-external humans and nonhumans but also by body-internal actants such as feelings, mental activities and reflections that may also mobilize the translator/ventriloquist to speak
- The construction of organizations as socio-material entities happens on the basis of translators who communicate and interact with, learn from and try to connect to body-external and body-internal human and non-human actants as they try to expand the number of actants that take part in and do the work that then – in practice – realizes/produces the effects that we associate with the organization

Stabilizing actants, relations and interactions

When a change idea/token has been translated and associated with humans and nonhuman actants in a certain way, the relations and interactions between the actants have been stabilized. According to ANT, the stabilizing of the actants, their relations and interactions, that realizes a given innovative and organizational idea or token, happens through the handling and settlement of controversies that take place during the translation process (Latour, 1988). Martha Feldman and Brian Pentland's ANT-inspired theory about routines (Feldman and Pentland, 2005) will now be presented and suggested as a more elaborate theory about how relations and interactions between humans and nonhumans are stabilized and thus about how innovative change ideas or other tokens are realized in practice in organizations.

Martha Feldman and Brian Pentland define their ANT-inspired routine concept in this way:

> The routine is an actor-network that consists of people, their performances and supporting artifacts held together by the narrative of the routine.
>
> (Feldman & Pentland, 2005, p. 94)

They explain what they mean by giving an example of a routine, which is used in connection with the recruitment of employees in organizations: 'Once we get the position approved, we advertise it, and then we screen the candidates...' (Feldman & Pentland, 2005, p. 94). Feldman and Pentland explain that this narrative is an idealized account of the activities that creates a sense that these activities fit together in a way that is 'natural' and taken for granted. They emphasize however also that this narrative must not be confused with the activities including humans (applicants, members of the employment committee, etc.) and things (job advertisements, applications, written formal rules, procedures related to employing new employees, etc.) which will also have to be handled as part of the employment process as a performance. Without these, the ideal narrative would be meaningless according to Feldman and Pentland. Rather the narrative, the activities and the humans and nonhumans (things) that are related to recruiting new employees are complementary and presuppose each other. Feldman and Pentland even go a step further and suggest that it is the narrative about the routine that 'holds' the activities and human and physical/material elements related to it 'together' (as suggested in the above-mentioned definition).

In this chapter, it will be assumed that Feldman and Pentlands ANT-inspired theory about routines is not just a theory about routines but about more general phenomena that in ANT have been labeled 'assemblies' (Latour, 1996). In ANT entities in the world – including routines – are thus assumed to be assemblies of human and nonhuman elements. These assemblies are assumed to perform the work that realizes the phenomena (routines, organizations, institutions, scientific knowledge, etc.) that ANT researchers study.

It will be suggested that a translation of an organizational change idea or token has been realized when there through the process of communication and translation is established one translation of the idea out of the probable and potentially many other ways it could have been translated. The organizational change idea/token will then have been associated with an actor-network that consists of people, their interactions and performances, supporting artifacts and a narrative about the assembly that explains it.

Contrary to Feldman and Pentland, however, it will not be suggested that it is the narrative that 'holds' the assembly (for instance a routine) together. It will instead be suggested that the assembly is an outcome of the joint work done by an actor-network of people, their interactions and performances, supporting artifacts and a narrative about the assembly. The assemblies that create phenomena in the world including organizations are thereby understood as 'co-constructed' and 'co-produced' by all the actants involved rather than 'held together' by humans through a narrative.

This also means that assemblies as defined above may be built up, changed or dissolved. Translators build up and construct new assemblies when new organizational change ideas or tokens are translated into an actor-network with a certain configuration of people interacting and performing in certain ways, with specific supporting artifacts and with a specific narrative about the assembly that explains it. Change of a phenomenon/an assembly thus occurs if the interaction between the above-mentioned elements of the actor-network that creates/performs the work that realizes it changes. Finally, the phenomenon/assembly ceases to exist if/when these relations and interactions between elements are no longer performed and dissolved.

The assumptions about how the relationships and interactions between actants stabilize during the translation process that is derived from Feldman and Pentland's theory may now be summarized as follows:

1 Innovative organizational change ideas and other tokens have been stabilized when the communication and translation process has resulted in the ideas/tokens having been translated into assemblies (actor-networks)
2 An assembly is an outcome of the joint work done by an actor-network of people, their interactions and performances, supporting artifacts and a narrative about the assembly that explains it
3 The relationship between the above-mentioned elements of the assembly is dynamical and interdependent. If one element of the assembly changes, the whole assembly changes. Therefore, the effects of the assembly also change
4 Assemblies can be constructed, changed or dissolved through building up, changing or dissolving the relationships established between people, their interactions and performances, supporting artifacts and the narrative about the assembly
5 Assemblies may however also be characterized by dynamic stability. This happens when certain organizational relationships between people, their interactions and performances, supporting artifacts and the narratives that explain them are produced and reproduced in a similar (but not identical) way across time and space

Using symbolic and socio-material tools to build assemblies

Translators are always designers. They intend to solve problems and realize specific wished-for outcomes, introduce new management ideas, share knowledge across social boundaries, implement policies or strategies in organizations, make doctors behave in accordance with evidence-based knowledge about treatments, build innovative and performative socio-technical IT and other types of systems, etc. In order to do so, it has been suggested that the object of the translators' design efforts is to build up socio-material assemblies with wished-for effects by establishing performative relationships and interactions between humans, objects and contexts in a way that makes the mobilized actants do the work that realizes the wished-for effects in question. It has moreover been specified that the performative assemblies that translators build up consist of an actor-network of people, their interactions and performances, supporting artifacts and a narrative about the assembly. In order to understand in more detail how such a social-material assemblage is built up, constructed and thus translated, professor Roger Säljös socio-cultural theory about humans' use of symbolic and socio-material tools (Säljö, 2003) will be looked into.

Symbolic and socio-material tools in the construction of assemblies

Roger Säljö suggests that humans contrary to other species are characterized by developing and using physical and language-based tools (Säljö, 2003, p. 79). Mediated through language, these tools are used to solve different types of practical problems that humans have in the world. The use of the concept of mediating means that humans are not assumed to be in a direct, spontaneous and uninterpreted contact with the environment. Rather, humans handle this environment through the use of different physical and intellectual tools that are developed by them over time in different types of problem situations. Säljö posits that the development of human tools as artifacts may be described on a scale from the concrete experience of individuals having a certain problem to the abstract codified symbolic knowledge of a collective about how to solve that type or category of problem.

Säljö uses the lever as an example. As demonstrated in Figure 20.1, the knowledge about the lever and how to use it starts out with a concrete problem. Humans having problems with lifting heavy objects like stones – perhaps in relation to building houses, monuments, etc.

The human will first find out that using a board of wood that is placed on a stone will make it easier to lift another stone in front of the setup. By collectively sharing and further experimenting with the technique, however, a more refined understanding of how to use the lever develops. Humans

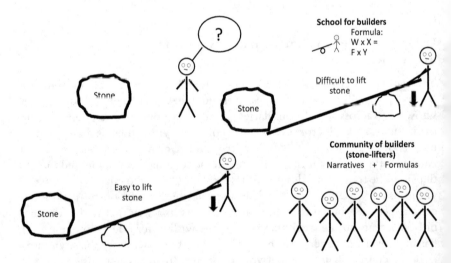

Figure 20.1 Using a lever to lift a stone

may thus make experiments where they move the stone on which the board of wood balances so that it is placed close or far from the human manually pushing the board down. In that case, the human will experience that he/she can lift heavier stones if the stone under the wooden board is placed far from compared to close to him/her when he/she pushes the lever down.

At an even later, stage, the community of practitioners of 'stone-lifters' (house or monument builders, etc.) may develop a codified and abstract form of knowledge – a formula that mathematically describes the physical and mechanical forces influencing the process of lifting objects with a lever (which is an entity consisting of a board of wood, a stone under it, a stone that is to be lifted in front of the setup and a person pushing the board of wood down in the other end of the setup). This formula may now be learned in a school far away in space and time from where the stone-lifting is practiced. Now however another problem arises; how humans translate the formula back to and use this abstract knowledge when again trying to lift stones in practice. Even though lifting stones using levers is understood as an abstract phenomenon (as forces described by a formula or as a narrative told by a more experienced stone-lifter), the student will miss the 'feeling' of physically lifting stones with such an instrument which leads Roger Säljö to conclude that the concrete and abstract knowledge related to lifting stones using levers are co-dependent. They must be learned by creating a communicative situation where the abstract knowledge – that is the narrative and the formula and the rules they describe – is demonstrated and learned by practically combining it with physical experiments with stone-lifting using a lever (Säljö, 2003, p. 84).

Now: What may we learn from this in relation to using symbolic and socio-material tools to build assemblies?

Using the theory and concepts developed earlier in this chapter to interpret (and thus translate) the above-mentioned example, you may suggest that what you see above is an actor-network – an assembly consisting of a narrative (in this case about how to lift stones using a lever practically and according to an abstract type of knowledge; a formula), people (the person or group trying to lift the stone), his/her performances (pushing the lever down, moving the stone and lever around, etc.) and supporting artifacts (the lever, the stone on which the lever balances, the stone that is to be lifted). In isolation, none of them are by themselves relevant in relation to stone-lifting. But put together in a certain type of assembly of humans, nonhumans and a narrative they are. And it is not the human actors' narrative about how to lift stones that 'hold' the assembly together (as suggested by Feldman and Pentland in their example of a routine above). It is rather the specific work done by the humans, nonhumans and the symbolic narrative/formula that have been related and made interact together (and thus been translated) in a certain way that creates the 'effect' of helping humans lift heavy stones.

But how do we know this? We know this because if just one of the actants mentioned above stops relating and interacting with the other actants in the network in the way ascribed to them by the translator (the person trying to lift heavy stones using a lever), the actor-network and thus the effects of the actor-network change. Different situations may arise where one of the actants involved stops relating and interacting with each other in the way ascribed to them by the translator. The stone may turn out to be much heavier than anticipated (perhaps it is made out of lead and is not a stone). Perhaps, the board of wood being used as part of the lever breaks. Or the stone we thought that we placed under the wooden board turns out to be a hard lump of clay that therefore breaks when being pressed down by the board when we try to lift the stone in front of the setup. The person may not have the strength to push down the board of wood – perhaps because the person is a child and therefore not very strong. Or the more experienced stone-lifter is not good at communicating his abstract knowledge about levers or the mathematical formula. Another possibility is that the mathematical formula may be wrong. In all of these situations, the relations and interactions of actants in the assembly/actor-network change and the effects of the assembly change.

A person interested in stone-lifting may thus approach the problem of stone-lifting using a practical and activity-based approach where he uses physical tools such as a board of wood and a stone assembled into a lever to do experiments with how it may be used to lift stones. As a consequence, the translator may experience and realize that placing the stone under the board/the lever near to him/her as he/she tries to lift the stone will make it difficult to lift it while placing it closer to the stone will make it easier. The person may also use an approach where he/she draws upon symbolic tools in the form of abstract narratives of 'more experienced' stone-lifters or a formula about the physics and mechanics related to using levers to lift stones. Or the person (the translator) may – as a third possibility – combine both approaches as suggested by Roger Säljö and combine both practical and experimental activities with physical tools with the use of symbolic tools in the form of narratives and formula. Either way the success of the assembly will depend on translating back and forth between a concrete socio-material practice (here of stone-lifting) and an abstract symbolic and narrative knowledge of how to understand and perform such a practice (or entity). The socio-material and symbolic tools used by the person to lift stones are thus co-dependent and the effect of the assembly (the ability to lift stones) is co-produced. The experience of 'what works' is thus produced in the encounter and intersection between the translators and their world.

Summing up the following assumptions may be derived from the above discussion:

- The actants of an assembly are co-dependent and co-produce the effects of the assembly
- Humans use both socio-material (humans and physical artifacts) and symbolic tools (narratives, formula, etc.) when they translate and construct performative assemblies

– Succeeding with translating and assembling actor-networks with wished-for effects (including lifting heavy stones) depends on learning what socio-material and symbolic tools may help translators accomplish such an aim
– Learning how to accomplish such an aim (an assemblage with wished-for effects) may be approached through practically experimenting with creating socio-material tools, through drawing upon or developing abstract symbolic tools (narratives, formula, etc.) or through combining these approaches
– Knowledge (about a certain type of assemblage) stored in a symbolic and narrative form needs to be translated back to the socio-material elements that it refers to. Knowledge obtained through experiments with tools made of socio-material assemblies needs to be supplemented with a symbolic tool – a narrative that helps making sense of the type of assembly needed to accomplish the task/wished-for aim
– Either way the success of the assembly will depend on translating back and forth between a concrete socio-material practice (here of stone-lifting) and an abstract symbolic and narrative knowledge of how to understand and perform such a practice (or entity)

Relational inertia in entity building

Schmid, Recker and Brocke (2017) have suggested a model of socio-technical inertia. The core propositions of the model are given as follows:

1 Inertia exists in structures, social and material, as well as in the interrelationships of those realms
2 The agential role of artifacts/materiality (as for instance information technology) contributes to the emergence of inertia
3 Inertia in the relationship between social and material entities takes meaning only in consideration of a socio-technical dimension, in which the two realms enact their agency upon each other

The authors define inertia as 'rigidity in the form and function of socio-technical systems' (Schmid et al., 2017, p. 4799). They suggest that socio-technical inertia is a result of path-dependent interactions of human actors with objects/materialities and that those interactions are constituted by three domains: The social, the material and the emerging socio-technical dimension. The realms are understood as interrelated and as mutually co-determining each other. According to Schmid et al. (2017), inertia may thus be present in the social and the material realm in isolation, but only in their enactment upon each other do they unfold into the socio-technical dimension.

Besides building on actor-network theory and the ventriloquist view on entity building, the concept of relational inertia suggested here is also related to and partly builds on the assumptions mentioned above. Relational inertia is thus defined as the accumulated and combined effect of conflicts and controversies that a translator meets and have to overcome as he/she tries to mobilize and assemble an actor-network of humans and nonhumans making it possible to perform and thus realize a given innovative change idea and its related supposed and intended effects in an organization. The types and forms of relational inertia are assumed to be as diverse and varied as the human and nonhuman actors involved and the types and forms of interactions, relationships and controversies that may develop between them during the introduction of an innovative organizational change idea.

During an organizational change project, thus a whole array of controversies may arise with many different human and nonhuman actors (actants) that may collectively hold the realization of the change idea/project back. 'What they may be' and 'what their collective effects on the change project are' are empirical questions and not reducible to social and material entities with certain characteristics. Rather, they depend on how these entities relate to and enact upon each other in practice in the socio-technical dimension.

Relational inertia thus has the same effect on organizational change and translation processes aimed at introducing innovative ideas as syrup or mud has on the movement of objects when they are submerged in it. That is, its collective molecular forces hold back the object/the idea when someone tries to move it from a given point A to another intended point B. As with objects moved through syrup or mud, the result of relational inertia in organizational change processes thus is an increase in the energy used and the amount of translation work needed to construct the socio-material relations and performative actor-networks that realize a given innovative idea, change project or effect.

The assumptions that may be derived from what was mentioned above are given as follows:

- Inertia may be present in the social and the material realm in isolation, but only in their enactment upon each other do they unfold into the socio-technical dimension. Inertia in entity building in organizations is therefore relational inertia
- Relational inertia is defined as the accumulated and combined effect of conflicts and controversies that a translator meets and have to overcome as he/she tries to mobilize and assemble an actor-network of humans and nonhumans, making it possible to perform and thus realize a given innovative change idea and its related, supposed and intended effects in an organization
- Relational inertia thus consists of the collective forces and combined effect of all the different controversies with humans and nonhumans that holds back and hinders the forming of the wished-for performative actor-network that is needed to translate and thus realize an innovative change idea

- The types and forms of relational inertia that may occur with humans and nonhumans during ventriloquist translation processes are diverse and varied and depend on how these entities relate to and enact upon each other in practice in the socio-technical dimension
- An increase in the number of controversies with humans and nonhumans related to the translation of an idea means an increase in relational inertia. Therefore, an increase in the energy used by and the amount of translation work done by the translators are needed. A decrease in the number of controversies has the opposite effect

References

Callon, M., & Latour, B. (1981). Unscrewing the big Leviathan: how actors macrostructure reality and how sociologists help them to do so. In K. Knorr-Cetina & A. V. Cicourel (Eds.), *Advances in social theory and methodology, toward an integration of micro and macro-sociologies*. Boston, MA: Routledge & Kegan Paul.

Clifton, J. (2017). Leaders as ventriloquists. Leader identity and influencing the communicative construction of the organisation. *Leadership, 13*(3), 301–319.

Cooren, F. (2008). The selection of agency as a rhetorical device: Opening up the scene of dialogue through ventriloquism. In E. Weigand (Ed.), *Dialogue and rhetoric* (pp. 23–37). Amsterdam: John Benjamins.

Cooren, F. (2010). *Action and agency in dialogue*. Amsterdam/Philadelphia, PA: John Benjamins Publishing Company.

Cooren, F., & Bencherki, N. (2010). How things do things with words: Ventriloquism, passion and technology. *Encyclopaideia, XIV*(28), 35–62.

Cooren, F. (2012). Communication theory at the center: ventriloquism and the communicative constitution of reality. *Journal of Communication, 68*, 1–20.

Cooren, F. (2018). Materializing communication: Making the case for a relational ontology. *Journal of Communication, 68*, 278–288.

Czarniawska, B., & Joerges, B. (1996). Travels of ideas. In B. Czarniawska & G. Sevon (Eds.), *Translating organizational change* (pp. 13–48). Berlin: de Gruyter.

Feldman, M., & Pentland, B. (2005). Organizational routines and the macro-actor. In B. Czarniawska & T. Hernes (Eds.), *Actor-network theory and organizing*. Lund: Liber & Copenhagen Business School Press.

Hacking, I. (1986). Making up people. In T. Heller, M. Sosna, & D. Wellbery (Eds.), *Reconstructing individualism: Autonomy, individuality, and the self in western thought*. Stanford, CA: Stanford University Press.

Hacking, I. (1999). *The social construction of what?* London: Harvard University Press.

Hébert, L. (2019). The actantial model. In L. Hebert (Ed.), *Tools for text and image analysis: An introduction to applied semiotics*. New York: Routledge.

Jarvis, P. (2006). *Towards a comprehensive theory of human learning*. New York: Routledge.

Latour, B. (1986). The powers of association. In J. Law (Ed.), *Power, action and belief – A new sociology of knowledge?* London: Routledge & Kegan Paul.

Latour, B. (1987). *Science in action*. Cambridge, MA: Harvard University Press.

Latour, B. (1988). *The pasteurization of France*. Cambridge, MA: Harvard University Press.

Latour, B. (1996). On actor-network theory A few clarifications. *Soziale Welt, 47* Jahrg., H.4, 369–381.

Love, T. (2002). Constructing a coherent cross-disciplinary body of theory about designing and designs: Some philosophical issues. *Design Studies, 23*, 345–361.

Martine, T., Cooren, F., Bénel, A., & Zacklad, M. (2016). What does really matter in technology adoption and use? A CCO approach. *Management Communication Quarterly, 30*(2), 164–187.

Meier, N., & Dopson, S. (2019). *Context in action and how to study It: Illustrations from health care*. Published to Oxford Scholarship Online: August 2019.

Murdoch, J. (2001). Ecologising sociology: Actor-network theory, co-construction and the problem of human exemptionalism. *Sociology, 35*(1), 111–133.

Romme, A. G. L. (2003). Making a difference: Organization as design. *Organization Science, 14*(5), 558–573.

Säljö, R. (2003). *Læring I Praksis – et sociokulturelt perspektiv*. Copenhagen: Hans Reitzels Forlag.

Scheuer, J. D., & Simonsen, J. (2021). Learning, co-construction, and socio-technical systems – Advancing classic individual learning and contemporary ventriloquism. In M. Lotz, N. C. Nickelsen, & B. Elkjaer (Eds.), *Current practices in workplace and organizational learning – Revisiting the classics and advancing knowledge: An anthology in the 'Lifelong Learning Book Series': Rethinking lifelong learning for the 21st century.* Springer.

Schmid, A. M., Recker, J., & Brocke, J. (2017). *The socio-technical dimension of inertia in digital transformations*. Proceedings of the 50th Hawaii International Conference on System Sciences, 2017, 4796–4805.

Simon, H. A. (1996). *The sciences of the artificial* (3rd ed.). Cambridge, MA: MIT Press.

Simonsen, J., Bærenholdt, J. S., Büscher, M., & Scheuer, J. D. (2010). *Design research – Synergies from interdisciplinary perspectives*. New York: Routledge.

21 Drawing it all together
The idea-practice-translation model

The idea-practice-translation model is related to practice theory in which practice is understood as

> a routinized type of behavior which consists of several elements, interconnected to one another: forms of bodily activities, forms of mental activities, 'things' and their use, a background knowledge in the form of understanding, know-how, states of emotion and motivational knowledge.
> (Reckwitz, 2002, p. 249)

The idea-practice-translation model theorizes what happens when an idea (or other token) is introduced and materialized by translators in a group of socio-materially embedded people in an organization. It theorizes how abstract ideas are turned into concrete practices in the form of routinized ways in which bodies are moved, objects are handled, subjects are treated, things are described and the world is understood (Reckwitz, 2002, p. 250). It also theorizes how such idea-related practices may change or be dissolved. In doing so, it draws upon the theoretical insights, assumptions and vocabularies that were presented in chapter 20– including those originating from actor-network theory and the ventriloquist view on the communicative constitution of organizations. The idea-practice-translation model is described in Figure 21.1.

In accordance with Czarniawska and Joerges, ideas are defined as '...images which become known in the form of pictures or sounds (words can be either one or another' (Czarniawska & Joerges, 1996, p. 20). Ideas may originate from fashionable management concepts like LEAN or AGILE organizing, a strategy, a policy, evidence-based knowledge about treatments, or from universities. Where the idea comes from does not really matter. But what matters and what all these ideas have in common is that they will all have to be translated locally by a translator and a group of people to have an effect on the organization. It may be a group of top managers who try to turn their software company into an 'AGILE' organization. It may be a group of middle managers: For instance doctors who are managing different departments in a hospital that tries to translate the concept of 'clinical pathways'. Or it may be a work group established in a service department in an airport that tries to translate an idea that some of the members heard about at a logistics

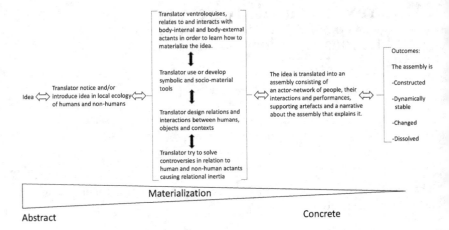

Figure 21.1 The idea-practice-translation model.

conference into a new way of transporting luggage. Or it may be researchers trying to move ideas from a university to a company.

The idea-practice-translation model builds on actor-network theory that theorizes organizations as heterogeneous assemblies of humans and nonhumans (actor-networks). It also builds on the idea that movement and realization of change ideas in organizations only happens if they are translated. Ideas are thus moved by humans who also have the power to influence what is moved:

> ...the spread in time and space of anything – claims, orders, artefacts, goods – is in the hands of people: each of these people may act in many different ways, letting the token drop, or modifying it, or deflecting it, or betraying it, or adding to it, or appropriating it.
>
> (Latour, 1986, p. 267)

The idea-practice-translation model also builds on the idea that some kind of work is involved when ideas move and are translated into assemblies (and thus actor-networks) in organizations. The process thus depends on 'all the negotiations, intrigues, calculations, acts of persuasion and violence, thanks to which an actor or force takes, or causes to be conferred on itself, authority to speak or act on behalf of another actor or force' (Callon & Latour, 1981, p. 279).

In contrast to actor-network theory however, the idea-practice-translation model builds on an asymmetric view on humans compared to nonhumans. It thus assumes that humans – including translators – are different from nonhumans because humans (and thus translators) can reflect upon their incorporation into socio-material relationships and can act upon these reflections in a way that nonhumans cannot (Hacking, 1986; Murdoch, 2001). It moreover assumes that this happens through the use of language and communication (as explained in chapter 20). As a consequence, Francois Cooren's (2010)

ANT-inspired ventriloquist view on the communicative constitution of organizations was introduced. According to ventriloquism, humans/translators ventriloquize – that is mobilize actants (human and nonhuman) as well as are being mobilized by actants (human and nonhuman) in the interactions and dialogues through which they learn about and 'constitute' the organization. According to ventriloquism, communication is defined as 'the materialization of relations through something or someone (an utterance, a force, a case, a spokesperson, a doorway, a website, etc.)' (Cooren, 2018, p. 279).

According to the idea-practice-translation model, the introduction of an idea in an organization starts with a translator who notices and then communicates the idea to group members embedded in a local ecology consisting of certain humans and nonhumans. What characterizes these humans and nonhumans and which of them that may be relevant to the project at hand (to introduce this particular idea) and which of them are not may not be determined with certainty a priori.

In order to explore and learn how the idea may be materialized and thus realized locally, the translator starts ventriloquizing, relating to and interacting with body-internal as well as body-external actants. As suggested by Jarvis (2006) and Scheuer and Simonsen (2021), the translator may thus identify and ventriloquize actants originating from his/her reflections upon wished-for future states, past experiences, personal knowledge, feelings and history that he/she finds relevant to materializing the idea. He/she may also explore and learn from relating to and interacting with body-external humans (like group members and other members of the organization) and nonhumans (physical objects, materials, IT and other materially based systems, etc.) present in the local ecology of humans and nonhumans in the organization.

The ecology of humans and nonhumans in which the translators and group members are embedded provides the context and thus background (Meier & Dopson, 2019) for the translators' and group members' attempts to co-design a local version of the idea. In order to translate the idea, the translators and the group try to learn how to design relations and interactions between humans, objects and the context (Love, 2002) so that the idea and wished-for effects of the idea are materialized (and thus realized). This learning and translation process happens through ventriloquist communication processes where humans/ translators mobilize actants (human and nonhuman) as well as are themselves being mobilized by actants (human and nonhuman) in the interactions and dialogues through which they learn about and try to materialize the idea and thus 'constitute' (Cooren, 2010) the organization. The translators and group members thus learn how to design and co-construct the assemblage that materializes (and thus realizes) the organizational idea in the intersection between them and the socio-material environment in which they are embedded in the organization. The learning process that unfolds in that connection is at the same time both an individual and a collective learning process (Jarvis, 2006; Scheuer & Simonsen, 2021).

An important task and challenge for the translators and the group is to solve controversies in relation to human and nonhuman actants that causes relational inertia. Relational inertia is defined as the accumulated and combined effect of conflicts and controversies that a translator meets and have to overcome as he/she tries to mobilize and assemble an actor-network of humans and nonhumans making it possible to perform and thus realize a given innovative change idea and its related, supposed and intended effects in an organization (as defined earlier in Chapter 20). Relational inertia thus consists of the collective forces and combined effect of all the different controversies with humans and nonhumans that holds back and hinders the forming of the wished-for performative actor-network that is needed to translate and thus realize the change idea. The types and forms of relational inertia that may occur with humans and nonhumans during ventriloquist translation processes are diverse and varied and depend on how these entities relate to and enact upon each other in practice in the socio-technical dimension (Schmid, Recker, & Brocke, 2017). An increase in the number of controversies with humans and nonhumans related to the translation of an idea means an increase in relational inertia. Therefore, an increase in the energy used by and the amount of communication and translation work done by the translators is needed. A decrease in the number of controversies has the opposite effect.

During the translation process, humans use or develop both socio-material (human and physical artifacts) and symbolic tools (narratives, formula, etc.) (Säljö, 2003) when they try to translate and construct performative assemblies. Succeeding with translating and assembling actor-networks with wished-for effects thus depends on learning what socio-material and symbolic tools may help translators accomplish such an aim. Learning how to accomplish such an aim (an assemblage with wished-for effects) may be approached through practically experimenting with creating socio-material tools, through drawing upon or developing abstract symbolic tools (narratives, formula, etc.) or through combining these approaches. Knowledge (about a certain type of assemblage) stored in a symbolic and narrative form needs to be translated back to the socio-material elements that it refers to. Knowledge obtained through experiments with tools made of socio-material assemblies needs to be supplemented with a symbolic tool – a narrative that helps making sense of the type of assembly needed to accomplish the task/wished-for aim. Either way the success of the assembly will depend on translating back and forth between a concrete socio-material practice and an abstract symbolic and narrative knowledge of how to understand and perform such a practice (or entity).

If the communication and translation process is successful, it will result in an assemblage consisting of an actor-network of people, their interactions and performances, supporting artifacts and a narrative about the assembly that explains it (Feldman & Pentland, 2005). When constructed this assembly may be produced and re-produced across a longer period of time in which case it has become stabilized and thus the way this idea and type of practice is performed in the organization. Later however one or more elements of the assembly may be changed in which case the performance and effects of the assembly and thus the idea also changes. Finally, the assembly may be dissolved in which case the idea ceases to influence the organization.

The idea-practice-translation model thus explains how an abstract cognitive idea is materialized through a communication and translation process that turns it into one type of assemblage of people, their interactions and performances, supporting artifacts and a narrative compared to the many other types of assemblages that may have been possible. It thus theorizes in more detail how the materialization (Czarniawska & Joerges, 1996) of ideas happens in organizations.

References

Callon, M., & Latour, B. (1981). Unscrewing the big Leviathan: How actors macro-structure reality and how sociologists help them to do so. In K. Knorr-Cetina & A. V. Cicourel (Eds.), *Advances in social theory and methodology, toward an integration of micro and macro-sociologies*. Boston, MA: Routledge & Kegan Paul.

Cooren, F. (2010). *Action and agency in dialogue*. Amsterdam/Philadelphia, PA: John Benjamins Publishing Company.

Cooren, F. (2018). Materializing communication: Making the case for a relational ontology. *Journal of Communication, 68*, 278–288.

Czarniawska, B., & Joerges, B. (1996). Travels of ideas. In B. Czarniawska & G. Sevon (Eds.), *Translating organizational change* (pp. 13–48). Berlin: de Gruyter.

Feldman, M., & Pentland, B. (2005). Organizational routines and the macro-actor. In B. Czarniawska & T. Hernes (Eds.), *Actor-network theory and organizing*. Lund: Liber & Copenhagen Business School Press.

Hacking, I. (1986). Making up people. In T. Heller, M. Sosna, & D. Wellbery (Eds.), *Reconstructing individualism: Autonomy, individuality, and the self in western thought*. Stanford, CA: Stanford University Press.

Jarvis, P. (2006). *Towards a comprehensive theory of human learning*. New York: Routledge.

Latour, B. (1986). The powers of association. In J. Law (Ed.), *Power, action and belief – A new sociology of knowledge?* London: Routledge & Kegan Paul.

Love, T. (2002). Constructing a coherent cross-disciplinary body of theory about designing and designs: Some philosophical issues. *Design Studies, 23*, 345–361.

Meier, N., & Dopson, S. (2019). *Context in action and how to study it: Illustrations from health care*. Published to Oxford Scholarship Online: August 2019.

Murdoch, J. (2001). Ecologising sociology: Actor-network theory, co-construction and the problem of human exemptionalism. *Sociology, 35*(1), 111–133.

Reckwitz, A. (2002). Toward a theory of social practices. *European Journal of Social Theory, 5*(2), 243–263.

Scheuer, J. D., & Simonsen, J. (2021). Learning, co-construction, and socio-technical systems – Advancing classic individual learning and contemporary ventriloquism. In M. Lotz, N. C. Nickelsen, & B. Elkjaer (Eds.), *Current Practices in workplace and organizational learning – Revisiting the classics and advancing knowledge: An anthology in the 'Lifelong Learning Book Series': Rethinking lifelong learning for the 21st century*. Cham: Springer.

Schmid, A. M., Recker, J., & Brocke, J. (2017) *The socio-technical dimension of inertia in digital transformations*. Proceedings of the 50th Hawaii International Conference on System Sciences, 2017, 4796–4805.

Säljö, R. (2003). *Learning in practice – a sociocultural perspective*. Copenhagen: Hans Reitzels Publishers.

22 Effects-driven socio-technical systems design as a method of translation

This section will introduce effects-driven socio-technical systems design as a method of translation. It discusses one way (but not the only way) that the idea-practice-translation model may be translated into a practical method that can be used to translate ideas and co-construct organizations. This happens through further development of a process model and method that has been developed in the area of effects-driven participatory IT design by Hertzum and Simonsen (2011). While Hertzum and Simonsen offer their model as an approach to development of IT systems, the effects-driven socio-technical systems design approach to translation is offered as a general model and method that may be used to translate ideas into socio-material assemblies in organizations. Here, it should be noticed that entities – including organizations – are assumed to be socio-material entities in practice, actor-network and ventriloquist theory. They are assumed to be socio-material assemblies constituted of humans and nonhumans and thus socio-technical systems.

Hertzum and Simonsen (2011) specify the core idea of their IT development model as follows:

> For customers information technology (IT) is a means to an end. This tight association between IT systems and their use is, however, often absent during their development and implementation, resulting in systems that may fail to produce desired ends. Effects driven IT development aims to avoid the chasm between development and implementation through a sustained focus on the effects to be achieved by users through their adoption and use of a system. This involves iteratively (a) specifying the purpose of the system in terms of effects, (b) developing an IT system and associated organizational change that realize the specified effects, and (c) measuring the absence or presence of the specified effects during pilot use of the system while also remaining alert to the emergence of beneficial but hitherto unspecified effects.
>
> (Hertzum & Simonsen, 2011, p. 3)

Ideas are most often translated to achieve certain wished-for effects in organizations, to achieve the beneficial effects promised by a new management

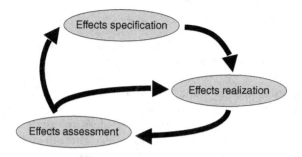

Figure 22.1 Effects-driven IT development.
Source: Simonsen and Hertzum, 2011, p. 6

idea (BPR, LEAN, Agile organizing, etc.), to implement a strategy or policy idea that is supposed to have certain effects that are important to the organization and to implement ideas derived from research evidence that will help the organization achieve certain wished-for effects (like using artificial intelligence to control important processes or analyzing information that is important and need to be integrated in decision-making in organizations). Like for users of new information technology, the sociotechnical system of the organization is a means to an end for the members of the organization. And like in relation to development of IT systems, the tight association between the organization as a sociotechnical system and its use risks being absent during its development and implementation, resulting in systems (and thus an organization) that may fail to produce desired ends. Like effects-driven IT development, the effects-driven sociotechnical systems design approach to translation tries to avoid this problem. In order to do so, it follows the same type of process and logic that is suggested by the model of effects-driven IT development by Hertzum and Simonsen (2011). This process and logic is described in Figure 22.1.

Thus, similar to Hertzum and Simonsen (2011) in their model, the effects-driven sociotechnical systems design approach to translation includes three activities that together form an iterative process:

1 Idea-related effects specification, which consists of identifying and aligning wished-for effects of introducing an idea across multiple stakeholders and hierarchical levels
2 Effects realization, which consists of constructing the organization as a sociotechnical system and of changing the organization in a way that allows for pilot implementation of the system while it is not yet finalized
3 Effects assessment, which consists of measuring the absence or presence of specified effects related to the idea while also remaining alert to emergent effects. Assessing effects during pilot implementations involves assessing the system, its adoption and use, and the outcome effects of the

system so that the assessments can provide guidance for the ongoing design of the system

When combined with the idea-practice-translation model, the different activities related to the model are distributed in the following way between the three phases.

The translation process – and thus phase 1 in the model – starts with a translator noticing an idea and introducing it in the local ecology of humans and nonhumans in the organization. Since ideas are always introduced in order to achieve some type of wished-for effect, this phase needs to include a process where the wished-for effects of the idea are identified and negotiated with relevant stakeholders within and across hierarchical levels in the organization. The process involves identifying, formulating and prioritizing effects with the stakeholders having an interest in the idea and its supposed effects. An effects hierarchy identifying wished-for effects on an environmental, business strategy, work task, work process and technological system level and specifying effects details (description of the effect, the responsible stakeholder, the measure, the target level of the measure, its present level and potential barriers related to performing the measure) may be used as a tool as suggested by Hertzum and Simonsen (2011, pp. 6–7) or some other type of tool may be applied. As suggested by Hertzum and Simonsen (2011), measurements should be (1) observable, (2) measurable, (3) quantifiable and, if possible, (4) financial (identify the economic outcome of introducing the idea).

This phase is followed by phase 2: The effects-realization phase. The phase starts out with the translator or translators' ventriloquizing, relating to and interacting with body-internal and body-external actants present in the workgroup and the local ecology of humans and nonhumans in which they are embedded. This in order to try to learn how the identified wished-for effects of the idea may be materialized. The translator(s) start designing relations and interactions between humans, objects and the local context that they think will make it possible for them to realize the wished-for effects that were identified during the first phase. Both symbolic tools (like abstract descriptions of LEAN in books or power point presentations, the effects hierarchy, etc.) and/or bottom-up learning from experiments with designing different configurations of humans and nonhumans that are then tried out in practice iteratively are or may be used in that connection. Through communicating, ventriloquizing and translating body-internal and body-external actants as well as using or developing appropriate tools during the translation process, the translators try to learn what type of configuration of humans and nonhumans and thus actor-network may achieve the wished-for effects of the idea that was identified in the first phase.

During the translation process, the translator(s) needs to solve all the controversies in relation to human and nonhuman actants that cause relational inertia and thus hinder the materialization of the wished-for effects of the idea identified in phase 1. During the process, the translator(s) needs to be aware of the three types of change that may occur during the translation process. As pointed out by Hertzum and Simonsen (2011, pp. 9–10), Orlikowski and Hofman (1997) identify three types of improvisational change management which are relevant in relation to design of sociotechnical systems. Anticipated change is planned ahead and occurs as intended by the originators of the change. Emergent change is defined as local and spontaneous changes, not originally anticipated or intended. Such changes do not involve deliberate action but grow out of practice. Opportunity-based changes are purposefully introduced changes resulting from unexpected opportunities, events or breakdowns that arise after the introduction of a new sociotechnical system. Opportunity-based change cannot influence the functionality of the sociotechnical system unless the process contains iterations from organizational implementation back to sociotechnical development.

Now if the translation and sociotechnical construction process are successful, an assembly consisting of an actor-network of people, their interactions and performances, supporting artifacts and a narrative about the assembly that explains it, will have been constructed. As a consequence, an abstract idea will have been translated and become materialized into one type of assembly compared to all the other ones that were or may have been possible. This assembly may now turn out to be dynamically stable and thus be produced and reproduced through the actants' work across time and space. It may however also be changed or dissolved later in which case the effects of the assembly change or cease to exist.

References

Hertzum, M., & Simonsen, J. (2011). Effects-driven IT development – Specifying, realizing, and assessing usage effects. *Scandinavian Journal of Information Systems, 232*(1), 3–28.

Orlikowski, W. J., & Hofman, J. D. (1997). An improvisational model for change management: The case of groupware technologies. *Sloan Management Review, 38*(2), 11–22.

Part 4

Consequences for researchers and practitioners

23 Scientific, humanistic, actualist and design approaches to the study of movement of ideas

You may distinguish between four ideal-typical modes of engaging in organizational research: A science mode, a humanities mode, an actualist mode and a design mode. Researchers in organizational translation studies have conducted research based on all these different modes (see Table 2.1 for an overview). And their ways of making 'truth statements' (Foucault, 1978) (Olsson, 2010) about translation processes are influenced by these modes. According to Foucault (1978) (Olsson, 2010), knowledge is intersubjective – a product of shared meanings, conventions and social practices operating within and between discourses, and to which an individual's sense-making processes are inextricably linked. Foucault thus argues that a discourse community – people who, at least in the context of a particular role (as for instance researchers in organization studies), share a recognized body of 'truth statements' – will not accept that a given statement is true in a random or ad hoc way. Rather, its members will have a set of conventions or 'discursive rules' – either formal or implicit, but widely recognized within the community by which a truth statement can be evaluated and validated or repudiated (Olsson, 2010, p. 66). What are the conventions or 'discursive rules' of researchers for making truth statements about organizational translation processes and their outcomes, and what may make them 'work better' within each of the four modes will now be analyzed. This in order to answer research questions 7 and 8 from the introduction.

The science mode

According to Romme (2003), the first mode has the natural sciences as a role model and emphasizes values such as disinterestedness and consensual objectivity. Researchers should protect the production of scientific knowledge from personal bias and other subjective influences by seeking consensus among peers about what 'counts' as research and scientific knowledge. Knowledge is about a world, which is 'out there' and may be studied from an outsider position. Thus, knowledge represents the world 'as it is' – i.e., knowledge is representational in nature. A key question that will have to be answered is whether or not general knowledge claims are valid. Organizational phenomena are seen as empirical objects characterized by an 'order' that is empirically manifested through stable regularities that may be expressed in the form of hypothetical statements. These statements are seen as revealing the 'objective mechanisms' underlying or resulting in that order. Theory development focuses on discovering causal relationships between dependent and independent variables (if x and y, then z). Relationships between variables are expressed in probabilistic equations or expressions (x is negatively related to y) since variations in effects may be due to other variables or causes than expressed in a given proposition. Data are (typically) analyzed by testing whether the values of certain variables are determined by the values of other variables. Research methods include the controlled experiment, field studies, mathematical simulation modeling and case studies.

Researchers working in the science mode believe in a probability logic (Polkinghorne, 2004). They assume that findings and knowledge obtained through typically quantitative but also sometimes qualitative and 'critical realist' (O'Mahoney, 2016) studies at a certain time with certain people in a certain context may be stable across groups of people of the same kind in similar contexts at other times. They thus assume that social systems like organizations have the same kind of regularity that you find in natural systems and bodies. In addition, such regularity may be detected through testing theories, models and hypothesis about diffusion of innovations (and other phenomena) on a large number of organizations. Therefore, what counts, as knowledge in relation to how ideas are moved in and between organizations, has to be confirmed in large-n studies or through systematic reviews of the accumulated body of knowledge present in the research literature.

Theories and models studying movement of ideas using the science mode

The research streams about movement of ideas that builds on the science mode include diffusion studies and knowledge translation studies in healthcare.

Diffusion studies

Diffusion studies of the movement of ideas belong to this 'archetype of scientism' (O'Mahoney, 2016).

They are based on statistical studies of the diffusion of innovations. According to O'Mahoney's (2016) analysis, they use variance-based theory and approaches where relationships between dependent and independent variables influencing the adoption of innovations are looked into. For instance, relationships between the adoption rate of innovations and independent variables like the perceived attributes of the innovation, the type of innovation-decision process, the type of communication channels used, characteristics of the social system like values, norms and interconnectedness and the extend of change agents' promotion efforts (Rogers, 2003). This form of studies concerns changes to the properties of an innovation at a population level, as it is communicated and diffuses through what is often presented as the rational choices of managers. These types of studies apply natural science methods to social science. Methodologically, the analysis tends to be based on statistical regression or correlation analysis which takes the relationship between empirical variables to illustrate generalizable laws that would be expected to apply to other examples of diffusion. In diffusion theory, change is depicted metaphorically as being subject to the laws of physics such that when variables A, B and C are in alignment, an innovation or idea will spread or be implemented successfully.

Knowledge translation studies in healthcare

Theories of knowledge translation in healthcare are also based on the science mode. They are based on the assumption that a scientific 'body of knowledge' concerning the movement of ideas/knowledge exists and that the best way to get access to this knowledge is to systematically review and synthesize the research literature. The results of these systematic reviews are then supposed to inform healthcare practitioners such as doctors, nurses and administrators in making 'evidence-based' decisions about how to introduce new ideas/ new types of knowledge in practice in these organizations (Straus, Tetroe, & Graham, 2013, pp. 9–12). Tricco, Tetzlaff and Moher (2013) explain that knowledge synthesis is a term used to describe the method of synthesizing results from individual studies and interpreting these results within the context of global evidence. These methods can be used to understand inconsistencies across studies and identify gaps in the literature for future research endeavors. They further explain:

> knowledge translation focusing on the results of individual studies may be misleading due to bias in their conduct or random variations in findings. As such, knowledge synthesis should be considered the base unit of knowledge translation. Synthesis provide the evidence base for knowledge translation tools, such as policy briefs, patient decision aids, and clinical practice guidelines…. Knowledge synthesis is central to knowledge translation, bridging the gap between research and decision-making.
>
> (Tricco et al., 2013, p. 30)

Like when doing research in how medicine affects bodies, the randomized controlled trial is considered the gold standard for evaluating the impact of interventions used to translate ideas/knowledge into practice in organizations (Bhattacharyya, Hayden, & Zwarenstein, 2013, p. 336).

The humanities mode

In the humanities mode, the purpose of the researcher is to portray, understand and reflect on the experience of human actors inside organized practices (Romme, 2003). It is assumed that the actual operations of scientific enquiry are socially constructed rather than representational and are embedded in a social process of negotiation rather than following the individual logic of hypothesis formulation and testing (Romme, 2003, p. 561). In the humanities mode, postmodernists and social constructivists have criticized representationalists using the science mode for suggesting that they are somehow able to stand outside language and the world when making their knowledge claims:

> ...since representationalists claim that their theories are "true" because they accurately match up with reality, this must imply that they are able somehow to stand outside language and the world (what Putnam, 1981, calls a "God's-eye point of view") in order to verify their claims. Clearly, this is a problematic stance.
>
> (Chia, 1996, p. 36)

Researchers in the humanist mode of research instead suggest that language actively configures entities and events in the world in the very act of representing. In our use of language as researchers, we do not just 'write about' our objects/subjects of analysis, but bring these objects into existence through representational acts of writing (Chia, 1996, p. 37). Therefore, knowledge in the humanist mode is seen as socially constructed narrative knowledge that arises from what actors think and say about the world as well as from how they critically reflect upon it.

A consequence of this view is that the role of the researcher as well as research changes. The researchers and communities of researchers claim that they have a privileged understanding of social events, and phenomena in the world are substituted by a situation where such claims become just one 'voice', just one type of (constructed) knowledge claim or discourse among others. As a consequence, it becomes difficult to judge whether one knowledge claim/discourse is 'better' and more 'true' than other knowledge claims/discourses. The consequence is eventually an 'anti-foundational' understanding of knowledge claims:

> ...questions of fact, truth, correctness, validity and clarity can neither be posed nor answered in reference to some extra contextual, a historical, non-situational reality, or rule, or law, or value; rather, anti-foundationalism asserts, all of these matters are intelligible and debatable only within the precincts of the contexts or situations or paradigms or communities that give them their local and changeable shape.
>
> (Tennert, 1998, p. 241)

Referring to Tennert, Bogason (2006) explains the consequences of such a view:

> Sentences are only true by their relations to other sentences; language cannot be isolated from the individuals who speak them. Science simply is a forum for unforced agreement, where communities test other beliefs against their own; thus we are bound to our language and our own web

of beliefs; our judgement of the beliefs of others are rational or reasonable depend on our attempt to weave their beliefs into our own (Tennert 1998, p. 237)...Social science, then, may be understood as a series of language games, none of which has beforehand greater value than others, and which can be defined and re-defined many times (Tennert 1998, p. 239).

(Bogason, 2006, p. 9)

As pointed out by Romme (2003), these ideas suggest that organizational research is better captured guided by more pluralistic and sensitive methodologies than by exclusive images of how science should be or is actually practiced (as preferred by researchers belonging to the science mode). In this respect, no discipline or method of enquiry should have a monopoly on wisdom in the social sciences, because there is no way to determine what constitutes better forms of meaning creation in either the epistemological or moral sense (Romme, 2003, p. 562). As a consequence, what knowledge claim/discourse is 'better' – for instance in relation to our understanding of translation processes – ends up depending on whether a certain category of human (researchers) experience in an organizational setting is perceived as being good, fair or in other ways valuable in the eyes and views of specific communities of organizational researchers when studying specific human actors and organizational contexts. According to Chia (1996), some meta-theorists thus suggest that theories of organizations in this mode are self-justifying 'intelligible narratives' which enable a community of inquirers to arrive at some consensus regarding their social experiences. Whether findings and knowledge obtained through studies of, for instance, translation processes at a certain time with certain people in a certain context are stable across groups of people of the same kind in similar contexts at other times are thus depending on whether researchers in a research community think they are. Or as expressed by Barbara Czarniawska in her book *Narrating the Organization* (Czarniawska, 1997, pp. 7–8):

Behind my present effort, and behind all my work, lies the idea of science not as an accumulating body of knowledge but as a conversation (Oakeshott 1959).....If science is conversation, then scientific texts are voices in it. In order to follow the conversation, it is important to know who is talking to whom, who is answering whose questions.

Another consequence of this view is that whether an idea 'works' as intended when being translated into practice depends on whether the organizational actors who have received the idea say that it works (O'Mahoney, 2016).

Theories/models studying movement of ideas using the humanities mode

The research streams studying translation of ideas in the humanities mode include Scandinavian institutionalism (the idea-model and theory about action nets), symbolic interactionist and knowledge-based theories/models of translation (including researchers studying policy translation, middle managers and consultants as translators as well as the knowledge translation value chain) and linguistic theories of translation (which include researchers studying strategy and instrumental translation).

Scandinavian institutionalism

According to O'Mahoney's (2016) analysis of the philosophy of social science of Scandinavian institutionalists, their perspective tends to focus on the local (re)construction or institutionalization of management innovations or fashions. They are close to social constructivist theorizing, rejecting empiricism and focusing on the discursive and political re-embedding of knowledge in local contexts. Translation for these writers is understood 'as a process wherein new practices or fashions become institutionalized in different fields at different points of time and space' (Morris & Lancaster, 2006, p. 209). Particularly, they focus upon the politics and rhetorics of legitimation that actors deploy in organizations when translating management ideas. Empirically, they focus on the translation activities of 'carriers' of management ideas such as management consultants, publishers, gurus and business schools as they seek to (re) package and sell ideas (e.g., Sahlin-Andersson and Engwall, 2002) or on what editing rules translators follow when they translate ideas into practice (Sahlin-Andersson, 1996). Researchers in this stream of research reject the 'grand narratives' or generalizable laws associated with scientism, and suggest that knowledge of an extra-discursive 'external' world is not possible, 'either because it is claimed there is no external reality outside of texts or discourses (strong social constructivism) or because, if there is an objective reality, we can know nothing about it (weak social constructivism)' (O'Mahoney, 2016; O'Mahoney & Vincent, 2014, p. 724). As a consequence,

> the characteristics of any particular innovation - its price, whether it works, whether it is easy to implement – are sacrificed to the discursive representation of the innovation: such as whether management say it works.
>
> (O'Mahoney, 2016)

Accordingly, the methods used are suited to identify and understand discourses, such as interviewing or discourse analysis that enables insights into how innovative management ideas are constructed as well as have effects through local discourses.

Symbolic interactionist theories of translation

The philosophy of the social sciences (or archetype) of the symbolic interactionist and knowledge-based perspective on organizational translation is also analyzed by O'Mahoney (2016). Symbolic interactionism focuses on the construction of meanings through human relationships and related emergent phenomena such as consciousness and language (Blumer, 1986). It has its theoretical roots in the American pragmatist tradition (Peirce, 1998), which emphasizes an epistemological emphasis on the usefulness of truth statements to the groups using them. According to the symbolic interactionist perspective on translation, translation is necessary as 'objects and methods mean different things in different worlds [and] actors are faced with the task of reconciling these meanings if they wish to cooperate' (Star & Griesemer, 1989, p. 388). Translation thus often involves 'boundary objects' situated in and between 'social worlds', which provide a basis for communication, as they 'inhabit several intersecting social worlds *and* satisfy the informational requirements of each of them' (Star & Griesemer, 1989, p. 393). Examples of such 'boundary objects' may for instance be engineering diagrams, accounting systems and strategy tools. Research may also include work on boundary brokers – usually individuals acting as translators between different communities (e.g., Pawlowski & Robey, 2004) – and common spaces, which promote communication between team members (Kellogg, Orlikowski, & Yates, 2006) (O'Mahoney, 2016). Empirically, the interactionist allows insights into the processes by which meanings are translated between groups to enable their cooperation, and especially the role of different boundary objects in achieving this. Since understanding human meanings is important in this perspective on translation, researchers tend to use methods from ethnomethodology, anthropology, ethnography or participant observation or other in-depth qualitative research suited to identify the meanings that different communities generate as ideas and boundary objects are translated. Whether an idea or boundary object 'works' thus depends on whether the communities of practitioners of the different groups translating these tokens say and think they work.

Linguistic theories

With the focus on the importance of language in the humanities mode, it is not surprising that some translation researchers have turned to linguistic theories about translation when trying to understand and theorize translation processes (Holden, Harald, & Kortzfleisch, 2004; Madsen, 2013; Røvik, 2007, 2016). Because as pointed out by Malmkjær (2017, p. 15), linguistics is the academic discipline that focuses on languages, and since translation can be seen, in Catford's (1965, p. 1) words as 'an operation performed on languages', many scholars interested in translation and interpreting have looked to linguistics for theoretical input. And as explained by Holden et al. (2004, p. 129), 'translation…is by far the oldest universal practice of conscientiously converting knowledge from one domain (i.e., a language group) to another'. The insights derived from linguistic translation theory in relation to translation in organizations by Holden et al. (2004) thus were given as follows:

- Translation is not just about the linguistic transcoding from one language to another but about integrating the translation into a wider network of social relations
- The quality of the final product and the translation process itself is what should be focused upon. The first aspect deals with issues of quality, accuracy and impact on readers; the second focuses on cognitive issues and the competencies of translators
- The level of accuracy of a translation is important. It may be communicated in four different ways: (1) the general idea is conveyed, (2) sufficient information is conveyed, (3) most of the information is conveyed and (4) virtually all the information is conveyed (Pinchuk, 1977)
- There are constraints on the production of good translations. They may be influenced by ambiguity (confusion at the source), interference (intrusive errors originating from one's own background), and a lack of equivalence (an absence of corresponding words or concepts)

A consequence of researchers adopting a linguistic perspective on translation processes in organizations is that they thereby also seem to adopt the idea that organizational translation processes are to some degree similar to the process that unfolds when translators translate books or other texts. When translating a book/text you have an author and a translator translating the text to a target language. You may thus say that there is an 'original' – the authors' text (or the original idea) – and that the task of the translator is to translate this original manuscript (or idea) into the target language in a way that represents that original work (idea) in the target language as faithfully to the original as possible. And in order to do so you need to be a multi-cultural translator. You need to know the social and cultural background and language of the group of the author as well as of the target group to be an efficient translator. It is implied that a successful translation is characterized by a translation of the original text or idea A being as similar as possible to successive translations B and C of that text/idea across social and cultural groups and boundaries. New themes with relevance to translation processes in organizations are introduced as a consequence of this view including the translatability of ideas, the competences of the translators and the interest in different degrees of similarity between an original idea and its different successive translations as well as in 'translation rules' (is the idea/text reproduced, modified or transformed/changed radically? If so why/in which situations?) (Røvik, 2016). With the explicit focus on language and the contributions of linguistic theory to translation studies, these authors use methods suitable to track how the translation of language and texts unfold in organizations including discourse, conversation and text analysis.

The actualist mode

Actualism is an ontology that acknowledges only events and happenings. Instead of trying to 'look into' people's heads in order to find out how they interpret or 'socially construct' the world, you – the researcher – should instead study only observable things, behaviors and activities of people (Porpora, 2018, pp. 417–418). Actualists such as Bruno Latour (1987, 2005) thus suggest that the actor-networks of which phenomena in the world are assumed to consist are not reducible to any inherent characteristics or a priori potentials of human and nonhuman actants. An actant is assumed to be an actant and a network at the same time and characteristics of actants are assumed to be network effects of relations and interactions with other actants rather than originate from potentials or characteristics that these actants possess within 'themselves' in advance (Harman, 2009, pp. 127–128). A person can thus not possess power. However, it may empirically be shown through what work of related and interacting humans and nonhumans in an actor-network that a person is in fact powerful. A strategy idea may have been communicated to the middle managers and employees but it may not be possible to show empirically that an actor-network performing the work necessary to realize the idea exists. An architect like Frank Gehry may be considered a genius. But when analyzed in more detail there may turn out to be chains of translators who translate Frank's abstract drawings into more refined physical objects like drawings, building plans and different concrete forms of building elements that later makes it possible for Frank to 'stand on their shoulders' and work and speak on their behalf and incarnate (Cooren, 2010) Frank Gehry the genius architect. Therefore, actualist researchers use for instance ethnographic methods that make them able to track empirically through what processes ideas/tokens are translated through time and space and turned into actor-networks.

Actor-network theory: The archetype of actualism

As explained by O'Mahoney's (2016), translation in ANT concerns primarily the attempts of actors to change the interests or representations of other actors in order to enroll them into an empirical network (e.g., Greener, 2006; Luoma-aho & Paloviita, 2010). Translation for ANT is profoundly anti-essentialist, acting on empirical relations (seen as temporary 'events') between actors that are accorded properties through these connections (Latour, 2005; Latour & Woolgar, 1986). The ontology of ANT, therefore, is actualist (Harman, 2009, p. 16), rejecting social structures or invisible motivations in favor of highly empiricist commitments to tracing 'what happens' in local contexts (Latour, 1987).While, ontologically realist, ANT is epistemologically constructivist (Lee & Hassard, 1999; see also, Elder-Vass, 2008), in that while real objects exist 'out there', they come into being through the practices of science (Latour & Woolgar, 1986). Humans and nonhumans are treated symmetrically: Things are only what they 'come to be in relational, multiple, fluid, and more or less unordered and indeterminate (set of) specific and provisional practices' (Law and Mol, 2008, p. 365).

According to O'Mahoney (2016), ANT studies use methods such as ethnomethodology to follow the actor and the network. Studies focus upon interessement for instance the use of rhetoric, persuasion and argument to shift the interests of actors in order to build alliances that enable successful implementation of innovations. They focus upon the establishment of obligatory points of passage where the representation and construction of actors are colonized by one group (Luoma-aho & Paloviita, 2010). They focus upon how management ideas such as the balance scorecard are translated through an actor–network (Sandhu, Baxter, & Emsley, 2008). Since following an actor–network necessitates methods that make it possible to follow the translation of tokens across geographical and temporal distances, many research papers focus instead on the translation of agentic interests in enrolling one specific actor. In highlighting the importance of empirical networks in enabling and constructing change, ANT's methodology provides powerful insights into how translation happens. However, by rejecting social structures, and the power that this implies, why translation happens is often left unanswered (Elder-Vass, 2008; O'Mahoney, 2016, p. 7).

The design mode

Historically, science researches and teaches about natural things while the engineering disciplines deal with artificial things, including how to design for a specified purpose and how to create artifacts that have desired properties (Romme, 2003, p. 562; Simon, 1996). Engineering is however not the only profession that does 'design work'. Since 'everyone designs who devises courses of action aimed at changing existing situations into preferred ones' (Simon, 1996), professionals in technical, managerial, social, healthcare and other domains all do design work. Engineering and other professional disciplines doing design work therefore serve as role models for designers. Following the ideas of Herbert Simon (1996) in 'The Sciences of the Artificial' design is 'the activity of changing existing situations into desired ones', it is the use of knowledge to create things that do not yet exist but that humans think should be created. The purpose of a design perspective in organizational studies is therefore to contribute to produce systems that do not yet exist or to change existing systems into desired ones (Romme, 2003). Its focus is on solving construction and improvement problems (Van Aken, 2004).

The design perspective is based on a pragmatic view on knowledge. It is 'normative and synthetic and directed toward desired situations and systems and toward synthesis in the form of actual actions' (Romme, 2003, p. 562).

According to Romme (2003), design scientists may learn from the normative ideas and values that characterize good practice in professions such as architecture, organization development and community development. The values and ideas identified by Romme (2003) in these communities of practitioners are related to (1) the content of design research and (2) the process of design.

The ideas and values related to content of design research are given as follows.

1 *Each situation is unique*: Each problem situation is unique and is embedded in a unique context of related problems requiring a unique approach
2 *Focus on purposes and ideal solutions:* This focus strips away non-essential aspects of the problem situation, opens up the door to the creative emergence of larger purposes and expanded thinking, and leads to an increase in considering possible solutions. It moreover puts a time frame on the system to be developed and guides long-term development and evolution
3 *Apply systems thinking:* It helps designers see that problems are embedded in larger systems of problems, and identifies relevant elements related to the problem, the relationships of elements as well as their interdependencies

The ideas and values related to the process of design are given as follows.

1 *Limited information:* Information about the current situation or system is considered limited
2 *Participation and involvement in decision-making and implementation:* If stakeholders have a stake in the design participate and are involved in the design process, this will lead to acceptance, commitment, dignity, meaning and a feeling of community
3 *Discourse as a medium for representing the world:* The use of language not to represent but to intervene in the world. Initiate and involve dialogue and discourse aimed at defining and assessing changes in organizational systems and practices
4 *Pragmatic Experimentation:* An emphasis on experimenting with new ways of organizing and searching for alternative and more liberating forms of discourse. An emphasis on future-oriented action experiments and research

Design focuses on organization issues and systems as artificial objects with descriptive as well as imperative properties, requiring non-routine action by agents in insider positions to be changed (Romme, 2003). In theory development, the key question is whether a particular design 'works' in a certain setting and problem situation (Romme, 2003). The translation theories/ models that are based on the design mode are Secundo et al. (2020) and the idea-practice-translation model.

Theories/models studying movement of ideas in the design mode

The idea-practice-translation model

Donald A. Schön was one of the most influential philosophers of design and design education of his generation (Waks, 2001). In his book *The Reflective Practitioner – How Professionals Think in Action* (Schön, 1983), he suggests that the scientific and rational approach to problem solving is not sufficient when professionals – for instance in medicine, engineering, management, teaching and music (and here; translators) – work with solving real-life practical problems. Citing Russell Ackoff, he points out that managers (as well as translators) are not confronted with problems that are independent of each other, but with dynamic situations that consist of complex systems of changing problems that interact with each other. Problems thus are abstractions extracted from messes by analysis, and thus what managers and translators do when they solve problems is managing messes (Schön, 1983, p. 16). Referring to Ackoff, he points out that 'what is called for, under these conditions, is not only the analytic techniques which have been traditional in operations research, but the active, synthetic skill of designing a desirable future and inventing ways of bringing it about' (Schön, 1983, p. 16). According to Schön, knowing-in-action and reflection-in-action are closely related. Knowing-in-action is characterized by the following (Schön, 1983, p. 54): There are actions, recognitions and judgments which we know how to carry out spontaneously; we do not have to think about them prior to or during their performance. We are often unaware of having learned to do these things; we simply find ourselves doing them. In some cases, we were once aware of the understandings which were subsequently internalized in our feeling for the stuff of action. In other cases, we may never have been aware of them. In both cases, however, we are usually unable to describe the knowing which our action reveals.

Reflecting-in-action means that even though we have knowledge-in-action, we as practitioners and professionals also think about or reflect upon what we are doing 'on-the-fly'. Schön thus explains reflecting-in-action and how it relates to knowledge-in-action in this way (1983, p. 62):

> When a practitioner reflects in and on his practice, the possible objects of his reflection are as varied as the kinds of phenomena before him and the systems of knowing-in-practice which he brings to them. He may reflect on the tacit norms and appreciations which underlie a judgment, or on the strategies and theories implicit in a pattern of behavior. He may reflect on the feeling for a situation which has led him to adopt a particular course of action, on the way in which he has framed the problem he is trying to solve, or on the role he has constructed for himself within a larger institutional context. Reflection-in-action, in these several modes, is central to the art through which practitioners sometimes cope with the troublesome "divergent" situations of practice.

The idea-practice-translation model suggests that an organizational change agent or translator is a reflective practitioner in the above-mentioned sense. The translator learns in the intersection between him and his world. But as explained in Chapters 20 and 21, translation and design of organizations as socio-material assemblies however involve at the same time both an individual (as suggested by Schön) and a collective learning process among people embedded in a particular socio-material context. To learn how to construct the organization as an assembly, the translators as reflective practitioners need to have an eye for and an understanding of the social and material contingencies and complexities of interacting body-external actants such as other humans and objects/materialities and of complexities originating from body-internal actants such as translators' personal histories, past experiences and images of imagined or wished-for futures and feelings (as proposed by Jarvis, 2006) (see Section 'How translators learn' in Chapter 20). It is thus through establishing relations to and interacting with such actants that the translator get to know and learn about the (body-external) phenomena before him and the (body-internal) systems of knowing-in-practice which he brings to them. And here as pointed out in Section 'The translator as a socio-material designer' in Chapter 20, the introduction of any idea or token in an organization will always include some types of attempts of translators to influence humans, objects (nonhumans), contexts and/or relations and interactions between them. Translators are therefore socio-technical and/or socio-material designers. They design and co-construct socio-material systems; that is, actor-networks. And during the translation process, the translation and design efforts of the translators are directed toward humans, objects, contexts or relations, and interactions between them.

The philosophy of the social sciences that the idea-practice-translation model builds on is partly old pragmatism, partly the ventriloquist perspective. To pragmatists true reality does not exist 'out there' in the real world; it 'is actively created as we act in and toward the world'. Second, people remember and base their knowledge of the world on what has proven to be useful to them. They are likely to alter what no longer 'works'. Third, people define the social and physical 'objects' that they encounter in the world according to their use for them (Ritzer, 2000, p. 338). Bogason (2006) explains how old and new pragmatists disagree on the role of language. In old pragmatism language is a tool used in experience, in new pragmatism language can only appeal to language. And therefore, a proposition may be verified in the old pragmatism by satisfying conditions that initiate a problem – while in new pragmatism propositions may only be verified by conversation that leads to linguistic devices that seem better (Bogason, 2006, p. 10). Bogason suggests that the controversy between old and new pragmatists may be related to one's understanding of the linguistic turn in the social sciences:

> To some degree, the controversy depends on one's understanding of the linguistic turn; if you understand experience as solely introspection,

experience becomes problematic because it is difficult to communicate in language. But if you understand experience as the intersection
between the conscious self and the world...., experience then may be
communicated to other people and put up for test in experimentation
(developing new practices) as well as in dialogue.

(Bogason, 2006, pp. 10–11)

Based on the second interpretation of the linguistic turn, Bogason (and this
author/the idea-practice-translation model) concludes that truth and objectivity must be sought in the specific characteristics of specific situations in
which action is required, and tested in communication and experimentation
by those who are committed to a sustainable outcome. During that process,
the meaning of experience is to be realized in an interaction between the individual and the world where it can then be used by communities of inquiry
for learning about the world and solving problems of the world (Bogason,
2006, p. 11).

Building on the Ventriloquist perspective, the philosophy of the social
sciences of the idea-practice-translation model however also partly diverges
from old pragmatism. Referring to the above-mentioned points of Bogason
(2006) and to identify the difference between a ventriloquist position and
that of old and new pragmatism, I (John Damm Scheuer) asked Francois
Cooren (from whom ventriloquism originates) the following question in a
personal email:

Would the ventriloquist perspective agree with new or old pragmatism
in its view on how humans relates to their environments. If you for instance interprete experience as solely introspection, experience becomes
problematic because it is difficult to communicate in language. You get
caught up in "language games" (new pragmatism) (Rorty). But if you
understand experience as the intersection between the conscious self and
the world, experience may then be communicated to other people and
put up for test in experimentation (developing new practices) as well as in
dialogue (old pragmatism) (Peirce). When reading about ventriloquism I
get the impression that ventriloquism suggests a kind of intermediate position between the two. And that it is implied that what we know about
our environment or world/reality is somehow co-constructed by us and
the actants in the world.

Francois Cooren answered as follows:

Yes, you are perfectly right and what you wrote beautifully summarizes
my position. Experience is what William James would call the double-
barreled character of experience. Experience is both in people's head, of
course, in what they say and do when experience appears to speak for
itself. When someone appears to speak by experience, it means that this

experience speaks through him or her and that s/he makes it say things to his/her interlocutors.

It may thus be suggested that no real separation exists between the translator and the world when a token (an idea, knowledge, etc.) is translated. When a translator communicates his/her experiences of the world in that connection, he/she does so through a momentary process where certain body-internal actants originating from his/her experiences with interacting with former ecologies of humans and nonhumans speak through him/her and he/she then make them (the experiences/actants) say things to his/her interlocutors just as certain body-external humans and nonhumans related to the situation may do. The knowledge translators have or develop about their world is thus continuously co-constructed by the translator, and body-internal and body-external human and nonhuman actants in the world during translation processes.

References

Bhattacharyya, O., Hayden, L., & Zwarenstein, M. (2013). Chapter 5.1: Methodologies to evaluate effectiveness of knowledge translation interventions. In S. E. Straus, J. Tetroe, & I. D. Graham (Eds.), *Knowledge translation in health care – Moving from evidence to practice* (pp. 331–348). Hobroken, NJ: Wiley Blackwell, BMJ Books.

Blumer, H. (1986). *Symbolic interactionism: Perspective and method*. Berkeley: University of California Press.

Bogason, P. (2006). *The new pragmatism and practice research*. Paper presented at the Second Organization Summer Workshop on Re-turn to Practice: Understanding Organization As it Happens 15–16 June 2006, Mykonos, Greece, Department of Social Sciences at Roskilde University, May 2006.

Catford, J.C. (1965) *A linguistic theory of translation*. Oxford: Oxford University Press.

Chia, R. (1996). The problem of reflexivity in organizational research: Towards a postmodern science of organization. *Organization, 3*(1), 31–59.

Cooren, F. (2010). *Action and agency in dialogue*. Amsterdam/Philadelphia, PA: John Benjamins Publishing Company.

Czarniawska, B. (1997). *Narrating the organization: Dramas of institutional identity*. Chicago, IL: The University of Chicago Press.

Elder-Vass, D. (2008). Searching for realism, structure and agency in actor-network-theory. *British Journal of Sociology, 59*, 455–473.

Foucault, M. (1978). Politics and the study of discourse. *Ideology and Consciousness, 3*, 7–26.

Greener, I. (2006). Nick Leeson and the collapse of Barings Bank: Socio-technical networks and the 'rogue trader'. *Organization, 13*, 421–441.

Harman, G. (2009). *Prince of networks –Bruno Latour and metaphysics*, re.press. Melbourne, Australia.

Holden, N. J, Harald, F. O., & Kortzfleisch, O. (2004). Why cross-cultural knowledge transfer is a form of translation in more ways than you think. *Knowledge and Process Management, 11*(2), 127–136.

Jarvis, P. (2006). *Towards a comprehensive theory of human learning*. New York, NY: Routledge.

204 *Consequences for researchers and practitioners*

Kellogg, K. C., Orlikowski, W. J., & Yates, J. (2006). Life in the trading zone: Structuring coordination across boundaries in postbureaucratic organizations. *Organization Science, 17*, 22–44.

Latour, B. (1987). *Science in action: How to follow scientists and engineers through society*. Cambridge, MA: Harvard University Press.

Latour, B. (2005). *Reassembling the social: An introduction to actor-network-theory*. Oxford: Oxford University Press.

Latour, B., & Woolgar, S. (1986). *Laboratory life: The construction of scientific facts*. Princeton, NJ: Princeton University press.

Law, J., & Mol, A. (2008). The actor-enacted: Cumbrian sheep in 2001. In C. Knappet & L. Malafouris (Eds.), *Material agency: Towards a non-anthropocentric approach* (pp. 57–96). New York, NY: Springer.

Lee, N., & Hassard, J. (1999). Organization unbound: Actor-network theory, research strategy and institutional flexibility. *Organizations, 6*, 391–404.

Luoma-aho, V., & Paloviita, A. (2010). Actor-networking stakeholder theory for today's corporate communications. *Corporate Communications, 15*, 49–67.

Madsen, S. O. (2013). The Leader as a Translator – A translation perspective on strategy work, Phd dissertation, Copenhagen Business School.

Malmkjær, K. (2017). Chapter 1: Theories of linguistics and of translation and interpreting. In *The Routledge handbook of translation studies and linguistics* (pp. 15–30). New York, NY: Routledge.

Morris, T., & Lancaster, Z. (2006). Translating management ideas. *Organization Studies, 32*, 187–210.

Olsson, M. R. (2010). Michel Foucault: Discourse, power/knowledge, and the battle for truth. In G. J. Leckie, L. M. Given, & J. E. Buschan (Eds.), *Critical theory for library and information science* (pp. 63–74). Libraries Unlimited.

O'Mahoney, J. (2016). Archetypes of translation: Recommendations for dialogue. *International Journal of Management Reviews, 18*(3), 333–350.

O'Mahoney, J., & Vincent, S. (Eds.) (2014). *Putting critical realism into practice: A guide to research methods in organization studies* (pp. 1–21). London: Oxford University Press.

Pawlowski, S. D., & Robey, D. (2004). Bridging user organisations: Knowledge brokering and the work of information technology professionals. *MIS Quarterly, 28*, 645–672.

Peirce, C. S. (1998). *The essential peirce, selected philosophical writings, Vol. 1 (1893–1913)*. Indianapolis: Indiana University Press.

Pinchuk, I. (1977). *Scientific and technical translation*. London: André Deutsch.

Polkinghorne, D. E. (2004). *Practice and the human sciences – The case for a judgment-based practice of care*. New York, NY: State University of New York Press.

Porpora, D. V. (2018). Critical realism as relational sociology. In F. Dépelteau (Ed.), *The Palgrave handbook of relational sociology* (pp. 414–429). Cham: Palgrave-Macmillan.

Ritzer, G. (2000). *Sociological theory* (5th ed.). New York: McGraw Hill Higher Education.

Rogers, E. (2003). *Diffusion of innovations* (5th ed.). New York, NY: Free Press.

Romme, A. G. L. (2003). Making a difference: Organization as design. *Organization Science, 14*(5), 558–573.

Røvik, K. A. (2007). *Trender og Translasjoner: Ideer som former det 21.Århundrets organisasjon*. Oslo: Universitetsforlaget.

Røvik, K. A. (2016). Knowledge transfer as translation: Review and elements of an instrumental theory. *International Journal of Management Reviews, 18*(3), 290–310.

Sahlin-Andersson, K. (1996). Imitating by editing success. In B. Czarniawska & G. Sevôn (Eds.), *Translating organizational change*. Berlin/New York, NY: Walter de Gruytér.Sahlin-Andersson, K., & Engwall, I. (2002). *The expansion of management knowledge: Carriers, flows, and sources*. Stanford, CA: Stanford University Press.

Sandhu, R., Baxter, J., & Emsley, D. (2008). The balanced scorecard and its possibilities: The initial experiences of a Singaporean firm. *Australian Accounting Review, 18*, 16–24.

Schön, D. A. (1983/1991). *The reflective practitioner – How professionals think in action*. Aldershot: Ashgate Publishing Limited.

Secundo, G., Del Vecchio, P., Simeone, L., & Schiuma, G. (2020). Creativity and stakeholder's engagement in open innovation: Design for knowledge translation in technology-intensive enterprises. *Journal of Business Research*, 272–282.

Simon, H. A. (1996). *The sciences of the artificial* (3rd ed.). Cambridge, MA: MIT Press.

Star, S. L., & Griesemer, J. (1989). Institutional ecology, 'translations', and boundary objects: Amateurs and professionals on Berkeley's museum of vertebrate zoology. *Social Studies of Science, 19*, 387–420.

Straus, S. E., Tetroe, J., & Graham, I. D. (2013). *Knowledge translation in health care – Moving from evidence to practice*. Hobroken, NJ: Wiley Blackwell, BMJ Books.

Tennert, J. R. (1998). Who cares about big questions? The search for the holy grail in public administration. *Administrative Theory & Praxis, 20*(2), 231–243.

Tricco, A., Tetzlaff, J., & Moher, D. (2013). Chapter 2.1: Knowledge synthesis. In S. E. Straus, J. Tetroe, & I. D. Graham (Eds.), *Knowledge translation in health care – Moving from evidence to practice* (pp. 29–49). Hobroken, NJ: Wiley Blackwell, BMJ Books.

Van Aken, J. E. (2004). Management research based on the paradigm of the design sciences: The quest for field-tested and grounded technological rules. *Journal of Management Studies, 41*(2), 219–246.

Waks, L. J. (2001). Donald Schon's philosophy of design and design education. *International Journal of Technology and Design Education, 11*, 37–51.

24 Practical consequences of a translation perspective on the movement of tokens

Often practitioners are interested in 'what works' in different situations. If the board of directors of a company has decided to introduce the idea of LEAN in their organization, they believe it will make their organization and its processes more effective or efficient if implemented. If the board of directors introduces a new strategy, they suppose that it is beneficial for the company and needs to be implemented. Politicians and public servants want their policies to be implemented because it is illegitimate and undemocratic if the policies that our elected representatives decide upon are not implemented in practice. In healthcare organizations, researchers who provide new evidence-based knowledge about what types of treatments 'work' expect this evidence-based knowledge to be used by the doctors who encounter the different patient groups for whom the knowledge is relevant. When people are collaborating and coordinating their actions across groups separated in space and time, you need to assure that what goes on makes sense to them. When relevant knowledge is produced at universities, you want that knowledge to 'travel' as far as possible through relevant knowledge translation value chains. And if you are a middle manager or a consultant, you want to be effective in what you are trying to do. So in all these situations where tokens (ideas, knowledge, texts, etc.) are moved: What difference does a translation perspective make?

As mentioned, the comparative analysis of theories and models in organizational translation studies above identified a number of focus points and themes that translation studies researchers in organizational studies share and 'look into' in their research. These included a focus on the token that is translated; the role of language and communication in the movement of tokens; a focus on the movement of tokens from a group of people A to another group of people B; the way tokens arrive in, leave groups or are negotiated between them; the role of translators, humans and objects in that connection; and how outcomes of translation processes are measured, evaluated and assumed to influence further translation processes. The comparative analysis also identified how these different focus points or elements related to translation processes were assumed to influence the translation process. What all these insights mean to practitioners who move ideas (or other tokes) and are interested in how to make them 'work' is what will be discussed next. The aim of this main section is to answer research question 9 from the introduction.

Translation of tokens is influenced by many factors

According to organizational translation studies researchers, the translation of tokens is influenced by many factors, including characteristics of the token, language and communication, differences between groups of people and how the token arrive in, leave or is negotiated between them; and by how outcomes are identified, measured, evaluated and assumed to influence further translation processes (see Table 17.1). As a consequence of the influence of these many factors, translation studies researchers assume that a translation process will never unfold in a linear manner where conceptual ideas (LEAN), strategy and policy ideas, and knowledge about practices or texts are simply loyally 'implemented' through a chain of command in a company, through a hierarchy in a public organization, through doctors' loyal identification and implementation of evidence-based knowledge or consultants' or middle managers' loyal implementation of their own or top managements ideas, etc. Rather, what happens with these tokens is influenced by the events, activities and choices (Langley, 1999) that unfold among translators and two or more groups (in a translation value chain (Thorpe et al., 2011)) who are 'mobilized' and participate in the translation process. It is moreover influenced by an ecology of humans and objects (nonhumans) that either present themselves as relevant to the translation process or are mobilized by the translators themselves in that connection.

When tokens are translated they change

Because of the many factors that influence translation processes, the tokens as well as those who translate them will always be changed as tokens move. A token (like a conceptual, strategy or policy idea, etc.) that has been translated may thus only be more or less like the original token in a relative sense, not in an absolute sense. The resemblance of a translated token compared to its original may only be interpreted and judged to be relatively (not exactly) similar, partly similar or not similar to the original token by the translator or group(s) of peopled involved in the translation process. The idea that evidence-based management (Rousseau, 2012), implementation science ideas (Nilsen and Birken, 2020) or knowledge developed in one organizational setting (a company) may easily be transferred, used and implemented as 'best practice' in another organizational setting is thereby problematized. The uncomplicated movement of innovative knowledge between universities and companies (Geuna & Muscio, 2009) is questioned. And the confidence some managers have in the adoption of traveling fashionable management ideas (Czarniawska & Joerges, 1996) (like BPR, LEAN, AGILE organizing etc.) when they want to realize certain organizational aims may (or may not) be misplaced. Just as strategy and policy ideas (also as texts) will be subject to transformations as they move.

The effects of translated tokens are uncertain

The effects of a token (idea, knowledge, text, etc.) that is translated in an organization are uncertain because of the many factors that influence the process – including the many people and groups of people the token moves through and the different types of 'nonhumans' (objects/things) that may play a role in that connection. It may however be suggested that the effects of a token depend especially on the last translation made of it in a chain of translations in the organization. An innovative token (like an idea or a knowledge construct) may thus have 'traveled' through many different people and groups of people outside as well as inside the organization before it reaches its final destination in a local department in some at this time still preliminary form. It is then how this (last) preliminary form is translated into a final local form that decides what effects the token will produce locally. Here, it should be noted that the different translation theories and models have different assumptions about when a token 'starts' producing its effects: Some theories and models assume that this happens when the text (talk or written) has been translated in a way that is meaningful to the receivers (Carlile, 2002, 2004; Star & Griesemer, 1989), others assume that it happens when the token (as an idea) 'materialize' into habitualized actions that are typified in the same way (Czarniawska & Joerges, 1996), yet others assume that it happens when an action-net (Czarniawska, 2014) or an actor-network (Callon, 1986; Latour, 1986) performs the work that 'realizes' the token has been established.

You can influence but not fully plan the translation process

Another consequence of the many factors that influence translation processes is that it is difficult to plan the process. Traditionally, theories in areas like organizational change, implementation science and strategy-and-policy implementation suggest that organizational change will be more successful if planned in the right way and if barriers and facilitators to change are identified and dealt with by change agents (Grimshaw, Eccles, Lavis, Hill, & Squires, 2012; Ngamo et al., 2016; Noble, 1999; Todnem, 2005; Winter, 2012). It is assumed that generalizable knowledge and rules about planning, use of interventions, types of facilitators and handling of typical barriers to change may be derived a priori from quantitative as well as qualitative studies of organizational change processes in a large number of organizations. Such a view is however untenable if change in organizations unfolds as translation processes and depends on establishing new situated types of (potentially very complex and always unique) relationships between a token (an idea, knowledge construct, etc.) and different types of 'humans' and for some translation researchers 'nonhumans'.

Here, it may be noted that the direct application of human science findings (from for instance research about organizational change, implementation science, strategy and policy implementation research, etc.) by practitioners working with people is limited in at least three ways (Polkinghorne, 2004, p. 94): (1) Findings are historically situated in that they have been obtained at a particular time with particular people. The projection by probability logic that these findings apply to people with the same characteristics, but who were not participants in the study is based on assumptions about the stability of findings across all the members of a certain type and about the stability of findings over time. A stability that you according to translation researchers will probably never find. (2) There are variations among the members of a type, and knowledge about what is generally so does not apply directly to the particular person that a practice (a token) is meant to assist. (3) As individuals are affected and changed by what they encounter, the impact of applications varies when they are used again with the same person.

This means that the general types of knowledge about how to plan, use interventions, facilitate and handle barriers to change that have been produced in organizational change management, implementation science, strategy and policy implementation research may at best be considered 'weak' evidence or general rules of thumb about how to handle organizational change rather than 'strong' evidence-based knowledge about these factors as usually assumed. While locally developed knowledge of translators built on experience and learning about what may make the translation and effects of a given token (an idea, a knowledge construct, etc.) materialize (Czarniawska & Joerges, 1996) in a given local context (ecology of humans and nonhumans) may be considered strong evidence.

In such a situation, a plan is not an intentional blueprint (Weick, 1995a) that creates order through deciding upon what acts should be performed by organizational members in the future to assure that a token is implemented. It is rather to be considered an interactive interpretative (or sense-making, Weick (1995b)) tool that practitioners may use to continuously reflect upon how wished-for changes may be accomplished; and to reflect on whether or not a translation process unfolds in a way that benefits the organization and has the potential to produce perhaps some of the wished-for changes that managers or translators associated with a given token (a fashionable management, strategy or policy idea, a knowledge construct, an order, etc.). For instance, through a process where local translators continuously shift between trying to perform (or enact, Weick (1979)) the plan and reflecting on and changing the plan.

The translator needs to do work in order to succeed with the translation

The organizational translation studies researchers agree that some kind of work is needed by translators to translate tokens. What types of work they focus on and think are needed varies however. Partly as a consequence of what philosophies of the social sciences and modes of research they 'believe in'. As shown in Chapter 17, these types of work include the following:

- Work aimed at creating links between and solving controversies with actants
- Work aimed at transferring, translating, bargaining, negotiating and learning
- Use of micro-practices
- Development and use of boundary objects
- Use of objects as intermediaries to mediate between idea and practice
- Use of design artifacts to ease communication
- Work aimed at collaborating with and making links to stakeholders situated differently across time and space
- Use of personal translation competences and insights in appropriate translation rules
- Work aimed at translating tokens as texts
- Work related to having a certain role or position in the organization (as manager or consultant) when the idea is translated
- Work related to learning how a token may be translated in a way that makes wished-for changes materialize in a particular local ecology of humans and nonhumans (as suggested by the idea-practice-translation model)

The success of the translation process will depend on translators doing the above-mentioned types of work. And changing an organization based on a new token will most often depend on a lot of work being done by the translators as well as others. Stubbornness, persistence and determination of translators as well as their translation competences (Røvik, 2016) may be important characteristics of translators in that connection. Just as setting aside sufficient economic, human and material resources to support the process will be important.

The kinds of translation work needed to construct relations and solve controversies with unique humans and nonhumans (objects) embedded in a certain unique contextual ecology of other humans and nonhumans (objects) (where some of them are, others are not related to the translation of the token) make what may make a translation process 'work' and be successful impossible to foresee and research a priori. Therefore, translators become especially dependent on what they may learn about what it takes to materialize (Czarniawska & Joerges, 1996) a token locally in their certain, particular and unique contextual ecology of humans and nonhumans (objects). What contributes to mobilizing and making actants (humans and/or objects) in that particular context assemble and do the work necessary to realize a given token will thus have to be experienced and learned in situ!

There are few translators

Since the above-mentioned translation work is complex and involves interacting with and learning about as well as influencing human and (for some translation researchers) nonhuman actants needed to introduce a wished-for token (an idea, a knowledge construct, etc.). And since this work often involves translating the token (idea) from a label and description of the token in symbolic form (as an image or a text) to other forms including meaningful constructs, habitualized and similar typified actions, action-nets or actor-networks, this complex work will probably often be done by one or a few people (a hypothesis that will need to be looked into in future research to be confirmed).

The translator may be the individual who writes down the project groups' local 'version' of LEAN as an idea and performs all the work needed to assure that the objects, humans and interactions between them in a local department unfold as agreed upon afterwards. Or it may be a smaller group of two or three persons who do so. Or it may be a middle manager who – based on an act of will – choose to do this type of work to materialize (Czarniawska & Joerges, 1996) a translated version of the company's strategy ideas in his local department. Or it may be two translators in two different organizations (a local council and a private company delivering healthcare services) who decide to do the translation work needed to realize a 'public-private' innovation (or idea) (for instance health schools for chronic diabetes patients).

Who these persons are may vary. But they may be identified. And if they are it will make sense to give these persons (types of humans) special attention and support (in the many different forms that may be needed). And it would make sense to look into whether they have or need to develop their translation competences (Røvik, 2016, 2007).

Power and effects depend on the number of actants performing the token

Organizational translation researchers share the idea that the power and effects of tokens depend on the number of humans and, for some researchers, also nonhumans (objects) (in Serres terminology 'actants' (Brown (2002)) that perform the work necessary to materialize (Czarniawska & Joerges, 1996) a given token. Translation work is thus aimed at expanding the number of human actors who participate in a social network or an action-net that performs the token; or is focusing on the expansion of the number of humans and nonhumans (objects) that participate in and through their work perform the token through an actor-network. Thus, the more people and objects (nonhumans) a translator mobilizes and succeeds with making do work to realize his/her token (idea) the more 'impact' it has and the more powerful it becomes.

Movement is not slowed down by resistance to change but relational inertia

Kurt Lewin theorized 'resistance' as social systems attempt to try to restore homeostasis and balance after a disturbance had occurred (Dent & Goldberg,

1999, p. 29). Chris Argyris (1990) introduced the psychological concept of 'defensive routines' to explain peoples' negative reactions to change. However, historically the term 'resistance to change' has gone through a transformation in meaning in organization studies (Dent & Goldberg, 1999, p. 39). Empirical evidence has built up that shows that the psychological concept of 'resistance to change' does not fully explain the varied types of reactions found among recipients of organizational change initiatives (Bareil, 2013; Dent & Goldberg, 1999; Piderit, 2000; Smollan, 2011). Instead of being only negative some change recipients' reactions have been found to be positive and constructive or simply different from psychological resistance (Bareil, 2013; Dent & Goldberg, 1999). The traditional idea that managers manage change which is implemented top-down and which employees resist is also questioned and is being replaced by more processual views that look at such processes as translation, sense-making and local organizing processes obtaining social order through improvisation and use of simple rules (Cunha, Clegg, Rego, & Story, 2013; Ford, Ford, & D'Amelio, 2008; Mcdermott, Fitzgerald, & Buchanan, 2013; Thomas & Hardy, 2011). Therefore, resistance to change is today suggested by several researchers to be a relational and socially interpreted rather than only a psychological phenomenon. If the unfolding of translation processes depends on translators overcoming 'controversies' with both humans and, for some researchers, nonhumans, it may be more appropriate to talk about 'relational inertia' (as suggested by the idea-practice-translation model) than 'resistance' when we try to identify what inhibits translation processes in unfolding as we want them to. Thus, according to Schmid, Recker and Brocke (2017), the social and material realms as well as the emergent socio-technical dimension are closely interlinked. Inertia might be present in the social and the material realm in isolation, *but only in their enactment upon each other* do they unfold into the socio-technical dimension. The enactment of the agency of social and material entities upon each other happens in the socio-technical dimension and as a consequence, rigidity or inertia in that realm arises from and within that enactment of agency. In the idea-practice-translation model, relational inertia was therefore defined as

> the accumulated and combined effect of conflicts and controversies that a translator meets and have to overcome as he/she tries to mobilize and assemble an actor-network of humans and non-humans making it possible to perform and thus realize a given innovative change idea and its related supposed and intended effects in an organization.
>
> (see Chapter 20)

For practitioners, this suggests that the concept of 'resistance to change' should probably be replaced with the concept of 'relational inertia' as they try to understand what may slow down translation processes in their organizations.

Differences in modes of research and philosophies of social science matter!

As mentioned at the beginning of this chapter, practitioners are interested in materializing (Czarniawska & Joerges, 1996) ideas or other tokens in different situations; when introducing a new management idea (like LEAN), strategy or policy ideas, knowledge constructs developed in evidence-based healthcare or by management or other types of scientists, etc. And practitioners often look for help from researchers in these endeavors. Here, practitioners should be aware that organizational translation studies researchers are biased by the different modes and philosophies of the social sciences they built on and therefore come up with different answers to the question of how and when tokens (ideas, knowledge constructs, etc.) have materialized. In the last chapter, four modes of engaging in social science and organizational translation research were identified: The science mode, the humanities mode, the actualist mode and the design mode.

Researchers working in the science mode including diffusion and knowledge translation in healthcare researchers believe in a probability logic (Polkinghorne, 2004). They assume that findings and knowledge obtained through typically quantitative but also sometimes qualitative and 'critical realist' (O'Mahoney, 2016) studies at a certain time with certain people in a certain context may be stable across groups of people of the same kind in similar contexts at other times. Therefore, what counts as knowledge and 'works' in relation to how ideas are moved in and between organizations has to be confirmed in large-n studies or through systematic reviews of the accumulated body of knowledge present in the research literature. Handling change and materializing knowledge in healthcare are thus supposed to depend on the knowledge creation and knowledge-to-action cycles (Graham et al., 2006) and on identifying 'barriers' 'facilitators' and 'intervention strategies' that systematic evidence show will probably contribute to translation of the token (knowledge) into action (Straus, Tetroe, & Graham, 2013).

As mentioned in the last chapter, however, this mode of research and philosophy of the social sciences was attacked by researchers in the humanities mode who suggested that 'critical realist' researcher in the science mode cannot assume that their theories are 'true' and accurately match up with or describe 'reality' because such descriptions are based on language and are culturally embedded. Being able to 'objectively' describe reality would thus suggest that these researchers would somehow be able to stand outside language and culture when they make their theories which would be an untenable position (Chia, 1996). Researchers in the humanities mode instead suggested that language actively configures entities and events in the world in the very act of representing. In our use of language, researchers do not just 'write about' our objects/subjects of analysis, but bring these objects into existence through representational acts of writing (Chia, 1996, p. 37). As a consequence, what knowledge claim/discourse is 'better' – for instance in relation to our understanding of translation processes or how they work or may work better – ends up depending on whether a certain category of human (researchers or practitioners) experience in an organizational setting is perceived as being good, fair or in other ways valuable in the eyes and views of these humans (researchers/practitioners).

In the actualist view on translation, actor-network researchers acknowledge only events and happenings. Instead of trying to 'look into' people's heads in order to find out how they interpret or 'socially construct' a token that is moved, the researcher should instead study only observable factors, behaviors and activities of people (Porpora, 2018, pp. 417–418). Actualists such as Bruno Latour (Latour, 1987) thus suggest that the actor-networks of which phenomena in the world are assumed to consist are not reducible to any inherent characteristics or a priori potentials of human and nonhuman actants. An actant is assumed to be an actant and a network at the same time and characteristics of actants are assumed to be network effects of relations and interactions with other actants rather than originate from potentials or characteristics that these actants possess within 'themselves' in advance (Harman, 2009, pp. 127–128). Actor-network researchers therefore produce descriptions of the actor-networks that are assembled and produce the effects related to tokens that are translated. But they do not offer any normative advice about how such actor-networks should be assembled or about what may facilitate or contribute to such a process (Vikkelsø, 2007). They moreover insist on an ontology where humans and objects at the outset of the analysis are assumed to be alike and not have certain characteristics that may influence the translation process a priori (Latour, 1987). Instead, such relationally produced characteristics will reveal themselves as the translation process and analysis of it unfolds. If a practitioner wants normative advice about how to succeed with the translation of a token, the actor-network researcher will give him/her a description of how such a token was translated by someone else before and ask the practitioner to draw his/her own conclusions and make further translations on that basis (Vikkelsø, 2007). Because according to the actor-network researcher what will happen to a given token in the future will depend on the practitioners' own and other humans' further translations of it in the future and on what human or nonhuman actants may be relevant and have an influence in that connection. And what may characterize this (future) translation process and these actants that may slow down or contribute to speed up the translation process or 'make it successful' may not be foreseen a priori.

Finally, the few researchers drawing on a design mode when theorizing or modeling translation processes adopt the idea that translation processes may be similar to design processes (see section "The translator as a socio-material designer" in chapter 20). According to the idea-practice-translation model, to learn how to construct the organization as an assembly (as when a token is translated), the translators as reflective practitioners need to have an eye for and an understanding of the social and material contingencies and complexities of interacting body-external actants such as other humans and objects/materialities and of complexities originating from body-internal actants such as translators' personal histories, past experiences and images of imagined or wished-for futures and feelings (as proposed by Jarvis, 2006). It is thus through establishing relations to and interacting with such actants that the translator gets to know and learn about the (body-external) phenomena before him/her and the (body-internal) systems of knowing-in-practice which he/she brings to them. And here the introduction of any idea or token in an organization will always include some types of attempts of translators to influence humans, objects (nonhumans), contexts and/or relations and interactions between them (Love, 2002). Translators are therefore assumed to be socio-technical and/or socio-material designers. They design and co-construct socio-material systems; that is, actor-networks. And during the translation process, the translation and design efforts of the translators are directed toward humans, objects, contexts and establishing relations and interactions between them. Consequently, tokens are assumed to be co-constructed through translators situated interaction with and translation of body-internal and body-external (human and nonhuman) actants that are relevant or make themselves relevant to the translation process. The philosophies of the social sciences and mode of research that was associated with this view were old pragmatism (Peirce, 1998). Here, truth and objectivity (experienced and created in translation processes) must be sought in the specific situations in which action is required to introduce a token and where these actions are tested in communication and experimentation by those who are committed to producing a sustainable outcome (for instance a certain wished-for effect) in that connection (Bogason, 2006). During the translation process, the meaning of experience related to the translation process is realized in an interaction between the individual translator(s) and the world where it can then be used by communities of inquiry (researchers and/or practitioners) for learning about the world and solving problems of the world (Bogason, 2006, p. 11). According to the idea-practice-translation model, communication is at the center of this process. Thus, according to Francois Cooren's (2010) ventriloquist view on communication processes, humans – including translators – are embedded in an ecology of human and nonhuman actants as they try to translate an idea into practice in organizations. And a translator may only learn about what is needed to materialize an idea in the intersection between him/her and the social and material entities (actants) in which he/she is embedded in the world by experiencing and identifying them through communication. Specific characteristics of body-internal and body-external humans as well as nonhuman actants that are relevant to materializing an idea at hand may therefore (only) be detected through the communication process. And that no matter whether these characteristics are specific to humans or nonhumans.

For a practitioner, the above-mentioned differences between modes of research result in different and biased answers to the question of what characterizes translation processes and how and when a token (ideas, knowledge constructs, etc.) is materialized (Czarniawska & Joerges, 1996). Is it when systematic reviews of research show that it is? Is it when a community of researchers or practitioners say that it is materialized? Is it when an actor-network researcher analyze and document that an actor-network that performs the token have been established? Or is it when the token have been designed, co-constructed and stabilized through a ventriloquist communication process involving translators, humans and nonhumans? As for researchers, what types of answers practitioners prefer will depend on their choice of scientific 'belief-system' and mode of doing science. Because there is no 'god's eye view' from where organizational translation researchers (or practitioners) may sit outside culture and language and claim that their way of producing science is the 'right' and 'better one'. What practitioners (and researchers) may and should be aware of however is what types of scientific 'belief systems' and modes of doing science they adopt and apply and why, when they try to come to some kind of understanding of organizational translation processes.

Conclusion

Practitioners are interested in making ideas and other tokens move and to make them 'work' in the contexts in which they are introduced. Therefore, the following research question was asked (research question 9 from the introduction):

What are the practical consequences of a translation perspective on the movement of tokens?

The chapter therefore discussed what are the consequences of adopting a translation perspective on change in organizations for practitioners. It was pointed out that the comparative analysis of theories and models of organizational translation processes shared some focus points and themes, including a focus on the token that is translated, the role of language and communication in the movement of tokens, a focus on the movement of tokens from a group of people A to another group of people B, the way tokens arrive in, leave groups or are negotiated between them, the role of translators, humans and objects in that connection, and how outcomes of translation processes are measured, evaluated and assumed to influence further translation processes. The comparative analysis also identified how these different focus points or elements related to translation processes were assumed to influence the translation process. Based on the comparative analysis of theories and models of translation in organizations, a number of practical consequences of a translation view on organizational change were pointed out:

- Translation of tokens is influenced by many factors
- When tokens are translated they as well as the translators change
- The effects of translated tokens are uncertain
- You can influence but not fully plan the translation process
- The translator needs to do many different types of work in order to succeed with the translation
- There are few translators

- Power and effects depend on the number of actants performing the token
- Movement is not slowed down by resistance to change but relational inertia
- Differences in modes of research and philosophies of social science matter!

Finally, it may be noticed that this is a preliminary list; and that an in-depth understanding of what a translation perspective means to practitioners will depend on further research. I hope that this book has created a better basis for such research to be performed in the future.

References

Argyris, C. (1990). *Overcoming organizational defenses: Facilitating organizational learning.* London; Allyn and Bacon.
Bareil, C. (2013). Two paradigms about resistance to change. *Organization Development Journal,* Fall, *31*(3), 59–71.
Bogason, P. (2006). *The new pragmatism and practice research.* Paper presented at the Second Organization Summer Workshop on Re-turn to Practice: Understanding Organization As it Happens 15–16 June 2006, Mykonos, Greece, Department of Social Sciences at Roskilde University, May 2006.
Brown, S. D. (2002). Michel Serres. Science, translation and the logic of the parasite. *Theory, Culture & Society, 19*(3), 1–28.
Callon, M. (1986). Some elements of a sociology of translation: Domestication of the scallops and the fishermen of St. Brieuc Bay. In J. Law (Ed.), *Power, action and belief – A new sociology of knowledge?* London: Routledge & Kegan Paul.
Carlile, P. R. (2002). A pragmatic view of knowledge and boundaries: Boundary objects in new product development. *Organization Science, 13,* 442–455.
Carlile, P. R. (2004). Transferring, translating, and transforming: An integrative framework for managing knowledge across boundaries. *Organization Science, 15*(5), 555–568.
Chia, R. (1996). The problem of reflexivity in organizational research: Towards a postmodern science of organization. *Organization, 3*(1), 31–59.
Cooren, F. (2010). *Action and agency in dialogue.* Amsterdam/Philadelphia, PA: John Benjamins Publishing Company.
Czarniawska, B. (2014). *A theory of organizing* (2nd ed.). Cheltenham, Northampton, MA: Edward Elgar Publishing Limited.
Czarniawska, B., & Joerges, B. (1996). Travels of ideas. In B. Czarniawska & G. Sevon (Eds.), *Translating organizational change* (pp. 13–48). Berlin: de Gruyter.
Cunha, M. P. E., Clegg, S. R., Rego, A., & Story, J. (2013). From the physics of change to realpolitik: Improvisational relations of power and resistance. *Journal of Change Management, 13*(4), 460–476.
Dent, E. B., & Goldberg, S. G. (1999). Challenging "resistance to change". *Journal of Applied Behavioral Science, 35*(25), 25–41.
Ford, J. D., Ford, L. W., & D'Amelio, A. (2008). Resistance to change: The rest of the story. *The Academy of Management Review, 33*(2), 362–377.
Geuna, A., & Muscio, A. (2009). The governance of university knowledge transfer: A critical review of the literature. *Minerva: A Review of Science, Learning and Policy, 47,* 93–114.

Graham, I. D., Logan, J., Harrison, M. b., traus, S. E., Tetroe, J., Caswell, W., & Robinson, N. (2006). Lost in knowledge translation: Time for a map? *The Journal of Continuing Education in the Health Professions, 26(1),* Winter, 13–24.

Grimshaw, J. M., Eccles, M. P., Lavis, J. N., Hill, S. J., & Squires, J. E. (2012). Knowledge translation of research findings. *Implementation Science,* 7(50), 1–17.

Harman, G. (2009). *Prince of networks –Bruno Latour and metaphysics,* repress. Melbourne, Australia.

Jarvis, P. (2006). *Towards a comprehensive theory of human learning.* New York: Routledge.

Langley, A. (1999). Strategies for theorizing from process data. *The Academy of Management Review, 24*(4), 691–710.

Latour, B. (1986). The Powers of association. In J. Law (Ed.), *Power, action and belief – A new sociology of knowledge?* London: Routledge & Kegan Paul.

Latour, B. (1987). *Science in action: How to follow scientists and engineers through society.* Cambridge, MA: Harvard University Press.

Love, T. (2002). Constructing a coherent cross-disciplinary body of theory about designing and designs: Some philosophical issues. *Design Studies, 23,* 345–361.

McDermott, A. M., Fitzgerald, L., & Buchanan, D. A. (2013). Beyond acceptance and resistance: Entrepreneurial change agency responses in policy implementation. *British Journal of Management, 24,* 93–115.

Ngamo, S. T., Souffez, K., Lord, C., & Dagenais, C. (2016). Do knowledge translation plans help to structure KT practices? *Health Research Policy and Systems, 14*(46), 1–12.

Nilsen, P., & Birken, S. A. (2020). *Handbook on implementation science.* Cheltenham, Northampton, MA: Edward Elgar Publishing.

Noble, C. H. (1999). The eclectic roots of strategy implementation research. *Journal of Business Research, 45*(2), 119–134.

O'Mahoney, J. (2016). Archetypes of translation: Recommendations for dialogue. *International Journal of Management Reviews, 18*(3), 333–350.

Peirce, C. S. (1998). *The essential peirce, selected philosophical writings, Vol. 1 (1893–1913).* Indianapolis: Indiana University Press.

Piderit, S. K. (2000). Rethinking resistance and recognizing ambivalence: A multidimensional view of attitudes toward an organizational change. *The Academy of Management Review, 25*(4), 783–794.

Polkinghorne, D. E. (2004). *Practice and the human sciences – The case for a judgment-based practice of care.* New York, NY: State University of New York Press.

Porpora, D. V. (2018). Critical realism as relational sociology. In F. Dépelteau (Ed.), *The Palgrave handbook of relational sociology* (pp. 414–429). Cham: Palgrave-Macmillan.

Rousseau, D. M. (2012). *The Oxford handbook of evidence-based management.* Oxford: Oxford University Press.

Røvik, K. A. (2007). *Trends and translations: Ideas that form the organization of the 21th century.* Oslo: Universitetsforlaget.

Røvik, K. A. (2016). Knowledge transfer as translation: Review and elements of an instrumental theory. *International Journal of Management Reviews, 18*(3), 290–310.

Schmid, A. M., Recker, J., & Brocke, J. (2017). *The socio-technical dimension of inertia in digital transformations.* Proceedings of the 50th Hawaii International Conference on system Sciences.

Smollan, R. K. (2011). The multi-dimensional nature of resistance to change. *Journal of Management & Organization, 17*(6), 828–849.

Star, S. L., & Griesemer, J. (1989). Institutional ecology, 'translations', and boundary objects: Amateurs and professionals on Berkeley's museum of vertebrate zoology. *Social Studies of Science, 19*, 387–420.

Straus, S. E., Tetroe, J., & Graham, I. D. (2013). *Knowledge translation in health care – Moving from evidence to practice.* Hobroken, NJ: Wiley Blackwell, BMJ Books.

Thorpe, R., Eden, C., Bessant, J., Ellwood, P. (2011) Rigour, relevance and reward: introducing the knowledge translation value-chain. *British Journal of Management, 22*, 420–431.

Thomas, R., & Hardy, C. (2011). Reframing resistance to organizational change. *Scandinavian Journal of Management, 27*, 322–323.

Todnem, R. (2005). Organizational change management: A critical review. *Journal of Change Management, 5*(4), 369–380.

Vikkelsø, S. (2007). Description as intervention: Engagement and resistance in actor-network analyses. *Science as Culture, 16*(3), 297–309.

Weick, K. E. (1979). *The social psychology of organizing* (2nd ed.). Reading, MA: Addison Wesley.

Weick, K. E. (1995a). Organizational redesign as improvisation. In W. H. Glick & G. P. Huber (Eds.), *Organizational change and redesign – Ideas and insights for improving performance.* Oxford: Oxford University Press.

Weick, K. E. (1995b). *Sensemaking in organizations.* Foundations for Organizational Science, A Sage Publication Series. Thousand Oaks, London, New Delhi: Sage Publications.

Winter, S. (2012). Implementation. In G. Peters & J. Pierre (Eds.), *The SAGE handbook of public administration* (pp. 265–278). Los Angeles, CA: Sage Publications.

Appendix 1
Moving translation studies forward through cross-fertilization

Wæraas and Nielsen (2016) systematically review and examine similarities and differences between three versions of translation theory (the actor-network, the knowledge-based and the Scandinavian institutional perspectives). They try to clarify where the perspectives overlap and where they differ concerning research focus and theory application, critically considering their insights and limitations. They notice that translation research in organization studies is far from being a cumulative science where authors build on each other's findings and theoretical propositions. Papers seeking to contribute to translation research rarely refer to other papers on translation. They find the general lack of cross-references and common language puzzling, considering that translation research in organization studies is a relatively young sub-discipline and the number of publications still fairly low. They suggest that this limits cross-fertilization and highlights the need for research that is guided by more than one perspective. Therefore, the main contribution of their literature review is that they identify the above-mentioned three distinct translation perspectives in organization studies and examine how they may contribute to cross-fertilizing each other. The characteristics of the three perspectives identified are the following according to Wæraas and Nielsen (2016).

Actor-network theory focuses upon a particular object (a token) that is traveling across different contexts. To translate something is to actively modify an object within the context and complexities of an actor-network. Studies inspired by Michel Callon's model of translation (Callon, 1986) emphasize the political and semiotic meanings of translation. They suggest that translation occurs in a setting characterized by diverging or conflicting meanings and interests; and that actors rely on various tactics, maneuvers, tricks and discursive techniques to convince others to embrace a certain point of view. Thus, translation is highly political and involves the mobilization of a network of actors supporting a particular claim or object, making it as permanent as possible. And when doing so, processes of problematization, interessement, enrollment and mobilization are involved (Callon, 1986). That which is translated during the processes are interests, claims, convictions and meanings. In another type of studies (inspired by Latour's model of translation (Latour, 1986), JDS), the geometric and semiotic dimensions of translation are emphasized. Translation is understood as a change process that occurs to a spreading construct. In this process, more than perceptions of a particular object or the interests of particular actors are at stake: Translation concerns the fate of management ideas, particularly with respect to intentional or unintentional modifications. The shared characteristic of these contributions is the focus on a particular object – for instance a management idea – that is traveling across different contexts. To translate something is thus to actively modify an object within the context and complexities of an actor-network (Wæraas & Nielsen, 2016).

The knowledge-based perspective on translation emphasizes the semiotic and geometric dimensions of translation and focus on organizational knowledge as the object of translation. The focus is on key concepts such as source, target, receiver, boundaries, peripheries and transfer. In most of the works, translation is portrayed as a boundary spanning activity undertaken to ensure the effective flow of critical information and domain-specific knowledge across organizational boundaries. Different meaning systems resulting from different group, organizational, professional and national cultures are assumed to limit the effective flow of knowledge (Merminod & Rowe, 2012). Knowledge translation, therefore, has a strategic importance for an organization; the need to translate grows out of differences in the form of requirements of actors or appears when innovation is a concern (Carlile, 2004). This means that the movement of knowledge and thus knowledge transfer from one place to another is relatively difficult, that translation requires bicultural translators who have expert knowledge of multiple contexts as well as organization-wide knowledge translation capabilities (Savory, 2006; Yanov, 2004). In such a view, brokers such as IT professionals, border crosses or peripheral workers, and project leaders and outsourcing engineers play an important role (Merminod & Rowe, 2012; Pawlowski & Robey, 2004; Yanov, 2004). There is an instrumental focus on effectiveness in terms of how translation may increase the effectiveness of knowledge management, how knowledge translation effectiveness may be increased by other factors, and how knowledge translation capability solves problems and contributes to competitive advantages (Merminod & Rowe, 2012; Pawlowski & Robey, 2004).

Finally, the Scandinavian institutionalist perspective has both a geometric and a semiotic meaning. Translation is associated with change in management ideas and models. Inspired by Sérres, Harari and Bell (1982) and Latour (1986), Czarniawska and Sevon (2005, p. 8) propose that translation attracts attention to the fact that the thing moved from one place to another cannot emerge unchanged: To set something in a new place or another point in time is to construct it anew. Translation is defined as the process in which ideas and models are adapted to local contexts as they travel across time and space (Lamb & Currie, 2012, p. 219). Spreading ideas are stripped of time- and space-bounded features before they are dis-embedded or de-contextualized from local contexts and start traveling (Czarniawska & Joerges, 1996). The lack of contextual features necessitates varying degrees of modification when the constructs enter a specific organization referred to as processes of re-embedding or contextualization or reconstruction whereby they acquire a new or modified meaning (Mazza, Sahlin-Andersson, & Pedersen, 2005; Özen & Berkman, 2007; Ritvala & Granqvist, 2009). The travel of ideas is suggested to having the potential to lead to both predicted and unpredictable outcomes. The translation of management ideas may thus result in both homogenization and variation (Wæraas & Nielsen, 2016).

Based on their analysis of the literature, Wæraas and Nielsen (2016) conclude the following:

- The three perspectives on translation in organizational research can be bridged via the central premise from the ANT perspective: That translations have a geometric, semiotic and political meaning[1]
- The perspectives are divided in their focus on translation into a source, brokering and recipient context

Actor-network theory has its strengths in the political dimension. The knowledge-based and Scandinavian institutionalist perspectives emphasize the geometric and semiotic meaning. The Scandinavian institutionalists have a preference for the source and recipient contexts, and the knowledge-based perspective has a preference for the brokering context, while the actor-network perspective emphasizes all three contexts.

Wæraas and Nielsen (2016) now suggest that the different translation perspectives may cross-fertilize each other by making it possible for researchers to ask new types of research questions about how ideas move between people and groups of people:

- Knowledge translation researchers may be inspired by Scandinavian institutionalists and ask: To what extent does the work of a broker or bicultural translator, who translates knowledge from a source to a recipient context, depend on the degree of de-contextualization that has already occurred in the source context? Which aspects of this embedding phase are likely to make brokering practices more complicated, and which aspects are likely to make them run more smoothly?
- Actor-network researchers may be inspired by Scandinavian institutionalists and ask: How is the formation of actor-networks in support of a certain object shaped by the de-contextualization and re-embedding processes? How are problematization, interessement, enrollment and mobilization activities constrained or enabled by these processes? How is translation affected when objects are stripped of their time- and space-bounded features as opposed to when they are not?
- Scandinavian institutionalists may inspire actor-network researchers to ask: Are there any 'translation rules' (Sahlin-Andersson, 1996) involved

during the moments of translation? Are they applied in similar or different ways? Do they lead to similar or different outcomes?

- If you look at disembedding and re-embedding processes suggested by Scandinavian institutionalists and combine with the knowledge-based perspective then: Who are the translators, and how do they negotiate between the source and the recipient context in translation processes? How are disembedding and re-embedding processes in intra-organizational translation of ideas and practices different from similar processes in interorganizational translation? How does distance between the source and the recipient end affect translations? What are the intra-organizational boundaries and who are the translators?

- If you combine the knowledge-based perspective with Scandinavian institutionalism, you may ask: Which are the factors that facilitate and determine translation effectiveness? Do translation competence requirements vary depending on the type of idea that is translated? What are the organizational consequences of bad translations? And, what are bad translations? What do they look like and how do we recognize them?

- Drawing on the knowledge-based perspective, you can ask: How do objects travel from a source to a recipient in organizations, how do their translations depend on the active role of mediators, and which are the characteristics of these contexts and mediators that facilitate or hinder the translation of the object?

- Combining the knowledge-based perspective/the concept of translation effectiveness with the ANT concept of successful or unsuccessful or failed translations, you may ask: How do translation outcomes end up as successes or failures? What does translation capability mean in the translation of interests and objects from an actor-network perspective? To what extent is translation success dependent on translation capability?

- The actor-network and the knowledge-based perspectives may make you ask: How does negotiations, power dynamics and micro-tactics unfold in the translation of managerial ideas and practices.

- Scandinavia institutionalist and actor-network perspectives may make you ask: To what degree are deinstitutionalization or institutionalization processes dependent on processes of problematization, interessement, enrollment and mobilization? What are the implications of inadequate enrollment of actors into a network that supports a specific interpretation of a construct?

- If you combine the actor-network perspective with knowledge translation theory, you may ask: To what extent do translation brokers promote a specific worldview of the boundary object in question? Whose worldview is promoted, whose interests are served in the translation of the object, and whose interests are ignored?

Note

1 The geometric meaning relates to the mobilization of human and nonhuman resources in different directions, the result of which is 'a slow movement from one place to another' (Latour, 1987, p. 117). The semiotic meaning concerns the transformation of meaning that occurs during the movement of the object in question. Finally, the political meaning refers to the pursuit of interests or specific interpretations, frequently involving acts of persuasion, power plays and strategic maneuvers (Nicolini, 2010; Wæraas & Nielsen, 2016).

References

Callon, M. (1986). Some elements of a sociology of translation: domestication of the scallops and the fishermen of st. Brieuc Bay. In J. Law (Eds.), *Power, Action and Belief – A New Sociology of Knowledge?* London: Routledge & Kegan Paul.

Carlile, P. R. (2004). Transferring, translating, and transforming: An integrative framework for managing knowledge across boundaries. *Organization Science, 15*(5), 555–568.

Czarniawska, B., & Joerges, B. (1996). Travels of ideas. In B. Czarniawska & G. Sevon (Eds.), *Translating organizational change* (pp. 13–48). Berlin: de Gruyter.

Czarniawska-Joerges, B., & Sevon, G. (2005). *Global ideas: How ideas, objects and practices travel in a global economy.* Copenhagen: Liber & Copenhagen Business School Press.

Lamb, P., & Currie, G. (2012). Eclipsing adaptation: the translation of the US MBA model in China. *Management Learning, 43,* 217–230.

Latour, B. (1986). The powers of association. In J. Law (Ed.), *Power, action and belief – A new sociology of knowledge?* London: Routledge & Kegan Paul.

Latour, B. (1987). *Science in action: How to follow scientists and engineers through society.* Cambridge, MA: Harvard University Press.

Mazza, C., Sahlin-Andersson, K., & Pedersen, J. S. (2005). European constructions of an American model – Developments of four MBA programmes. *Management Learning, 36,* 471–491.

Merminod, V., & Rowe, F. (2012). How does PLM technology support knowledge transfer and translation in new product development? Transparency and boundary spanners in an international context. *Information and Organization, 22,* 295–322.

Nicolini, D. (2010). Medical innovation as a process of translation: A case from the field of telemedicine. *British Journal of Management, 21,* 1011–1026.

Özen, S., & Berkman, U. (2007). Cross-national reconstruction of managerial practices: TQM in Turkey. *Organization Studies, 28,* 825–851.

Pawlowski, S., & Robey, D. (2004). Bridging user organizations: Knowledge brokering and the work of information technology professionals. *MIS Quarterly, 28,* 645–672.

Ritvala, T., & Granqvist, N. (2009). Institutional entrepreneurs and local embedding of global scientific ideas – The case of preventing heart disease in Finland. *Scandinavian Journal of Management, 25,* 133–145.

Sahlin-Andersson, K. (1996). Imitating by editing success. In B. Czarniawska & G. Sevón (Eds.), *Translating organizational change.* Berlin/New York, NY: Walter de Gruyter.

Savory, C. (2006). Translating knowledge to build technological competence. *Management Decision, 44*, 1052–1075.

Sérres, M., Harari, J. V., & Bell, D. F. (1982). *Hermes*. Baltimore, MD: Johns Hopkins University Press.

Wæraas, A., & Nielsen, J. A. (2016). Translation theory 'translated': Three perspectives on translation in organizational research. *International Journal of Management Reviews, 18*(3), 236–270.

Yanov, D. (2004). Translating local knowledge at organizational peripheries. *British Journal of Management, 15*, 9–25.

Appendix 2
Moving translation studies forward through critical realism

Like Wæraas and Nielsen (2016), O'Mahoney (2016) points out that there is considerable variation in what translation researchers claim translation is and does, in terms of both the object and the process of translation. He thus identifies four different perspectives on translation in his review of the translation studies literature: The diffusion, the actor-network, the Scandinavian institutionalist and the organizational boundaries/symbolic interactionist perspectives. He argues that an important reason for the differences in interpretations of translation is the variety of theoretical archetypes by which they are underpinned. 'Theoretical archetypes' means the assumptions that inform the ontological, epistemological and methodological choices that researchers make (Parker, 1998, p. 33). These archetypes form guiding principles for researchers rather than strict templates, but provide relatively coherent logics by which the world is understood and described by researchers (Al-Amoudi & O'Mahoney, 2015, pp. 1–2). The theoretical archetypes identified by O'Mahoney (2016) have the following characteristics:

Diffusion studies (Rogers, 1995 and others) are based on the theoretical archetype of scientism. This form of studies concerns changes to the properties of an innovation at a population level, as it is communicated and diffuses through what is often presented as the rational choices of managers. These types of studies apply natural science methods to social science. Methodologically, the analysis tends to be based on statistical regression or correlation analysis which takes the relationship between empirical variables to illustrate generalizable laws that would be expected to apply to other examples of diffusion.

Actor-network theory belongs to the archetype of 'actualism'. While ontologically realist, ANT is epistemologically constructivist (Lee & Hassard, 1999; see also Elder-Vass, 2008), in that, while real objects exist 'out there', they come into being through the practices of science (Latour & Woolgar, 1986). Humans and nonhumans are treated symmetrically: Things are only what they 'come to be in a relational, multiple, fluid, and more or less unordered and indeterminate (set of) specific and provisional practices' (Law & Mol, 2008, p. 365). ANT studies use methods such as ethnomethodology to follow the actor and the network. Studies focus upon interessement for instance the use of rhetoric, persuasion and argument to shift the interests of actors in order to build alliances that enable successful implementation of innovations.

Scandinavian institutionalists understand translation 'as a process wherein new practices or fashions become institutionalized in different fields at different points of time and space' (Morris & Lancaster, 2006, p. 209). Their studies tend to focus on the local (re)construction or institutionalization of management innovations or fashions, often through micro-politics or discourse (e.g., Czarniawska, 2012). While many authors claim a Latourian heritage (e.g., Lindberg and Czarniawska, 2006; Malsch, Gendron, & Grazzini, 2011), O'Mahoney (2016) thinks that they are actually much closer to social constructivist theorizing, rejecting empiricism and focusing on the discursive and political re-embedding of knowledge in local contexts. They are thus using methods suited to identifying and understanding discourses, such as interviewing or discourse analysis that enables insights into how innovative management ideas are constructed as well as have effects through local discourses.

The researchers belonging to the organizational boundaries/archetype of symbolic interactionism use translation to explore how groups communicate and cooperate across organizational boundaries (Bechky, 2003; Wenger, 1998). According to these researchers, translation is necessary as 'objects and methods mean different things in different worlds [and] actors are faced with the task of reconciling these meanings if they wish to cooperate' (Star & Griesemer, 1989, p. 388). Methodologically, these papers tend toward interpretivist methods such as ethnography or participant observation, which are suited to understanding the meanings that different communities generate. Empirically, the researchers focus upon different understandings of (boundary) objects and concepts in communities of practice.

O'Mahoney (2016) points out that there are few examples of papers in one archetype citing those from another. He moreover states that these siloes matter because they have resulted in a 'colonization' of translation types by archetype: Evolutionary or population-level forms of translation (diffusion) are the domain of scientism, the translation of actors' interests is dominated by actor-network theorists, the translation of management ideas into local contexts is primarily undertaken by social constructivists and the translation of meanings across disparate groups seeking to cooperate is colonized by interactionists. O'Mahoney (2016) notes that 'philosophical incommensurability can mean that some perspectives miss out on important or useful analytical insights that their own perspective cannot provide'.

According to O'Mahoney (2016), each archetype has limitations. In diffusion studies, explanations only come in the form of statistical correlations. ANT denies any reality other than events and their relations, and treats all actors as symmetrical. This means that the translation of actors' interests can only be explained with reference to their actions rather than their thoughts, interests, identities or motivations (McLean & Hassard, 2004). Moreover, ANT rejects social structures, and the power that this implies. Therefore, why translation happens is often left unanswered (Elder-Vass, 2008; Porpora,

2005) (p. 7). In Scandinavian institutionalism, non-discursive factors are downplayed and the potential of workers to resist the translations of managers and consultants is often ignored (Fleetwood & Ackroyd, 2004). The Scandinavian institutionalists are also criticized for focusing on the local and discursive and thus for missing the nonlocal, structural and population-level framing of an innovation that can help explain its success or failure (Fleetwood, 2005). Similarly, in the organizational boundaries and symbolic interactionist perspective its focus on communication means that it is overly focused on the micro-level and misses the macro-level structures that can influence the ability of groups to communicate (Porpora, 2015).

O'Mahoney (2016) presents critical realism as a foundation for 'ontological dialogue' between researchers in translation studies. He explains the position as follows:

> Critical realism is an ontology holding that reality exists at different emergent levels, which are dependent on, but irreducible to each other (e.g. atoms, cells, organisms, minds, teams, organizations, society). It argues that reality is stratified, and distinguishes between the real (underlying causal mechanisms), the actual (empirical epiphenomena) and the empirical (perceptions of the actual). It therefore distinguishes between the 'transitive' (our theories and talk about the world) and the 'intransitive' (the world itself). While critical realism is ontologically realist, it is epistemologically relativist, but with a commitment towards judgmental rationality (the ability to judge between better and worse theories about the world).
>
> (O'Mahoney, 2016, p. 7)

O'Mahoney (2016) then offers critical realism as a way of asking questions about the ontology and epistemology of the different theoretical archetypes in translation studies and as a way to solve the problems identified with each of the three archetypes he has identified. This by asking and making a critical realist study and assessment of these types of questions: What is the thing being translated? What are its properties and which of these changes? What causes these changes to occur? What are the possibilities and limits of the translation process – and how are these known (O'Mahoney, 2016, p. 9)? According to O'Mahoney (2016):

> These (questions, JDS) both challenge the archetypes to ask 'what makes a difference?', rather than starting with an apriori answer (i.e. Discourse, communication or networks), and also encourage a greater variety of methods to provide insights into a number of potential causal factors, not simply those that are traditionally important within that archetype.
>
> (O'Mahoney, 2016, p. 9)

References

Al-Amoudi, I., & O'Mahoney, J. (2015). Ontology: Philosophical discussions and implications for organization studies. In H. Willmott, W. Mir, & M. Greenwood

(Eds.), *Routledge companion to philosophy in organization studies* (pp. 1–26). London: Routledge.

Bechky, B. (2003). Sharing meaning across occupational communities: The transformation of understanding on the production floor. *Organization Science, 14,* 312–330.

Czarniawska, B. (2012). New plots are badly needed in finance: Accounting for the financial crisis of 2007–2010. *Accounting, Auditing and Accountability Journal, 25*(5), 756–775.

Elder-Vass, D. (2008). Searching for realism, structure and agency in actor-network-theory. *British Journal of Sociology, 59,* 455–473.

Fleetwood, S. (2005). Ontology in organization and management studies: A critical realist perspective. *Organization, 12,* 197–222.

Fleetwood, S., & Ackroyd, S. (2004). *Critical realist applications in organisation and management studies.* London: Routledge.

Latour, B., & Woolgar, S. (1986). *Laboratory life: The construction of scientific facts.* Princeton, NJ: Princeton University Press.

Law, J., & Mol, A. (2008). The actor-enacted: Cumbrian sheep in 2001. In C. Knappet & L. Malafouris (Eds.), *Material agency: Towards a non-anthropocentric approach* (pp. 57–96). New York, NY: Springer.

Lee, N., & Hassard, J. (1999). Organization unbound: Actor-network theory, research strategy and institutional flexibility. *Organizations, 6,* 391–404.

Lindberg, K., & Czarniawska, B. (2006). Knotting the action net, or organizing between organizations. *Scandinavian Journal of Management, 22,* 292–306.

Malsch, B., Gendron, Y., & Grazzini, F. (2011). Investigating interdisciplinary translations: the influence of Pierre Bourdieu on accounting literature. *Accounting, Auditing & Accountability Journal, 24,* 194–228.

McLean, C., & Hassard, J. (2004). Symmetrical absence/symmetrical absurdity: Critical notes on the production of actor-network accounts. *Journal of Management Studies, 41,* 493–519.

Morris, T., & Lancaster, Z. (2006). Translating management ideas. *Organization Studies, 32,* 187–210.

O'Mahoney, J. (2016). Archetypes of translation: Recommendations for dialogue. *International Journal of Management Reviews, 18*(3), 333–350.

Parker, I. (1998). *Social constructionism, discourse and realism (Inquiries in Social Construction series).* London: Sage.

Porpora, D. (2005). Do realists run regressions? In J. Lopez and G. Potter (Eds.), *After postmodernism: An introduction to critical realism* (pp. 260–269). London: Athlone Press.

Porpora, D. V. (2015). *Reconstructing sociology: The critical realist approach*: Cambridge: Cambridge University Press.

Rogers, E. M. (1995). *Diffusion of innovations.* New York, NY: Free Press.

Star, S. L., & Griesemer, J. (1989). Institutional ecology, 'translations', and boundary objects: Amateurs and professionals on Berkeley's museum of vertebrate zoology. *Social Studies of Science, 19,* 387–420.

Wenger, E. (1998). *Communities of practice: Learning, meaning and identity.* Cambridge: Cambridge University Press.

Wæraas, A., & Nielsen, J. A. (2016). Translation theory 'translated': Three perspectives on translation in organizational research. *International Journal of Management Reviews, 18*(3), 236–270.

Appendix 3

Making citation networks and lists using Web of Science and CitNetExplorer

By Mirlinda Kreci[1] and John Damm Scheuer

A systematic literature review was conducted defining translation research's boundaries in organization, actor-network, Scandinavian institutionalist, symbolic interactionist, linguistic, and policy, strategy and innovation studies. The time span used for the research goes from 1960 to 2020. The review included both articles and book chapters.

We used the universal databases ProQuest, Google Scholar and Web of Science. We utilized research queries that included in the title and abstract the following keywords: 'translation', 'translation theory' and 'organization'.

We created different queries for each area of translation theory (those mentioned above), limiting the area of study. For each query, the process was the following: On Web of Science we selected the relevant articles, and added the ones present on the other databases, limiting the language to 'English'. Afterward, we moved the results in the marked list and from there we made an analysis of the most cited articles exporting data to Microsoft Excel. The same marked list was also exported into a txt file that was used to make a citation network analysis using CitNetExplorer software, which provided a visual result of the most cited authors. Both the results were then combined, and we were able to extract the key authors for each area of translation theory.

We started our review with two general queries and then we made an individual search for each area.

The general query 1: TS= (translation* theory * AND organization*) gave us 441 results, with 25 of these cited at least 100 times, 47 at least 50 times, 201 at least 10 times and 390 at least one time.

Figure A.3.1 shows the result from the citation network analysis and the most cited articles are the ones with most connections.

The general query 2 was more specific because we delimited the area of studies: TI = (translation) AND TS = (organization *) AND WC = (HEALTH CARE SCIENCES SERVICES OR HEALTH POLICY SERVICES OR POLITICAL SCIENCE OR MANAGEMENT OR PRIMARY HEALTH CARE OR PUBLIC ENVIRONMENTAL OCCUPATIONAL HEALTH OR COMPUTER SCIENCE THEORY METHODS OR BEHAVIORAL SCIENCE OR COMPUTER SCIENCE INTERDISCIPLINARY APPLICATIONS OR ENVIRONMENTAL STUDIES OR SOCIAL

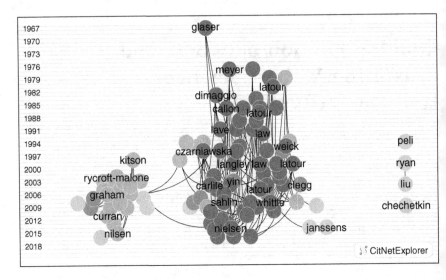

Figure A.3.1 General query 1.

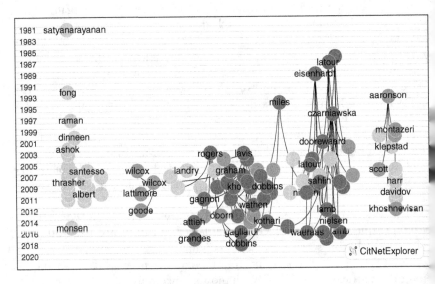

Figure A.3.2 General query 2.

WORK OR PSYCHOLOGY APPLIED OR COMPUTER SCIENCE SOFTWARE ENGINEERING OR PUBLIC ADMINISTRATION OR COMPUTER SCIENCE CYBERNETICS OR MEDICAL INFORMATICS OR PSYCHOLOGY RESULTS).

The search gave 209 results, with 4 articles cited at least 4 times, 14 at least 50 times, 93 at least 10 times and 187 articles cited at least 1 time.

Appendix 3 233

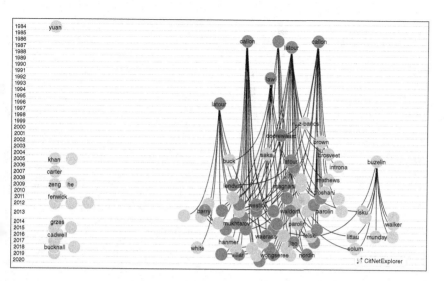

Figure A.3.3 Actor-network theory network analysis.

Figure A.3.2 shows the result from the citation network analysis and the most cited articles are the ones with most connections.

Actor-Network Theory (ANT)

We used the following query to search ANT related articles: TI= (translation) AND TS= (ANT OR ACTOR NETWORK OR ACTOR NETWORK THEORY). The query gave us 90 results, with 2 of them cited at least 100 times, 7 at least 50 times, 33 at least 10 times and 65 at least 1 time.

Figure A.3.3 shows the citation network analysis of the ANT articles, and the authors with most connections are the ones most cited. The pattern of citations confirmed our existing knowledge about this research area.

Scandinavian Institutionalism

We used the following query to search Scandinavian Institutionalism-related articles: (TI=(translation) AND TS=(SCANDINAVIAN INSTITUTIONALISM OR INSTITUTIONAL THEORY OR TRAVEL OF IDEA★)) AND LANGUAGE: (English). We obtained 68 results, with 2 of them cited at least 50 times, 23 at least 10 times and 49 at least 1 time.

Figure A.3.4 shows the citation network analysis of the Scandinavian Institutionalism articles, and the authors with most connections are the most cited.

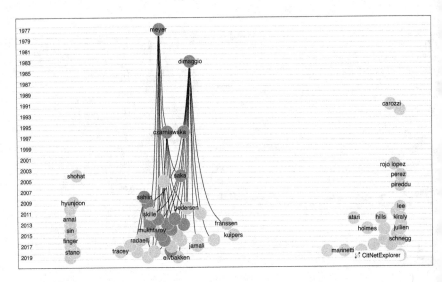

Figure A.3.4 Scandinavian Institutionalism network analysis.

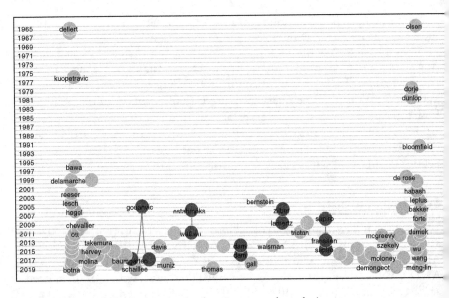

Figure A.3.5 Symbolic interactionist theories network analysis.

Symbolic interactionist theories

We used the following query to search symbolic interactionist-related articles: (TI=(translation) AND TS=(symbolic OR symbolic interactionism OR interactionist theory OR organizational boundaries)) AND LANGUAGE

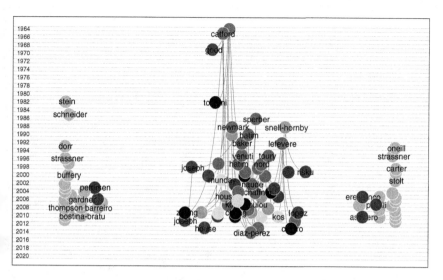

Figure A.3.6 Linguistic theories network analysis.

(English). The query gave us 93 results, with 2 of them cited at least 100 times, 4 at least 50 times, 15 at least 10 times and 69 at least 1 time.

Figure A.3.5 shows the citation network analysis of the symbolic interactionist articles, and authors with most connections are the most cited.

Linguistic theories

We used the following query to search linguistic theory-related articles: TI=(translation) AND TS=(linguistic AND theory). We obtained 296 results, with 1 of them cited at least 100 times, 6 at least 50 times, 22 at least 10 times and 125 at least 1 time.

Figure A.3.6 shows the citation network analysis of the linguistic theory articles, and the authors with the most connections are the most cited.

Policy-translation

We used the following query to search policy-translation–related articles: (TI=(policy AND translation) AND WC= (HEALTH POLICY SERVICES OR POLITICAL SCIENCE OR MANAGEMENT OR COMPUTER SCIENCE THEORY METHODS OR BEHAVIORAL SCIENCES OR COMMUNICATION OR BUSINESS OR COMPUTER SCIENCE INTERDISCIPLINARY APPLICATIONS OR ENVIRONMENTAL STUDIES OR SOCIAL WORK OR PSYCHOLOGY APPLIED OR COMPUTER SCIENCE SOFTWARE ENGINEERING OR PUBLIC ADMINISTRATION OR COMPUTER SCIENCE CYBERNETICS

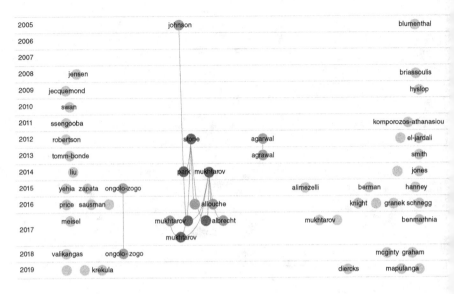

Figure A.3.7 Policy translation network analysis.

OR MEDICAL INFORMATICS OR PSYCHOLOGY MULTIDISCI-
PLINARY OR OPERATIONS RESEARCH MANAGEMENT SCI-
ENCE OR SOCIOLOGY)) AND LANGUAGE: (English). The query gave
us 56 results, with 1 of them cited at least 100 times, 3 at least 50 times, 22 at
least 10 times and 43 at least 1 time.

Figure A.3.7 shows the citation network analysis of the policy-translation
theory articles, and the authors with most connections are the most cited.

Strategy translation

We used the following query to search strategy translation-related ar-
ticles: (TI = (strategy AND translation) AND WC = (HEALTH CARE
SCIENCES SERVICES OR HEALTH POLICY SERVICES OR POLITI-
CAL SCIENCE OR MANAGEMENT OR PRIMARY HEALTH CARE
OR PUBLIC ENVIRONMENTAL OCCUPATIONAL HEALTH OR
COMPUTER SCIENCE THEORY METHODS OR BEHAVIORAL
SCIENCE OR COMPUTER SCIENCE INTERDISCIPLINARY APPLI-
CATIONS OR ENVIRONMENTAL STUDIES OR SOCIAL WORK
OR PSYCHOLOGY APPLIED OR COMPUTER SCIENCE SOFT-
WARE ENGINEERING OR PUBLIC ADMINISTRATION OR COM-
PUTER SCIENCE CYBERNETICS OR MEDICAL INFORMATICS
OR PSYCHOLOGY RESULTS).) AND LANGUAGE: (English).

The query gave 45 results, with 2 of them cited at least 150 times, 2 cited
at least 100 times, 1 cited at least 50 times, 7 cited at least 20 times, 5 cited

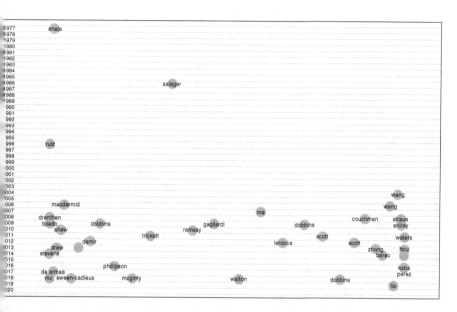

igure A.3.8 Strategy translation network analysis.

at least 10 times and 14 cited at least 1 time. Figure A.3.8 shows the citation network analysis of the strategy-translation theory articles, and the authors with most connections are the most cited.

Innovation translation

We used the following query to search innovation translation-related articles: (TI = (translation) AND TS = (innovation) AND WC = (HEALTH CARE SCIENCES SERVICES OR HEALTH POLICY SERVICES OR POLITICAL SCIENCE OR MANAGEMENT OR PRIMARY HEALTH CARE OR PUBLIC ENVIRONMENTAL OCCUPATIONAL HEALTH OR COMPUTER SCIENCE THEORY METHODS OR BEHAVIORAL SCIENCE OR COMPUTER SCIENCE INTERDISCIPLINARY APPLICATIONS OR ENVIRONMENTAL STUDIES OR SOCIAL WORK OR PSYCHOLOGY APPLIED OR COMPUTER SCIENCE SOFTWARE ENGINEERING OR PUBLIC ADMINISTRATION OR COMPUTER SCIENCE CYBERNETICS OR MEDICAL INFORMATICS OR PSYCHOLOGY RESULTS)) AND LANGUAGE: (English)

The query gave 98 results, with 2 articles cited at least 200 times, 1 article cited at least 150 times, 1 article cited at least 100 times, 6 articles cited at least 50 times, 24 articles cited at least 20 times, 12 articles cited at least 10 times and 36 articles cited at least 1 time. Figure A.3.9 shows the citation network

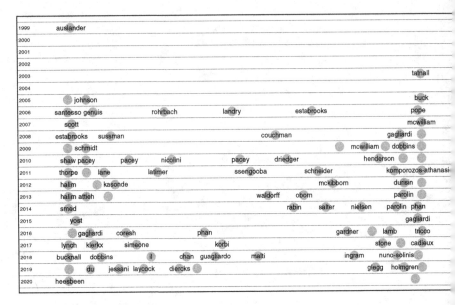

1999	auslander						
2000							
2001							
2002							
2003							tatnall
2004							
2005	johnson						buck
2006	santesso genuis		rohrbach	landry	estabrooks		pope
2007	scott						mcwilliam
2008	estabrooks sussman			couchman			gagliardi
2009	schmidt					mcwilliam	dobbins
2010	shaw pacey	pacey	nicolini	pacey	driedger		henderson
2011	thorpe lane	latimer		ssengooba	schneider		komporozos-athanasi
2012	halim kasonde				mckibborn		durisin
2013	halim attieh			waldorff oborn			parolin
2014	smed			rabin salter	nielsen		parolin phan
2015	yost						gagliardi
2016	gagliardi coresh		phan		gardner	lamb	tricco
2017	lynch klerkx	simeone	korbi			stone	cadieux
2018	bucknall dobbins	il	chan guagliardo	malti	ingram	nuno-solinis
2019	du	jessani laycock	diercks			glegg	holmgren
2020	heesbeen						

Figure A.3.9 Innovation translation network analysis.

analysis of the innovation–translation theory articles and citation connections
between authors.

Note

1 Mirlinda Kreci is a master student in Economics and Business Administration
and Leadership at Roskilde University. She worked for me as research assistant as
part of her internship at the university in spring 2020.

Index

acquisition of idea 104, 105
action 24, 27, 29–31, 35, 39, 40, 42–45,
  47, 51, 54, 57–61, 70, 86, 94–99, 108,
  110, 118, 120–123, 128, 129–132,
  146, 147, 155–157, 160, 163, 166, 185,
  193, 198–200, 202, 206, 208, 211, 213,
  215, 228
  cycle 95–97, 128, 146, 213
  types of 59, 156
action-net, definition of 57–61
actor
  as actant 30–31, 155–156
  in policy translation 87–88
  role of 39–40
actor-network 6, 29, 30–35, 51, 52,
  119–121, 123, 128, 130, 132, 133, 140,
  146, 147, 155, 156, 158–160, 164, 165,
  167–169, 171–174, 178, 180, 182,
  184, 185, 197, 198, 201, 208, 211, 212,
  214–216, 221–224, 227, 228, 231
actor-network theory (ANT) 8, 28–35,
  51, 67, 91, 118, 123, 130–132, 135,
  145, 148, 151, 155–160, 164, 165, 167,
  168, 173, 177–179, 197–198, 221, 223,
  224, 227, 228, 233
acts of translation 67, 68
actualist mode 5, 140, 189, 197–198, 213
adoption, rate of 8, 22, 24, 26–27, 190
alignment of actors 105
ambiguity 4, 62, 63, 65, 68, 123, 196
ANT *see* actor-network theory (ANT)
appropriation of translation role 105
articulation 91, 92
artifacts 44, 59, 86, 101, 102, 118, 122,
  130, 132, 167–173, 180, 181, 185,
  198, 210
association 28, 33, 60, 91, 92, 120,
  182, 183
assumptions 4, 6, 43, 47, 57, 67, 75, 82,
  87, 123, 133–134, 140, 145–146, 149,
151–162, 164, 167, 169, 172, 174, 179,
  191, 208, 209, 227
  about human communication
    156–158
  about humans as translators 158–162
  about learning 165–167
  challenge of 133–134
  and designers 162–165
  of entity building (ANT) 155–156
  of idea-practice translation model
    145–146, 151–154
  of instrumental theory 67–68
  and relational inertia in entity building
    173–175
  stabilizing of relations and interactions
    167–169
  use of symbolic and socio-material
    tools 169–173
  and ventriloquism 161–162
assumptions and values, of author
  145–146

Bainton, D. 85, 91, 92, 118
barriers, to knowledge use 95–97
behavior, institutionalized 58
Bessant, J. 113, 118
boundaries
  pragmatic 48, 49
  semantic 48, 49
  syntactic 48, 49
boundary objects 47–52, 114, 115,
  120, 122, 130, 131, 148, 195, 210,
  224, 228
  definition of 50–52

Callon, M. 28, 29, 31–35, 51, 52,
  118–121, 123, 127, 128, 130–132, 145,
  147, 155, 178, 208, 221
Carlile, P.R. 47–49, 115, 118, 121, 122,
  127, 128, 130, 132, 146, 148, 208, 222

Ellwood, P. 113, 118
embeddedness 68, 69, 107, 123, 129, 148
enrollment 52, 105, 107, 119, 147, 221, 223, 224
equivalence, definition of 63
evidence 7, 94, 97–99, 108, 114, 128, 183, 191, 209, 212, 213
explicit knowledge 64, 65, 69, 128
explicitness 68, 69, 123, 148
exploitation 102, 110
exploration 110
externalization 64

facilitators 96–99, 130, 208, 213
factors, influencing knowledge translation 65–66
factors influencing translation 128, 140, 207, 208, 216
fashion 40, 42–45, 129, 136, 162, 194, 228
focus points 5, 6, 13, 117–137, 140, 141, 206, 216
formal structure 40, 69, 129
forming action nets 58–60
Foucault, M. 5, 87, 189
four basic systems of language 63
four perspectives of translation 81, 82
friction, when ideas travel 58
functional perspective 80

gabs 4, 6, 13, 117–137, 141, 145
general symmetry, principle of 29
good translation 62, 67, 196
Graham, I.D. 94–97, 100, 118, 120, 128, 129, 146, 191, 213
Greima, A.J. 29, 30, 158, 160
Griesemer, J. 47, 50–52, 118–122, 127, 128, 130–132, 146, 148, 195, 208, 228
Grimshaw, J.M. 94, 97, 98, 208
group A and B 118–119, 128, 130
guideline (policy) to practice 91

habits 58
Harald, F.O. 62, 118, 195
heterogeneity 26, 30, 38–39
Holden, N.J. 62–65, 118–123, 127, 128, 130, 132, 148, 195, 196
homogeneity 26
humanities mode 5, 189, 191–203, 213

idea
    definition of 42, 104, 177
    stabilization 105, 108
    variation 105, 108

idea-model 41, 118, 123, 132, 147, 193
idea-practice-translation model 4, 6, 140, 145, 151–154, 177–182, 184, 199–203, 210, 212, 214, 215
ideological perspective 75, 79, 80–81
impact, of research 115
influence, on translation processes 5, 6, 8, 68, 70, 78, 121, 122–133, 135, 136, 140, 141, 147, 148, 206–208, 214, 216
informal structure 23
information, different ways of conveying it 62, 66, 196
innovation 3, 4, 8, 13, 21–27, 41, 48, 70, 75, 86, 90, 100–102, 114, 121, 190, 191, 194, 198, 211, 222, 227–229, 231, 237–238
innovation-decision 23–26, 190
innovators 8, 25
institution 39, 42, 44–45, 50, 58, 101, 102, 115, 121, 129, 130, 147, 168
institutionalization 40, 42, 43, 45, 194, 224, 228
instrumental theory of translation 67–73, 137
instrumental thinking 67
intermediary, designer as 101
intermediate position 104, 105, 202
internalization 64
international organizations as intermediaries 88–89
interpretation 47, 48, 57, 65, 68, 69, 85, 89, 90, 101, 108, 119, 120, 123, 146, 147, 202, 224, 225, 227
interpretive templates 59
intertextuality of texts 79
intervention 96–99, 110, 111, 130, 191, 208, 209, 213
intervention strategies 96–99, 213
invention 32, 33, 111, 120
isomorphism 38–39, 87

Joerges, B. 4–6, 38, 40–45, 58, 86, 90, 105, 111, 118, 120–123, 127, 129–132, 136, 145–147, 151, 160, 177, 181, 207–211, 213, 216, 222
Johnson, B. 85–87, 118, 119, 121, 122, 128–130, 132, 145

knowing, way of 53
knowledge 3, 7, 8, 24–26, 28–31, 47–55, 57, 59, 61–71, 73, 79, 89, 94–102, 104, 105, 110, 112–115, 117, 118, 120–123, 128–133, 137, 140, 145, 146, 148, 155, 156, 158, 160, 165–173, 177, 179, 180,

Printed in the United States
by Baker & Taylor Publisher Services